3,000
Quotations
on
Christian Themes

3,000
Quotations
on
Christian Themes

compiled by
Carroll E. Simcox

BAKER BOOK HOUSE
Grand Rapids, Michigan 49506

ISBN 0-8010-8286-2

Formerly published under the title,
A Treasury of Quotations on Christian Themes

Copyright © 1975 by The Seabury Press, Inc.

Reprinted 1988 by Baker Book House
with permission of copyright owner

Third printing, November 1989

Designed by Publishing Synthesis
Printed in the United States of America

This book is gratefully dedicated to
the people I have worked with
in the Foundation for Christian Theology
and in loving remembrance of our "founding mother"
the Dragon Lady Dorothy Faber
quondam editor of *The Christian Challenge*
Defuncta adhuc loquitur!

CONTENTS

PREFACE

Solomon found a "word fitly spoken" delectable as a golden apple on a silver platter (Proverbs 25:11). Sir Winston Churchill found refreshment in browsing through *Bartlett's Quotations.* If you share their taste I hope you will find this book delightful and useful.

Over many years I have been collecting words fitly spoken on the great themes of God, Creation, Man, Christ and His Church, Life in the Spirit, and The End. The quotations in this collection are not all from Christian sources, nor all expressive of Christian truth. They are included because they are "ponderabilia," pertinent to their subjects, and in one way or another fitly spoken.

One practical suggestion: If you want to find all of the quotations on a particular subject turn to the subject index at the end.

"Next to the originator of a good sentence is the first quoter of it," Emerson said. Perhaps you can find some things in this book that you can first-quote to your friends, and even better, to yourself. I hope so.

All biblical quotations in this book are from the Authorized or King James Version unless otherwise indicated, and quotations from the psalms are from the version of the Psalter in the Book of Common Prayer, also unless otherwise indicated.

C.E.S.

I

God

In the beginning, God. . . .

Oh thou that art! Ecclesiastes names thee the
Almighty. Maccabees names thee Creator; the
Epistle to the Ephesians names thee Liberty;
the Psalms name thee Wisdom and Truth; John
names thee Light; the Book of Kings names thee
Lord; Exodus calls thee Providence; Leviticus,
Holiness; Esdras, Justice; Creation calls thee God;
Man names thee Father; but Solomon names thee
Compassion, and that is the most beautiful of all
thy names.

Victor Hugo

And we must dare to affirm that the Creator, by
reason of love, is drawn from his transcendent
throne above all things to dwell within the heart of
all things, while he yet stays within himself.

Dionysius the Areopagite

ATHEISM

1 The worst moment for the atheist is when he is really thankful and has nobody to thank.
DANTE GABRIEL ROSSETTI

2 The religion of the atheist has a God-shaped blank at its heart.
H.G. WELLS

3 The atheists have not got around to answering Huxley's self-critical confession that neither he nor his followers have succeeded in showing how you can deduce Hamlet from the molecular structure of a mutton⸱ chop.
WILLIAM F. BUCKLEY, JR.

4 An atheist is a man without invisible means of support.
JOHN BUCHAN

5 My atheism, like that of Spinoza, is true piety towards the universe and denies only gods fashioned by men in their own image, to be servants of their human interests.
GEORGE SANTAYANA

6 I am an atheist, thank God!
Anonymous

7 "There are no atheists in foxholes!" What a mean tribute this turns out to be once you have come to think of it!
EMILE CAILLET

8 I had rather believe all the fables in the legends and the Talmud and the Alcoran, than that this universe is without a mind.
FRANCIS BACON

9 A little philosophy inclineth a man's mind to atheism, but depth in philosophy bringeth men's minds about to religion.
FRANCIS BACON

10 We shall say without hesitation that the atheist who is moved by love is moved by the spirit of God; an atheist who lives by love is saved by his faith in the God whose existence (under that name) he denies.
WILLIAM TEMPLE

11 Christianity founds hospitals, and atheists are cured in them, never knowing that they owe their cure to Christ.
WILLIAM TEMPLE

12 The unbelieving epochs are the cradles of new superstitions.
HENRI FRÉDÉRIC AMIEL

13 The three great apostles of practical atheism that make converts without persecuting, and retain them without preaching, are health, wealth, and power.
CHARLES CALEB COLTON

14 God does not die on the day when we cease to believe in a personal deity, but we die on the day when our lives cease to be illumined by the steady radiance, renewed daily, of a wonder, the source of which is beyond all reason.
DAG HAMMARSKJÖLD

ATTRIBUTES OF GOD

15 Always active, always quiet *(semper agens, semper quietus)*.
AUGUSTINE OF HIPPO

16 I will tell you, scholar, I have heard a grave divine say, that God has two dwellings, one in heaven, and the other in the meek and thankful heart.

IZAAK WALTON

17 God is within all things but not included; outside all things, but not excluded; above all things, but not beyond their reach.

POPE GREGORY I

18 A God all mercy is a God unjust.

EDWARD YOUNG

19 Some of us believe that God is almighty and may do all, and that he is all-wisdom and can do all; but that he is all-love and will do all— there we stop short.

LADY JULIAN OF NORWICH

20 A comprehended God is no God at all.

GERHARD TERSTEEGEN

21 God is an unutterable sigh, planted in the depths of the soul.

JEAN PAUL RICHTER

22 One might lay it down as a postulate: All conceptions of God which are incompatible with a movement of pure charity are false. All other conceptions of him, in varying degree, are true.

SIMONE WEIL

23 We are all strings in the concert of his joy.

JAKOB BOEHME

24 There is but one living and true God, everlasting, without body, parts, or passions; of infinite power, wisdom, and goodness; the Maker, and Preserver of all things both visible and invisible. And in unity of this Godhead there be three Persons, of one substance, power, and eternity; the Father, the Son, and the Holy Ghost.

Articles of Religion (I)

Does God seem far away? Guess 25 who moved.

Anonymous

God does not offer himself to our 26 finite beings as a thing all complete and ready to be embraced. For us he is eternal discovery and eternal growth. The more we think we understand him, the more he reveals himself as otherwise. The more we think we hold him, the further he withdraws, drawing us closer into the depths of himself. The nearer we approach him through all the efforts of nature and grace, the more he increases in one and the same movement, his attraction over our powers, and the receptivity of our powers to that divine attraction.

PIERRE TEILHARD DE CHARDIN

God is that, the greater than which 27 cannot be conceived.

ANSELM OF CANTERBURY

God is that indefinable something 28 which we all feel but which we do not know. To me God is truth and love, God is ethics and morality, God is fearlessness, God is the source of light and life, and yet he is above and beyond all these. He is even the atheism of the atheist.

MOHANDAS GANDHI

God is not patient in the sense that 29 we are when we wait our turn at the dentist's. His patience is an active power which (in both senses) bears the world, causing it to move to a fixed end, and which also bears each individual, making him advance in the way of God. His patience is also a power which gives the world and each individual enough time for this advance to be their own act, the fruit of their experience, investigation, and choice.

JACQUES ELLUL

30 God is not a cosmic bellboy for whom we can press a button to get things.

HARRY EMERSON FOSDICK

31 Belief in a cruel God makes a cruel man.

THOMAS PAINE

32 It is essential that God be conceived as the deepest power in the universe; and second, that he be conceived under the form of a mental personality. God's personality is to be regarded, like any other personality, as something lying outside my own and other than me, and whose existence I simply come upon and find.

WILLIAM JAMES

33 Beware of the man whose God is in the skies.

GEORGE BERNARD SHAW

34 Brothers, the God of the universe has need of nothing.

CLEMENT OF ROME

BELIEF

(See also *Creeds, Faith*)

35 Lord, I believe; help thou my unbelief.

Mark 9:24

36 Belief consists in accepting the affirmations of the soul; unbelief in denying them.

RALPH WALDO EMERSON

37 To believe means to recognize that we must wait until the veil shall be removed. Unbelief prematurely unveils itself.

EUGEN ROSENSTOCK-HUESSY

38 With most men, unbelief in one thing springs from blind belief in another.

GEORG CHRISTOPH LICHTENBERG

39 It is as absurd to argue men, as to torture them, into believing.

JOHN HENRY NEWMAN

40 If you believe in the Gospel what you like, and reject what you don't like, it is not the Gospel you believe, but yourself.

AUGUSTINE OF HIPPO

41 Belief in God means believing that the ideals we cherish are real, that justice, peace, brotherhood, compassion and honesty actually emerge out of the very structure of the universe.

IRA EISENSTEIN

42 I have never discarded beliefs deliberately. I left them in the drawer, and, after a while, when I opened it, there was nothing there at all.

WILLIAM GRAHAM SUMNER

43 It hurts more to have a belief pulled than to have a tooth pulled, and no intellectual Novocain is available.

ELMER DAVIS

44 I believe in God as I believe in my friends, because I feel the breath of his affection, feel his invisible and

intangible hand, drawing me, leading me, grasping me, because I possess an inner consciousness of a particular providence and of a universal mind that marks out for me the course of my destiny.

MIGUEL DE UNAMUNO

45 You never know how much you really believe anything until its truth or falsehood becomes a matter of life and death to you.

C.S. LEWIS

46 We have only to believe. And the more threatening and irreducible reality appears, the more firmly and desperately must we believe. Then, little by little, we shall see the universal horror unbend, and then smile upon us, and then take us into its more human arms.

PIERRE TEILHARD DE CHARDIN

47 The point of having an open mind, like having an open mouth, is to close it on something solid.

GILBERT KEITH CHESTERTON

48 More persons, on the whole, are humbugged by believing nothing, than by believing too much.

P.T. BARNUM

49 *Credo Deum!* That is a fine, a worthy thing to say; but to recognize God where and as he reveals himself, is the only true bliss on earth.

JOHANN WOLFGANG VON GOETHE

50 Why abandon a belief merely because it ceases to be true? Cling to it long enough, and . . . it will turn true again, for so it goes. Most of the change we think we see in life is due to truths being in and out of favor.

ROBERT FROST

51 Whatever the queer little word "God" means, it means something we can none of us quite get away from, or at; something connected with our deepest explosions.

D.H. LAWRENCE

52 I wonder whether Peter, Paul, Moses, and all the saints fully and thoroughly understood a single word of God so that they had nothing more to learn from it, for the understanding of God is beyond measure. To be sure, the saints understood the Word of God and could also speak about it, but their practice did not keep pace with it. Here one forever remains a learner. The scholastics illustrated this with a ball which only at one point touches the table on which it rests, although the whole weight of the ball is supported by the table.

Though I am a great doctor, I haven't yet progressed beyond the instruction of children in the Ten Commandments, the Creed, and the Lord's Prayer. I still learn and pray these every day with my Hans and my little Lena. Who understands in all of its ramifications even the opening words, "Our Father who art in heaven"? For if I understand these words in faith—that the God who holds heaven and earth in his hand is my Father—I would conclude that therefore I am lord of heaven and earth, therefore Christ is my brother, therefore all things are mine, Gabriel is my servant, Raphael is my coachman, and all the other angels are ministering spirits sent forth by my Father in heaven to serve me in all my necessities, lest I strike my foot against a stone. In order that this faith should not remain untested, my Father comes along and allows me to be thrown into prison or to be drowned in water. Then it will finally become apparent how well we understand these words. Our faith wavers. Our weakness gives rise to the question, "Who knows if it is true?" So this one word "your" or "our" is the most difficult of all in the whole Scripture. It's like the word "your" in the first commandment, "I am the Lord your God" (Exod. 20:2).

MARTIN LUTHER

BIBLE

(See *God's Word*)

53 In the Old Testament the New lies hidden, in the New Testament the Old is laid open.

AUGUSTINE OF HIPPO

54 Whoever seems to himself to have understood the divine scriptures in such a way that he does not build up that double love of God and neighbor has not yet understood.

AUGUSTINE OF HIPPO

55 The Bible is like a telescope. If a man looks *through* his telescope, then he sees worlds beyond; but if he looks *at* his telescope, then he does not see anything but that. The Bible is a thing to be looked through, to see that which is beyond; but most people only look at it; and so they see only the dead letter.

PHILLIPS BROOKS

56 Caiaphas was in his own mind
A benefactor of mankind,

And read the Bible day and night.

WILLIAM BLAKE

Most people are bothered by those 57 passages in Scripture which they cannot understand; but as for me, I always noticed that the passages in Scripture which trouble me most are those that I do understand.

MARK TWAIN

The Bible is alive, it speaks to me; it 58 has feet, it runs after me; it has hands, it lays hold on me.

MARTIN LUTHER

The dogma of the infallibility of the 59 Bible is no more self-evident than is that of the infallibility of the popes.

THOMAS HENRY HUXLEY

It has been truly said that any 60 translation of the Bible must be a failure.

EDGAR J. GOODSPEED

This Bible is for the government of 61 the people, by the people, and for the people.

JOHN WYCLIFFE

Political freedom is only a political 62 reading of the Bible.

WHITTAKER CHAMBERS

There must always have been Nazis, 63 or how would it be possible for the Bible to be so full of warnings against them?

THEODOR HAECKER

What you bring away from the 64 Bible depends to some extent on what you carry to it.

OLIVER WENDELL HOLMES

If thou knewest the whole Bible by 65

heart, and the sayings of all the philosophers, what would it profit thee without the love of God and without grace?

THOMAS À KEMPIS

66 It is impossible to enslave mentally and socially a Bible-reading people.

HORACE GREELEY

67 England has two books: the Bible and Shakespeare. England made Shakespeare but the Bible made England.

VICTOR HUGO

68 Odd, the way the less the Bible is read the more it is translated.

C.S. LEWIS

69 Whatsoever things were written aforetime were written for our learning, that we through patience and comfort of the scriptures might have hope.

Romans 15:4

COMMUNION WITH GOD

(See *God and Man, Knowledge of God*)

70 The chief end of man is to glorify God, and to enjoy him forever.

Westminster Catechism

71 There is always something dark, hidden, secret, about our real intercourse with God. In religion we should always distrust the obvious and the clear. The closet where we speak to God is not very well lit—

but the light that filters into it has a quality of its own; it is a ray of the Eternal Light on which we cannot easily look; but as we get used to it, sun ourselves in its glow, we learn, as we can bear it, to see more and more. Therefore we must be content to dwell with God in that dim silence. Gaze at him *darkly,* as the mystics say, offer yourselves again and again to him.

EVELYN UNDERHILL

To have found God is not an end in itself but a beginning. 72

FRANZ ROSENZWEIG

It is not by driving away our brother that we can be alone with God. 73

GEORGE MAC DONALD

All the doors that lead inward, to the sacred place of the Most High, are doors outward—out of self, out of smallness, out of wrong. 74

GEORGE MAC DONALD

Whosoever walks towards God one cubit, God runs towards him twain. 75

Jewish proverb

Live with men as if God saw you; converse with God as if men heard you. 76

SENECA

Each conception of spiritual beauty is a glimpse of God. 77

MOSES MENDELSSOHN

Man only of a softer mould was made 78
Not for his fellows' ruin but their aid:
Created kind, beneficent and free,

The noble image of the Deity.

JOHN DRYDEN

79 That which is our beginning, regeneration, and happiest end—likeness to God.

JOHN MILTON

80 As no man is found, however barbarous and even savage he may be, who is not touched with some idea of religion, it is clear that we all are created in order that we may know the majesty of our Creator, that having known it, we may esteem it above all and honor it with all awe, love, and reverence.

JOHN CALVIN

81 O God of peace, who hast taught us that in returning and rest we shall be saved, in quietness and in confidence shall be our strength; by the might of thy Spirit lift us, we pray thee, to thy presence, where we may be still and know that thou art God; through Jesus Christ our Lord.

Book of Common Prayer

CREEDS

(See *Belief, Faith*)

82 A man's liberty to travel is not cramped by signposts: on the contrary, they save his time by showing what roads he must avoid if he wishes to reach his destination. The creeds perform the same function.

C.B. MOSS

83 When once one believes in a creed, one is proud of its complexity, as scientists are proud of the complexity of science. It shows how rich it is in discoveries. If it is right at all, it is a compliment to say that it's elaborately right. A stick might fit a hole or a stone a hollow by accident. But a key and a lock are both complex. And if a key fits a lock, you know it is the right key.

GILBERT KEITH CHESTERTON

If only a single congregation could 84 enter into a full possession of all that lies in this acknowledgement of the divine allegiance which we agree to profess: if we could each feel, and then all act together as feeling, that faith in God as he has revealed himself as the foundation, the rule, the life of our lives: there would be a force present to move the world.

B.F. WESTCOTT

The proper question to be asked 85 about any creed is not, "Is it pleasant?" but, "Is it true?"

DOROTHY L. SAYERS

Thomas Carlyle and his friend 86 Bishop Wilberforce were talking about death, and Carlyle asked, "Bishop, have you a creed?" "Yes," Wilberforce replied, "I have a creed, and the older I grow the firmer it becomes; there is only one thing that staggers me." "What is that?" asked Carlyle. "It is the slow progress," said the bishop, "that that creed seems to make in the world." Carlyle was silent for a moment, then said gravely, "Ah, but if you have a creed you can afford to wait."

Anonymous

FEAR OF GOD

87 We should not forget that in Psalm 130 God pardons in order that we may fear him. This fear comes from accomplished grace. The condemned man who is pardoned is seized by fear at the power which has caused death to retreat.

JACQUES ELLUL

88 I fear God, yet am not afraid of him.

THOMAS BROWNE

89 To fear God is to stand in awe of him; to be afraid of God is to run away from him.

CARROLL E. SIMCOX

90 Here in Geneva [at the League of Nations] we have every fear except the fear of God.

H.K. HAMBRO

91 Whoso feareth the Lord shall not fear nor be afraid.

Ecclesiasticus 34:14

92 Now the gist of true piety does not consist in a fear which would gladly flee the judgment of God but, being unable to do so, has horror in it. True piety consists rather in a pure and true zeal which loves God altogether, and reveres him truly as Lord, embraces his justice and dreads to offend him more than to die.

JOHN CALVIN

93 Sanctify the Lord of hosts himself; and let him be your fear, and let him be your dread. And he shall be for you a sanctuary.

Isaiah 8:13–14

94 To fear God is never to pass over any good thing that ought to be done.

POPE GREGORY I

95 Holy fear is a loving anxiety to please God.

FRANCIS J. HALL

96 Let us hear the conclusion of the whole matter: Fear God, and keep his commandments: for this is the whole duty of man.

Ecclesiastes 12:13

GOD'S GOODNESS

97 I shall never believe that God plays dice with the world.

ALBERT EINSTEIN

98 The Lord God is subtle, but malicious he is not.

ALBERT EINSTEIN

99 Everybody will cry up the goodness of men; but who is there that is, as he should, affected with the goodness of God?

JOHN BUNYAN

100 Reason cries: "If God were good, he could not look upon the sin and misery of men and live! It would break his heart!"
The church points to the crucifixion and says: "God's heart did break."
Reason cries: "Born and reared in sin and pain as we are, how can

we keep from sin? It is the Creator who is responsible; it is God who deserves to be punished."

The church kneels by the cross and whispers: "God takes the responsibility and bears the punishment."

Reason cries: "Who is God? What is God? The Name stands for the unknown. It is blasphemy to say we know him."

The church kisses the feet of the dying Christ and says: "We must worship the Majesty we see."

That, I think, is to speak good of his name.

ROBERT NELSON SPENCER

101 When God elects us it is not because we are handsome *(ce n'est pas pour nos beaux yeux)*.

JOHN CALVIN

102 The ministering angels wanted to sing a hymn at the destruction of the Egyptians, but God said: "My children lie drowned in the sea, and you would sing?"

RABBI JOHANAN

103 Remember that God loves your soul, not in some aloof, impersonal way, but passionately, with the adoring, cherishing love of a parent for a child. The outpouring of his Holy Spirit is really the outpouring of his love, surrounding and penetrating your little soul with a peaceful, joyful delight in his creature: tolerant, peaceful, a love full of longsuffering and gentleness, working quietly, able to wait for results, faithful, devoted, without variableness or shadow of turning. Such is the charity of God.

ABBÉ HENRI DE TOURVILLE

The Infinite Goodness has such 104 wide arms that it takes whatever turns to it.

DANTE ALIGHIERI

GOD'S JUDGMENTS

(See *Justice*)

You have ordained, Lord, and so it 105 is: that every man's inordinate affection is his own punishment.

AUGUSTINE OF HIPPO

Fondly do we hope, fervently do we 106 pray, that this mighty scourge of war may speedily pass away. Yet, if God wills it to continue until all the wealth piled by the bondsman's two hundred and fifty years of unrequited toil shall be sunk, and until every drop of blood drawn with the lash shall be paid by another drawn with the sword, as was said three thousand years ago, so still must it be said, "The judgments of the Lord are true, and righteous altogether."

ABRAHAM LINCOLN

Shall not the judge of all the earth 107 do right?

Genesis 18:25

Stevenson has made a study of the 108 breakdown of a good man's character under a burden for which he is not to blame, in the tragedy of Henry Durie in *The Master of Ballantrae.* Yet he has added, in the mouth of Mackellar, the exact common sense and good theology of the matter, saying "It matters not a jot; for he that is to pass judgment upon the records of our life is the same that formed us in frailty."

GILBERT KEITH CHESTERTON

109 My son, despise not the chastening of the Lord, neither be weary of his correction: for whom the Lord loveth he correcteth; even as a father the son in whom he delighteth.

Proverbs 3:11–12

GOD'S PROVIDENCE

(See *God and His Creation, God and Man*)

110 God's providence is not in baskets lowered from the sky, but through the hands and hearts of those who love him. The lad without food and without shoes made the proper answer to the cruel-minded woman who asked, "But if God loved you wouldn't he send you food and shoes?" The boy replied, "God told someone, but he forgot."

GEORGE A. BUTTRICK

111 Judge not the Lord by feeble sense,
But trust him for his grace;
Behind a frowning providence
He hides a smiling face.

WILLIAM COWPER

112 Providence has at all times been my only dependence, for all other resources seem to have failed us.

GEORGE WASHINGTON

It is a perfectly correct view of 113 things—and strictly consonant with the Gospel—to regard providence across the ages as brooding over the world in ceaseless effort to spare that world its bitter wounds and to bind up its hurts. Most certainly it is God himself who, in the course of the centuries, awakens the great benefactors of mankind, and the great physicians, in ways that agree with the general rhythm of progress. He it is who inspires, even among those furthest from acknowledging his existence, the quest for every means of comfort and every means of healing.

PIERRE TEILHARD DE CHARDIN

"Any news down t'th' village, 114 Ezra?"
"Nuthin' a tall, nuthin' a tall, 'cept for a new baby down t' Tom Lincoln's. Nuthin' ever happens out here."

Dialogue in a cartoon published on Lincoln's birthday

Trusting in him who can go with 115 me, and remain with you, and be everywhere for good, let us confidently hope that all will yet be well.

ABRAHAM LINCOLN

In some good time, his good time, I 116 shall arrive: He guides me and the bird. In his good time!

ROBERT BROWNING

A man's heart deviseth his way: but 117 the Lord directeth his steps.

Proverbs 16:9

118 I came about like a well-handled ship. There stood at the wheel that steersman whom we call God.

ROBERT LOUIS STEVENSON

119 I claim credit for nothing. Everything is determined, the beginning as well as the end, by forces over which we have no control. It is determined for the insect as well as for the star, human beings, vegetables, or cosmic dust, we all dance to a mysterious tune, intoned in the distance by an invisible piper.

ALBERT EINSTEIN

120 The longer I live, the more faith I have in Providence, and the less faith I have in my interpretation of Providence.

JEREMIAH DAY

121 And I said to the man who stood at the gate of the year:
"Give me a light, that I may tread safely into the unknown!"
And he replied:
"Go out into the darkness and put your hand into the Hand of God.
That shall be to you better than light and safer than a known way."

So I went forth, and finding the Hand of God, trod gladly into the night.
And he led me toward the hills and the breaking of day in the lone East.

So, heart, be still!
What need our little life,
Our human life, to know,
If God hath comprehension?
In all the dizzy strife
Of things both high and low
God hideth his intention.

M. LOUISE HASKINS

GOD'S WILL

(See *Acceptance, Communion with God, Faith, Fear of God, Godliness, Obedience, Religion*)

In his will is our peace.   *122*

DANTE ALIGHIERI

Of course, not everything that hap- *123* pens is simply "God's will," and yet in the last resort nothing happens "without your Father's will" (Matt. 10:29), *i.e.* through every event, however untoward, there is access to God.

DIETRICH BONHOEFFER

A man's heart is right when he wills *124* what God wills.

THOMAS AQUINAS

I find that doing the will of God *125* leaves me no time for disputing about his plans.

GEORGE MAC DONALD

There was a man here last night— *126* you needn't be afraid that I shall mention his name—who said that his will was given up to God, and who got mad because the omnibus was full and he had to walk to his lodgings.

DWIGHT L. MOODY

It sometimes comes into my head to *127* wonder whether I have ever properly confessed my sins, whether God has ever forgiven me my sins, whether I am in a good or bad spiritual state. What progress have I made in prayer or the interior life? When this happens I say to myself at once, God has chosen to hide all this from me, so that I may just blindly abandon myself to his mercy. So I submit myself and I adore his decision. . . . He is the Master: may all that he wills be accomplished in me; I want no grace, no merit, no perfection but that which shall please him. His will alone is sufficient for me and that will always be the measure of my desires.

JEAN PIERRE DE CAUSSADE

128 Let us remember these great truths: (1) there is nothing, however small or apparently indifferent, which has not been ordained or permitted by God—even to the fall of a leaf. (2) God is sufficiently wise, good, powerful and merciful to turn those events which are apparently the most calamitous to the good and the advantage of those who know how to adore and accept with humility all that his divine and adorable will permits.

JEAN PIERRE DE CAUSSADE

129 The will of God is not always clear, especially with regard to the intricacies of daily conduct in our baffling world. But often the will is clear, and its main directions are always clear. A man ought not to expect light on God's will in life's intricacies of conduct if he is unwilling to follow a clear will in life's simplicities. Thus when a jaunty skeptic admitted his grave doubts about the Trinity, a man of simple faith rightly answered, "But aren't you weak also on the Ten Commandments?

GEORGE A. BUTTRICK

130 I am approached with the most opposite opinions and advice, and that by religious men, who are equally certain that they represent the divine will. I am sure that either the one or the other' class is mistaken in that belief, and perhaps, in some respects, both. I hope it will not be irreverent for me to say, that if it is probable that God would reveal his will to others, on a point so connected with my duty, it might be supposed that he would reveal it directly to me; for, unless I am more deceived in myself than I often am, it is my earnest desire to know the will of Providence in this matter. And if I can learn what it is, I will do it. These are not, however, the days of miracles, and I suppose it will be granted that I am not to expect a direct revelation. I must study the plain, physical facts of the case, ascertain what is possible, and learn what appears to be wise and right.

ABRAHAM LINCOLN

"The Almighty has his own purposes," said Lincoln in one of his immortal speeches. We should note the profound force of the little word "own" in that statement. Lincoln understood, as too few others do, that *our* purpose may be one thing— and a most high and holy thing, as we see it, that must surely coincide with that of the Almighty himself, while in truth God's "own" purpose is a very different thing, possibly flatly contrary to ours. "The Almighty has *his own* purposes," and we are not privy to them, and he does not seek our counsel.

131

CARROLL E. SIMCOX

GOD'S WORD

(See *Bible*)

132 The word of God is quick, and powerful, and sharper than any two-edged sword, piercing even to the dividing asunder of soul and spirit, and of the joints and marrow, and is a discerner of the thoughts and intents of the heart.

Hebrews 4:12

133 The highest and most satisfactory expression which the New Testament reaches for the true understanding of Jesus is to call him the *Word* of God: he is God's means of communication with the world, God's rational address to mankind.

ALAN RICHARDSON

134 The Lord hath more light and truth yet to break forth out of His Holy Word.

PASTOR JOHN ROBINSON

135 The word of God came to me,
Sitting alone among the multitudes;
And my blind eyes were touched with light.
And there was laid upon my lips a flame of fire.

I laugh and shout for life is good,
Though my feet are set in silent ways.
In merry mood I leave the crowd
To walk in my garden. Ever as I walk
I gather fruits and flowers in my hands.
And with joyful heart I bless the sun
That kindles all the place with radiant life.

I run with playful winds that blow the scent
Of rose and jessamine in eddying whirls.
At last I come where tall lilies grow,
Lifting their faces like white saints to God.
While the lilies pray, I kneel upon the ground;
I have strayed into the holy temple of the Lord.

HELEN KELLER

Christ is God's self-disclosure. He is *136* God showing himself to us in such a way that he leaves no room for doubt or error in our minds as to what God is like. This is why we call him the word of God. A word is a true word only as it reveals him who speaks it. In Christ we do not see all that there is of God; but all that we see in him is God, and it is enough for our present need.

CARROLL E. SIMCOX

GOD'S WRATH

The wrath of God is never thought *137* of in scripture as opposed to his holiness. It is a necessary part of it. Christ would have lost my soul if he had not refused to compromise with me.

ARTHUR J. GOSSIP

Love can forbear, and Love can *138* forgive . . . but Love can never be reconciled to an unlovely object. He can never therefore be reconciled to your sin, because sin itself is incapable of being altered; but he may be reconciled to your person, because that may be restored.

THOMAS TRAHERNE

139 Sometimes my confessor said to me when I repeatedly discussed silly sins with him, "You are a fool. God is not incensed against you, but you are incensed against God. God is not angry with you, but you are angry with God." This was magnificently said.

MARTIN LUTHER

140 God cannot dispel the cowardly thought, that he is anxious only to punish, except by letting his heavy hand abide till it purify also. The permanence of God's wrath is thus an ennobling, not a stupefying doctrine.

GEORGE ADAM SMITH

141 *The wrath of God abideth in him* (St. John 3:36). A sentimental and hedonist generation tries to eliminate "wrath" from its conception of God. Of course, if "anger" and "wrath" are taken to mean the emotional reaction of an irritated self-concern, there is no such thing in God. But if God is holy love, and I am in any degree given to uncleanness or selfishness, then there is, in that degree, stark antagonism in God against me.

WILLIAM TEMPLE

142 The idea of the divine wrath has become strange to our time. We have rejected a religion which seemed to make God a furious tyrant, an individual with passions and desires who committed arbitrary acts. This is not what the wrath of God means. It means the inescapable and unavoidable reaction against every distortion of the law of life, and above all against human pride and arrogance. That reaction, through which man is thrown back into his limits, is not a passionate act of punishment or vengeance on the part of God. It is the re-establishment of the balance between God and man, which is disturbed by man's elevation against God.

PAUL TILLICH

GOD AND HIS CREATION

Any flea as it is in God is nobler 143 than the highest of angels in himself.

MEISTER ECKHART

Every visible or invisible creature is 144 a theophany or appearance of God.

JOHN SCOTUS ERIGENA

Whatever weaknesses, miscalcula- 145 tions, and guilt there are in what precedes the facts, God is in the facts themselves.

DIETRICH BONHOEFFER

The finger of God never leaves iden- 146 tical fingerprints.

STANISLAW J. LEC

The atoms of Democritus   147
And Newton's particles of light
Are sands upon the Red sea shore
Where Israel's tents do shine by
  night.

WILLIAM BLAKE

To look away from the world, or to 148 stare at it, does not help a man to reach God; but he who sees the world in God stands in God's presence.

MARTIN BUBER

149 Earth's crammed with heaven,
And every common bush afire with
  God;
But only he who sees takes off his
  shoes;
The rest sit round it and pluck
  blackberries.
ELIZABETH BARRETT BROWNING

150 Every day God makes silk purses
out of sows' ears.
Anonymous

151 Thus does the world forget thee, its
creator, and falls in love with what
thou hast created instead of with
thee.
AUGUSTINE OF HIPPO

152 The end of God's creating the world
was to prepare a kingdom for his
Son.
JONATHAN EDWARDS

153 The essence of the doctrine of Creation is not that God inaugurated the
existence of the world at a particular
moment of time, but that the world
owes its existence—not only its beginning—to his volitional activity.
WILLIAM TEMPLE

154 How the world is managed, and
why it was created, I cannot tell; but
it is no feather-bed for the repose of
sluggards.
A.E. HOUSMAN

155 I hold there is a general beauty in
the works of God, and therefore no
deformity in any kind or species of
creature whatsoever. I cannot tell by
what logic we call a toad, a bear, or
an elephant ugly, they being created
in those outward shapes and figures
which best express the actions of
their inward forms, and having

passed that general visitation of
God, who saw that all that he had
made was good, that is, conforma-
ble to his will, which abhors deformity and is the rule of order and
beauty.
THOMAS BROWNE

The whole difference between con- **156**
struction and creation is exactly
this: that a thing constructed can
only be loved after it is constructed;
but a thing created is loved before it
exists.
GILBERT KEITH CHESTERTON

The creation of the world—that is to **157**
say, the world of civilized order—is
the victory of persuasion over force.
ALFRED NORTH WHITEHEAD

No rain, no mushrooms. No God, **158**
no world.
African saying

God was making you ten billion **159**
years ago, and he knew what he was
doing: setting up a world you could
live in and lining up an ancestry for
you. He is making you now, and
knows what he is doing. He will be
making you ten billion years from
now, and knowing what he is doing.
CARROLL E. SIMCOX

GOD AND MAN

Where there is no God, there is no **160**
man.
NICHOLAS BERDYAEV

The weakest of sinners can either **161**
frustrate or crown a hope of God.
CHARLES PÉGUY

162 Woe unto him that striveth with his Maker! Let the potsherd strive with the potsherds of the earth. Shall the clay say to him that fashioneth it, What makest thou? or thy work, he hath no hands?

Isaiah 45:9

163 For my thoughts are not as your thoughts, neither your ways my ways, saith the Lord.

Isaiah 55:8

164 A man with God is always in the majority.

JOHN KNOX

165 Man is man's A.B.C. There is none that can
Read God aright, unless he first spell Man.

FRANCIS QUARLES

166 Only a person can truly utter a person. Only from a character can a character be echoed. You might write it all over the skies that God was just, but it would not burn there. It would be, at best, only a bit of knowledge; never a Gospel; never something which it would gladden men's hearts to know. That comes only when a human life, capable of a justice like God's, made just by God, glows with his justice in the eyes of men, a candle of the Lord.

PHILLIPS BROOKS

167 Full of Zeus are all the streets and all the marketplaces of men.

ARATUS

168 Do everything as though success depended on you alone, but expect nothing save from God.

IGNATIUS LOYOLA

169 For God made man (as it were) for his play-fellow.

THOMAS VAUGHAN

170 What else can I, a lame old man, do but sing hymns to God? If, indeed, I were a nightingale, I should be singing as a nightingale; if a swan, as a swan. But as it is, I am a rational being, therefore I must be singing hymns of praise to God. This is my task; I do it, and will not desert my post, as long as it may be given me to fill it; and I exhort you to join me in this same song.

EPICTETUS

171 God be praised,
Antonio Stradivari has an eye
That winces at false work and loves the true . . .
And for my fame—when any master holds
'Twixt chin and hand a violin of mine,
He will be glad that Stradivari lived,
Made violins, and made them of the best . . .

I say not God himself can make man's best
Without best men to help him . . .
'Tis God gives skill,
But not without men's hands: he could not make
Antonio Stradivari's violins
Without Antonio.

GEORGE ELIOT

172 When God wishes to perform in us, through us, and with us some act of great charity, he first proposed it to us by his inspiration, then we favor it, and finally we consent to it.

FRANCIS DE SALES

173 There is in this world no gulf between higher and lower human

beings. To each is the highest open. Each life has its entrance to reality, each kind of man has his eternal right. From each thing does a way lead to God.

MARTIN BUBER

174 God wants only one thing in the whole world—to find the innermost part of the spirit of man clean and ready for him to accomplish the divine purpose therein. He has all power in heaven and earth, but the power to do his work in man against man's will he has not got.

JOHN TAULER

175 Without God, we cannot. Without us, God will not.

AUGUSTINE OF HIPPO

176 The compassion that you see in the kindhearted is God's compassion: he has given it to them to protect the helpless.

SRI RAMAKRISHNA

177 God is complete for himself, while for us he is continually being born.

PIERRE TEILHARD DE CHARDIN

178 Behold, I stand at the door, and knock: if any man hear my voice, and open the door, I will come in to him, and will sup with him, and he with me.

Revelation 3:20

HOLY SPIRIT

179 The fruit of the Spirit is love, joy, peace, longsuffering, gentleness, goodness, faith, meekness, temperance.

Galatians 5:22–23

God hath not given us the spirit of 180 fear; but of power, and of love, and of a sound mind.

II Timothy 1:7

The Holy Spirit is the living interior- 181 ity of God.

ROMANO GUARDINI

No, I do not think that any man 182 may ever expect to know God and to define him. But there is an extraordinary something which happens now and then in the human spirit. There comes to the soul a second wind. A man gets a chance to say to himself, and to say truthfully: "This thing I have done is magnificent. I didn't know I had it in me."

HEYWOOD BROUN

The Spirit of God first imparts love; 183 he next inspires hope, and then gives liberty; and that is about the last thing we have in many of our churches.

DWIGHT L. MOODY

I should as soon attempt to raise 184 flowers if there were no atmosphere, or produce fruits if there were neither light nor heat, as to regenerate men if I did not believe there was a Holy Ghost.

HENRY WARD BEECHER

Our prayer will certainly gain in 185 depth and aliveness, if we continually think of God as the true inspirer of our most original-seeming thoughts and wishes, whensoever these are good and fruitful—as him who secretly initiates what he openly crowns.

FRIEDRICH VON HÜGEL

186 Before Christ sent the church into the world he sent the Spirit into the church. The same order must be observed today.

JOHN R.W. STOTT

187 He does not take the place of an absent Christ, or work in his stead; his mission is to bring Christ, to ensure his Presence. Before, Christ had been *with* them; now, through the agency of the Holy Ghost, he is to be *in* them; his Presence and action is central, not on the circumference as before. The descent of the Holy Ghost at Pentecost was a change in the manner of his working, a change which may be described as both an extension and an intensification.

FRANK H. HALLOCK

188 Cleanse the thoughts of our hearts by the inspiration of thy Holy Spirit, that we may perfectly love thee, and worthily magnify thy holy name.

Book of Common Prayer

189 The Comforter, which is the Holy Ghost, whom the Father will send in my name, he shall teach you all things, and bring all things to your remembrance, whatsoever I have said unto you.

John 14:26

190 I am sure there is a common Spirit that plays within us, yet makes no part of us; and that is the Spirit of God, the fire and scintillation of that noble and mighty essence which is the life and radical heat of spirits, and those essences that know not the virtue of the sun; a fire quite contrary to the fire of hell. This is the gentle heat that brooded on the waters, and in six days hatched the world; this is that irradiation that dispels the mists of hell, the clouds of horror, fear, sorrow, despair, and preserves the region of the mind in serenity. Whosoever feels not the warm gale and gentle ventilation of this Spirit, though I feel his pulse I dare not say he lives: for truly, without this, to me there is no heat under the tropic, nor any light, though I dwelt in the body of the sun.

THOMAS BROWNE

191 The gift of the Holy Ghost closes the last gap between the life of God and ours. . . . When we allow the love of God to move in us, we can no longer distinguish ours and his; he becomes us, he lives us. It is the firstfruits of the Spirit, the beginning of our being made divine.

AUSTIN FARRER

192 The Holy Ghost is that which is good in everything. In every object, in every man, in every event, there is something good, not in a philosophical and not in a mystical sense, but in the simplest psychological and everyday sense. If a man does not see this good, if he condemns everything irrevocably, if he seeks and sees only the bad, if he is incapable of seeing the good in things and people—then this is the blasphemy against the Holy Ghost.

P.D. OUSPENSKY

193 The Spirit also helpeth our infirmities: for we know not what we should pray for as we ought: but the Spirit itself maketh intercession for us with groanings which cannot be uttered.

Romans 8:26

194 Pure and genuine love always desires above all to dwell wholly in the
truth, whatever it may be, uncondi-
tionally. Every other sort of love
desires before anything else means
of satisfaction, and for this reason is
a source of error and falsehood.
Pure and genuine love is in itself
spirit of truth. It is the Holy Spirit.
The Greek word which is translated
spirit means literally fiery breath,
breath mingled with fire, and it
represented, in antiquity, the notion
which science represents today by
the word energy. What we translate
by "spirit of truth" signifies the
energy of truth, truth as an active
force. Pure love is this active force,
the love that will not at any price,
under any condition, have anything
to do with either falsehood or error.

SIMONE WEIL

195 Those who have the gale of the Holy
Spirit go forward even in sleep.

BROTHER LAWRENCE

196 Every time we say "I believe in the
Holy Spirit" we mean that we believe there is a living God able and
willing to enter human personality
and change it.

J.B. PHILLIPS

HOLY TRINITY

197 We are enclosed in the Father, and
we are enclosed in the Son, and we
are enclosed in the Holy Ghost.
And the Father is enclosed in us,
and the Son is enclosed in us, and
the Holy Ghost is enclosed in us:
Almightiness, All Wisdom, All
Goodness: one God, one Lord.

LADY JULIAN OF NORWICH

God dwells in our heart by faith, *198*
and Christ by his Spirit, and the
Spirit by his purities: so that we are
also cabinets of the mysterious Trinity: and what is this short of heaven
itself, but as infancy is short of
manhood, and letters of words?

JEREMY TAYLOR

It (Christ's incarnate life) was a life *199*
of self-giving in response to the
Father's love, through the Spirit.
The doctrine of the Trinity is the
projection into eternity of this essential relationship, the assertion that
eternally the Divine Life is a life of
mutual self-giving to one another of
Father and Son through the Spirit
who is the *vinculum* or bond of love
between them.

LEONARD HODGSON

An ordinary simple Christian kneels *200*
down to say his prayers. He is trying
to get into touch with God. But if he
is a Christian he knows that what is
prompting him to pray is also God:
God, so to speak, inside him. But he
also knows that all his real knowledge of God comes through Christ,
the Man who was God—that Christ
is standing beside him, helping him
to pray, praying for him. You see
what is happening. God is the thing
to which he is praying—the goal he
is trying to reach. God is also the
thing inside him which is pushing
him on—the motive power. God is
also the road or bridge along which
he is being pushed to that goal. So
that the whole threefold life of the
three-personal Being is actually
going on in that ordinary little bed-
room where an ordinary man is
saying his prayers. The man is being
caught up into the higher kind of
life—what I call *Zoe* or spiritual life:

he is being pulled into God, by God, while still remaining himself.

C.S. LEWIS

201 Think of the Father as a spring of life begetting the Son like a river and the Holy Ghost like a sea, for the spring and the river and the sea are all one nature. Think of the Father as a root, of the Son as a branch, and of the Spirit as a fruit, for the substance in these three is one. The Father is a sun with the Son as rays and the Holy Ghost as heat. The Holy Trinity transcends by far every similitude and figure. So, when you hear of an offspring of the Father, do not think of a corporeal offspring. And when you hear that there is a Word, do not suppose him to be a corporeal word. And when you hear of the Spirit of God, do not think of wind and breath. Rather, hold your persuasion with a simple faith alone. For the concept of the Creator is arrived at by analogy from his creatures.

JOHN OF DAMASCUS

202 The Father's is the goodwill and command. The Son executes and fabricates. The spirit nourishes and increases.

G.L. PRESTIGE

KNOWLEDGE OF GOD

(See *Faith*)

203 All living knowledge of God rests upon his foundation: that we experience him in our lives as Will-to-Love.

ALBERT SCHWEITZER

It is easy to know God so long as 204 you do not tax yourself with defining him.

JOSEPH JOUBERT

Men may tire themselves in a laby- 205 rinth of search, and talk of God: but if we would know him indeed, it must be from the impressions we receive of him; and the softer our hearts are, the deeper and livelier those will be upon us.

WILLIAM PENN

For we behold him but asquint, 206 upon reflex or shadow; our understanding is dimmer than Moses' eye; we are ignorant of the back-parts or lower side of his divinity; therefore to pry into the maze of his counsels is not only folly in man, but presumption even in angels.

THOMAS BROWNE

We can no more find a method for 207 knowing God than for making God, because the knowledge of God is God himself dwelling in the soul. The most we can do is to prepare for his entry, to get out of his way, to remove the barriers, for until God acts in us there is nothing positive that we can do in this direction.

ALAN W. WATTS

Canst thou by searching find out 208 God? canst thou find out the Almighty unto perfection? It is as high as heaven; what canst thou do? deeper than hell; what canst thou know?

Job 11:7–8

By faith we know his existence; in 209 glory we shall know his nature.

BLAISE PASCAL

210 I myself believe that the evidence for God lies primarily in inner personal experiences.

WILLIAM JAMES

211 God is more truly imagined than expressed, and he exists more truly than he is imagined.

AUGUSTINE OF HIPPO

212 God never meant that man should scale the heavens
By strides of human wisdom. In his works,
Though wondrous, he commands us in his word
To seek him rather where his mercy shines.

WILLIAM COWPER

213 The best way to know God is to love many things.

VINCENT VAN GOGH

214 Men talk of "finding God," but no wonder it is difficult; he is hidden in that darkest hiding-place, your heart. You yourself are a part of him.

CHRISTOPHER MORLEY

215 God often visits us, but most of the time we are not at home.

JOSEPH ROUX

LOVE FOR GOD

216 The Lord direct your hearts into the love of God, and into patient waiting for Christ.

II Thessalonians 3:5

217 God does not need us to say many words to him, nor to think many thoughts. He sees our hearts, and that is enough for him. He sees very well our suffering and our submission. We have only to repeat continuously to a person we love, "I love you with all my heart." It even often happens that we go a long time without thinking that we love him, and we love him no less during this period than in those in which we make him the most tender protestations. True love rests in the depths of the heart.

FRANÇOIS FÉNELON

218 The reason why God's servants love creatures so much is that they see how much Christ loves them, and it is one of the properties of love to love what is loved by the person we love.

CATHERINE OF SIENA

219 Love of God is the root, love of our neighbor the fruit, of the Tree of Life. Neither can exist without the other; but the one is cause and the other effect, and the order of the Two Great Commandments must not be inverted.

WILLIAM TEMPLE

220 It is always springtime in the heart that loves God.

JEAN VIANNEY, the Curé d'Ars

221 You want to compete with his affection before you have understood it; that is your mistake. . . . Come, then! Show a little more deference to our Lord and allow him to go first. Let him love you a great deal before you have succeeded in loving him even a little as you would wish to love him. That is all that our Lord asks of you.

HENRI DE TOURVILLE

222 To believe in God is to love him.
     MIGUEL DE UNAMUNO

223 If a man say, I love God, and hateth
     his brother, he is a liar: for he that
     loveth not his brother whom he hath
     seen, how can he love God whom he
     hath not seen?
     I John 4:20

224 God forces no one, for love cannot
     compel, and God's service, there-
     fore, is a thing of perfect freedom.
     HANS DENK

225 Some people want to see God with
     their eyes as they see a cow, and to
     love him as they love their cow—for
     the milk and cheese and profit it
     brings them. This is how it is with
     people who love God for the sake of
     outward wealth or inward comfort.
     They do not rightly love God, when
     they love him for their own advan-
     tage. Indeed, I tell you the truth,
     any object you have in your mind,
     however good, will be a barrier
     between you and the inmost Truth.
     MEISTER ECKHART

226 There is scarcely anything which the
     understanding can know about
     God, but the will can love him most
     deeply. Let a man imprison himself
     within himself, in the center of his
     soul, where the image of God is, and
     there let him wait upon God, as one
     listens to another speaking from
     some high tower, or as though one
     had him within his heart, and as if in
     all creation there were nothing else
     save the soul and God. He should
     even forget himself and what he is
     doing, for, as one of the Fathers
     said, "perfect prayer is that in which
     he who is praying is unaware that he
     is praying at all."
     PETER OF ALCÁNTARA

227 When I think upon my God, my
     heart is so full of joy that the notes
     dance and leap from my pen; and
     since God has given me a cheerful
     heart it will be pardoned me that I
     serve him with a cheerful spirit.
     FRANZ JOSEF HAYDN

228 Too late I loved you, O beauty so
     ancient yet ever new! Too late I
     loved you! And, behold, you were
     within me, and I out of myself, and
     there I searched for you.
     AUGUSTINE OF HIPPO

MYSTICISM

(See *Communion with God, Faith, God and Man, Holy Spirit, Love for God, Meditation, Prayer, Religion, Worship*)

229 Mysticism keeps men sane. As long
     as you have mystery you have
     health; when you destroy mystery
     you create morbidity. The ordinary
     man has always been a mystic. He
     has permitted the twilight. He has
     always had one foot in earth and the
     other in fairyland. He has always
     left himself free to doubt his gods;
     but (unlike the agnostic of today)
     free also to believe in them. He has
     always cared more for truth than for
     consistency. If he saw two truths
     that seemed to contradict each
     other, he would take the two truths
     and the contradiction along with
     them.
     GILBERT KEITH CHESTERTON

230 Of all things good and fair and holy
     there is a spiritual cognisance which
     precedes and is independent of that

knowledge which the understanding conveys.

JOHN CAIRD

231 "What," it will be questioned, "when the sun rises, do you not see a round disc of fire somewhat like a guinea?" "O no, no, I see an innumerable company of the heavenly host crying, 'Holy, Holy, Holy, is the Lord God Almighty!' "

WILLIAM BLAKE

232   I have seen
A curious child, who dwelt upon a tract
Of inland ground, applying to his ear
The convolutions of a smooth-lipped shell;
To which, in silence hushed, his very soul
Listened intensely; and his countenance soon
Brightened with joy; for from within were heard
Murmurings, whereby the monitor expressed
Mysterious union with its native sea.
Even such a shell the universe itself
Is to the ear of Faith; and there are times,
I doubt not, when to you it doth impart
Authentic tidings of invisible things;
Of ebb and flow, and ever-during power;
And central peace, subsisting at the heart
Of endless agitation.

WILLIAM WORDSWORTH

PEACE OF GOD

233 God's peace is that existence-form in which our lives as Christians, in all their totality, are set. We like to imagine that peace is a delicate thing, which we must lock up within ourselves, and protect, and hide in the depths of our hearts, so that it may not be lost or be evaporated. But in the Scriptures peace is spoken of in an utterly different way. There it is said that God's peace is a mighty power, which of itself can keep our hearts and our thoughts. God's peace is a mighty fortress, in which we are well defended and safe against all hostile powers of destruction. It is not we who are to protect peace, but rather it is peace which is to protect us.

ANDERS NYGREN

Peace may be translated "har- 234 mony." Harmony with one's self is integrity; harmony with life itself is gratitude; harmony with people is brotherhood; harmony with God is faith. All this adds up to the meaning of peace. It is the gift of Christ.

OSCAR F. BLACKWELDER

A great many people are trying to 235 make peace, but that has already been done. God has not left it for us to do; all we have to do is to enter into it.

DWIGHT L. MOODY

They cast their nets in Galilee   236
Just off the fields of brown;
Such happy, simple fisher folk,
Before the Lord came down.

Contented, peaceful fishermen,
Before they ever knew
The peace of God that filled their hearts
Brimful, and broke them too.

Young John who trimmed the flapping sail,

Homeless, in Patmos died.
Peter, who hauled the teeming net,
Head-down was crucified.

The peace of God, it is no peace,
But strife closed in the sod.
Yet, brothers, pray for but one
    thing—
The marvelous peace of God.

WILLIAM ALEXANDER PERCY

237 The more a man gives up his heart
to God, to his vocation and to men,
forgetful of himself and of that
which belongs to him—the greater
poise he will acquire, until he
reaches peace, quiet, joy: the apan-
age of simple and humble souls.

FATHER YELCHANINOV

238 The Stoics of old used to debate
whether a good and wise man could
be happy while stretched out on a
rack. An English wag once com-
mented: "Well, maybe a very good
man on a very bad rack!" This
question is better pondered in a
classroom or over the tea cups than
on a real rack in good working
order. But in any case the Stoic's
question envisions a peace funda-
mentally different from the peace of
God. The peace of God is that
peace with God which is given to
him who finds his sole joy in doing
God's will. Paul had no peace with
God until he gave himself over to
the complete obedience of Christ.
Then his peace began—and also his
troubles. The peace of God in this
world does not provide a happy
adjustment to the circumstances of
this world. That happy adjustment
will come only in heaven. But the
real, all-out Christian is content to
have it so.

CARROLL E. SIMCOX

PRAYER

I have lived to thank God that all 239
my prayers have not been answered.

JEAN INGELOW

He who rises from his knees a better 240
man, his prayer has been granted.

GEORGE MEREDITH

Christians and camels receive their 241
burdens kneeling.

AMBROSE BIERCE

Pray not for lighter burdens but for 242
stronger backs.

THEODORE ROOSEVELT

Prayer is the effort to live in the 243
spirit of the whole.

SAMUEL TAYLOR COLERIDGE

In prayer it is better to have a heart 244
without words, than words without
a heart.

JOHN BUNYAN

God only comes to those who ask 245
him to come; and he cannot refuse
to come to those who implore him
long, often, and ardently.

SIMONE WEIL

If your prayer is selfish, the answer 246
will be something that will rebuke
your selfishness. You may not recognize it as having come at all, but it
is sure to be there.

WILLIAM TEMPLE

In our Lord's teaching about peti- 247
tionary prayer there are three main
principles. The first is confidence,
the second is perseverance, and the
third, for lack of a better word, I will
call correspondence with Christ.

WILLIAM TEMPLE

248 God answers sharp and sudden on some prayers,
And thrusts the thing we have prayed for in our face,
A gauntlet with a gift in't.
ELIZABETH BARRETT BROWNING

249 Prayer does not change God, but it changes him who prays.
SØREN KIERKEGAARD

250 He gave them their request; but sent leanness into their soul.
Psalm 106:15

251 I would have no desire other than to accomplish thy will. Teach me to pray; pray thyself in me.
FRANÇOIS FÉNELON

252 I love to pray at sunrise—before the world becomes polluted with vanity and hatred.
THE KORETSER RABBI

253 A Master said: "Mankind thinks it prays to God; it is not so, for prayer itself is the Divine."
MARTIN BUBER

254 Deep down in me I knowed it was a lie, and He knowed it. You can't pray a lie—I found that out.
MARK TWAIN *(Huck Finn)*

255 Do I want to pray or only to think about my human problems? Do I want to pray or simply kneel there contemplating my sorrow? Do I want to direct my prayer towards God or let it direct itself towards me?
HUBERT VAN ZELLER

256 Prayer is for the religious life what original research is for science—by it we get direct contact with reality . . . We pray because we are made for prayer, and God draws us out by breathing himself in.
P.T. FORSYTH

257 You need not cry very loud: he is nearer to us than we think.
BROTHER LAWRENCE

258 Prayer from the heart can achieve what nothing else can in the world.
MOHANDAS GANDHI

259 They tell about a fifteen-year-old boy in an orphans' home who had an incurable stutter. It was agony for him to talk to strangers. One Sunday the minister who came out regularly from town was detained, and the boy, to the surprise of the people in charge, volunteered to say the prayer in his stead. He did it perfectly, too, with the proper reverence and without a single stutter. Later, he explained, "I don't stutter when I talk to God. He loves me."
BENNETT CERF

260 There is nothing that makes us love a man so much as praying for him.
WILLIAM LAW

261 I asked for strength that I might achieve.
  He made me weak that I might obey.
I asked for health that I might do greater things.
  I was given grace that I might do better things.
I asked for riches that I might be happy.
  I was given poverty that I might be wise.
I asked for power that I might have the praise of men.

I was given weakness that I might feel the need of God.
I asked for all things that I might enjoy life.
I was given life that I might enjoy all things.
I received nothing that I asked for.
All that I hoped for.
My prayer was answered.

*Found on the body
of a Confederate soldier*

RELIGION

262 When God reveals himself to man, then a characteristic disturbance is set up in the human soul and in the life of our human society, and that disturbance is what we mean by religion.

JOHN BAILLIE

263 Were one asked to characterize the life of religion in the broadest and most general terms possible, one might say that it consists of the belief that there is an unseen order, and that our supreme good lies in harmoniously adjusting ourselves thereto. This belief and this adjustment are the religious attitude in the soul.

WILLIAM JAMES

264 Religion is the love of life in the consciousness of impotence.

GEORGE SANTAYANA

265 Good men use the world in order to enjoy God, whereas bad men want to use God in order to enjoy the world.

AUGUSTINE OF HIPPO

Men never do evil so completely 266 and cheerfully as when they do it from religious conviction.

BLAISE PASCAL

Religion consists in believing that 267 everything that happens is extraordinarily important. It can never disappear from the world, precisely for this reason.

CESARE PAVESE

Faith is never identical with piety. 268

KARL BARTH

Religion is a process of turning your 269 skull into a tabernacle, not of going up to Jerusalem once a year.

AUSTIN O'MALLEY

The publicity surrounding religious 270 activities is usually in inverse ratio to their intrinsic importance.

AELRED GRAHAM

Religion is what the individual does 271 with his own solitariness.

ALFRED NORTH WHITEHEAD

Religion is world loyalty. 272

ALFRED NORTH WHITEHEAD

All divinity is love or wonder. 273

JOHN DONNE

Religion has not civilized man, man 274 has civilized religion.

ROBERT G. INGERSOLL

A religious life is a struggle and not 275 a hymn.

MME. GERMAINE NECKER DE STAËL

Science without religion is lame; 276 religion without science is blind.

ALBERT EINSTEIN

277 That religion cannot be right that a man is the worse for having.
WILLIAM PENN

278 Those who say that religion has nothing to do with politics do not know what religion means.
MOHANDAS GANDHI

279 Pure religion and undefiled before God and the Father is this, To visit the fatherless and widows in their affliction, and to keep himself unspotted from the world.
James 1:27

REVELATION

280 Unless all things are revelation, nothing can be revelation. Unless the rising of the sun reveals God, the rising of the Son of Man from the dead cannot reveal God.
WILLIAM TEMPLE

281 The knowledge of man is as the waters, some descending from above, and some springing up from beneath; the one informed by the light of nature, the other inspired by divine revelation.
FRANCIS BACON

282 It [the church] is . . . a community of faith grounded in a certain revelation of God. Now, if this revelation is analyzed, it is found to be understood by the Bible (the accepted norm of the church's belief) as imparted, not as proposition, but as presence. It is not the communication of oracles about things in heaven, on earth, and under the earth, past, present, and future; rather, it is encounter with the living God, who discloses himself for what he is in the act of answering man's need and demanding his obedience in the here and now of his personal and social existence. It speaks to him of a Presence and therefore of the present, of an insistent succor and demand confronting him for acceptance or rejection. All revelation is of a now and for a now. It is not in itself information about the past or the future.
JOHN A.T. ROBINSON

283 A Revelation is religious doctrine viewed on its illuminated side; a Mystery is the self-same doctrine viewed on the side unilluminated.
JOHN HENRY NEWMAN

284 Revelation is not information about divine things; it is the ecstatic manifestation of the Ground of Being in events, persons, and things. Such manifestations have shaking, transforming, and healing power. They are saving events in which the power of the New Being is present.
PAUL TILLICH

285 We do not believe that God has added, or ever will add, anything to his revelation in his Son. But we can now see many things in that revelation which could not be seen by those who first received it. Each generation of Christians, and each people to which the Christian Gospel is preached, makes its own contribution to the understanding of the riches of Jesus Christ.
C.B. MOSS

REVERENCE

286   Our courteous Lord willeth that we
should be as homely with him as
heart may think or soul may desire.
But let us beware that we take not
recklessly this homeliness as to leave
courtesy.

LADY JULIAN OF NORWICH

287   Fear God, and where you go men
will think they walk in hallowed
cathedrals.

RALPH WALDO EMERSON

288   With the people, and especially with
the clergymen, who have God daily
upon their tongues, God becomes a
phrase, a mere name, which they
utter without any accompanying
idea. But if they were penetrated
with his greatness, they would rather
be dumb, and for very reverence
would not dare to name him.

JOHANN WOLFGANG VON GOETHE

289   Lambs have the grace to kneel while
nursing.

Chinese proverb

290   O my Lord! If I worship thee from
fear of hell, burn me in hell. If I
worship thee from hope of paradise,
exclude me thence. But if I worship
thee for thine own sake, then with-
hold not from me thine eternal
beauty.

Moslem prayer

291   I will give thanks unto thee, for I am
fearfully and wonderfully made:
marvellous are thy works, and that
my soul knoweth right well.

Psalm 139:13

A deep reverence for human life is   292
worth more than a thousand executions for the prevention of murder;
and is, in fact, the great security of
human life. The law of capital punishment, whilst pretending to support this reverence, does in fact tend
to destroy it.

JOHN BRIGHT

Be reverent before the dawning day.   293
Do not think of what will be in a
year, or in ten years. Think of today.
Leave your theories. All theories,
you see, even those of virtue, are
bad, foolish, mischievous. Do not
abuse life. Live in today. Be reverent
towards each day. Love it, respect it,
do not sully it, do not hinder it from
coming to flower. Love it even when
it is gray and sad like today. Do not
be anxious. See. It is winter now.
Everything is asleep. The good earth
will wake again. You have only to
be good and patient like the earth.
Be reverent. Wait.

ROMAIN ROLLAND

Christians often talk far too glibly   294
and easily about God. "I have heard
students," says Professor Eugen
Rosenstock-Huessy, "talking about
the attributes of God in a way that
made me feel ashamed. They knew
everything 'about' God, except that
he was listening to them. They
showed no signs of shame. They
were theological students." Dietrich
Bonhoeffer says more than once in

his letters from prison that he finds a continually deepening meaning in the fact that the Israelites never allowed themselves to pronounce the name of God.

J.H. OLDHAM

295 Reverence is the attitude which can be designated as the mother of all moral life, for in it man first takes a posi..on toward the world which opens his spiritual eyes and enables him to grasp values.

DIETRICH VON HILDEBRAND

296 God is in heaven, and thou upon earth: therefore let thy words be few.

Ecclesiastes 5:2

297 Orthodoxy is reticence.

Anonymous

298 How can you expect God to speak in that gentle and inward voice which melts the soul, when you are making so much noise with your rapid reflections? Be silent, and God will speak again.

FRANÇOIS FÉNELON

299 Dangerous it were for the feeble brain of man to wade far into the doings of the Most High; whom although to know be life, and joy to make mention of his name; yet our soundest knowledge is to know that we know him: and our safest eloquence concerning him is our silence, when we confess without confession that his glory is inexplicable, his greatness above our capacity and reach. He is above, and we upon earth; therefore it behoveth our words to be wary and few.

RICHARD HOOKER

THEOLOGY

(See *God and His Creation, God and Man, Knowledge of God*)

Theology is a science, but at the 300 same time how many sciences? A man is a substance, but if you dissect him what is he? Head, heart, stomach, veins, each vein, each bit of vein, blood, each humor of blood?

BLAISE PASCAL

It has not pleased God to save his 301 people by dialectic *(Non in dialectica placuit Deo salvum facere populum suum).*

AMBROSE OF MILAN

Theology is but an appendix to love, 302 and an unreliable appendix!

TOYOHIKO KAGAWA

There used to be a thing called 303 theology, which is the Greek for thinking about God. It is very old-fashioned now. Instead there is a thing called the philosophy of religion, which means thinking about your own nice feelings. It's very popular.

FATHER KELLY,
*quoted by William Temple
in* The Universality of Christ

It is the heart that makes the theolo- 304 gian.

MARCUS FABIUS QUINTILIAN

The reason why the churches are 305 discredited today is not that they are too bigoted about theology, but that they have run away from theology.

DOROTHY L. SAYERS

306 Inspiration without theology is like the grin of the cat without the cat.
Anonymous

307 Theology is but our ideas of truth classified and arranged.
HENRY WARD BEECHER

308 Love is the abridgement of all theology.
FRANCIS DE SALES

309 As the grave grows nearer my theology is growing strangely simple, and it begins and ends with Christ as the only Savior of the lost.
HENRY BENJAMIN WHIPPLE

WORSHIP

310 Have I knowledge? confounded it shrivels at Wisdom laid bare.
Have I forethought? how purblind, how blank, to the Infinite Care!
Do I task any faculty highest, to image success?
I but open my eyes,—and perfection, no more and no less,
In the kind I imagined, full-fronts me, and God is seen God
In the star, in the stone, in the flesh, in the soul and the clod.
And thus looking within and around me, I ever renew
(With that stoop of the soul which in bending upraises it too)
The submission of man's nothing-perfect to God's all-complete,
As by each new obeisance in spirit, I climb to his feet.
ROBERT BROWNING

311 Vainly we offer each ample oblation,
Vainly with gifts would his favor secure;
Richer by far is the heart's adoration,
Dearer to God are the prayers of the poor.
REGINALD HEBER

312 Nothing is so deadening to the divine as an habitual dealing with the outsides of holy things.
GEORGE MAC DONALD

313 The gods we worship write their names on our faces, be sure of that. And a man will worship something —have no doubt about that, either. He may think that his tribute is paid in secret in the dark recesses of his heart—but it will out. That which dominates will determine his life and character. Therefore, it behooves us to be careful what we worship, for what we are worshipping we are becoming.
RALPH WALDO EMERSON

314 The true inner life is no strange or new thing; it is the ancient and true worship of God, the Christian life in its beauty and in its own peculiar form. Wherever there is a man who fears God and lives the good life, in any country under the sun, God is there, loving him, and so I love him too.
GERHARD TERSTEEGEN

315 Ceremony keeps up all things. 'Tis like a penny glass to a rich spirit, or some excellent water. Without it the water were spilt, the spirit lost.
JOHN SELDEN

316 At my devotion I love to use the civility of my knee, my hat, and hand.
THOMAS BROWNE

317 The more beautiful and elaborate our worship becomes, the greater is the danger of formalism. No worship, indeed, is free from this danger: the Puritan may be as superstitious in his use of the Bible as any ceremonialist in his use of ornaments; but if our worship is elaborate, and requires a great deal of time and attention to be given to its performance, the spirit, without which all ceremonies are useless, may be neglected. Therefore there must be in all Christian worship an element of puritanism. The true puritan does not despise or reject the use of material beauty in worship, but he uses it with restraint. The Cistercians were the great puritans in the medieval church.

C.B. MOSS

318 To this purpose of exciting love it is good that we transplant the instruments of fancy into religion; and for this reason music was brought into churches, and ornaments, and perfumes, and comely garments, and solemnities, and decent ceremonies, that the busy and less discerning fancy, being bribed with its proper objects, may be instrumental to a more celestial and spiritual love.

JEREMY TAYLOR

319 God is the supreme artist. He loves to have things beautiful. Look at the sunset and the flowers and the snow-capped mountains and the stars. They are beautiful because they come from God. God loves to have things beautiful in church, too. And the same goes for church courtesies. To show our reverence for the Cross on which he died for us, and for the Sacrament in which he comes to our hearts, is just to be polite to God. This is not required, but it is the part of Christian good breeding. It has the importance that courtesy has the world over.

JOHN S. BALDWIN

RITUALISM, *n.* A Dutch Garden *320* of God where He may walk in rectilinear freedom, keeping off the grass.

AMBROSE BIERCE,
The Devil's Dictionary

The Curé of Ars noticed a peasant *321* farmer frequently kneel in church for long periods without the slightest movement of his lips, and asked him: "What do you say to our Lord during these long visits?" He replied: "I say nothing to him. I look at him and he looks at me."

A. MONNIN

They that wait upon the Lord shall *322* renew their strength; they shall mount up with wings as eagles; they shall run, and not be weary; and they shall walk, and not faint.

Isaiah 40:31

II

Creation

When God began to create. . . .

Genesis 1:1
(*translated by Theodore J. Meek,*
in The Complete Bible).

Glory be to God for dappled things—
   For skies of couple-color as a brindled cow;
     For rose-moles all in stipple upon trout that
swim;
Fresh fire-coal chestnut-falls; finches' wings;
   Landscape plotted and pieced—fold, fallow, and
plow;
     And all trades, their gear and tackle and trim.

All things counter, original, spare, strange;
   Whatever is fickle, freckled (who knows how?)
     With swift, slow; sweet, sour; adazzle, dim;
He fathers-forth whose beauty is past change:
     Praise him.

Gerard Manley Hopkins

It is quite certain that we must not lay any vileness
to the charge of the All.

Plotinus

ANGELS

323 Be not forgetful to entertain
strangers: for thereby some have
entertained angels unawares.
Hebrews 13:2

324 It is not because angels are holier
than men or devils that makes them
angels, but because they do not
expect holiness from one another,
but from God alone.
WILLIAM BLAKE

325 Messengers clad in the swiftness of
   light,
Subtle as flame, and creative in
   might,
Helmed with the truth and with
   charity shod,
Wielding the wind of the purpose of
   God!
PERCY DEARMER

326 The virtue of angels is that they
cannot deteriorate; their flaw is that
they cannot improve. Man's flaw is
that he can deteriorate; and his
virtue is that he can improve.
Hasidic saying

327 Through intelligence and knowledge
man comes to resemble the character of the angels.
SOLOMON IBN GABIROL

328 The question of how many angels
could dance on the point of a pin no
longer is absurd in molecular phys-
ics, with its discovery of how broad
that point actually is, and what a
part invisible electronic "messengers" play in the dance of life.
LEWIS MUMFORD

329 Man is neither angel nor beast; and

the misfortune is that he who would
act the angel acts the beast.
BLAISE PASCAL

330 O everlasting God, who hast ordained and constituted the service
of angels and men in a wonderful
order; mercifully grant that, as thy
holy angels always do thee service in
heaven, so, by thy appointment,
they may succor and defend us on
earth; through Jesus Christ our
Lord.
Book of Common Prayer

ANIMALS

331 Tyger! Tyger! burning bright
In the forests of the night,
What immortal hand or eye
Could frame thy fearful symmetry?
WILLIAM BLAKE

332 The lions, roaring after their prey,
do seek their meat from God.
Psalm 104:21

333 It was quite incomprehensible to
me—this was before I began going
to school—why in my evening
prayers I should pray for human
beings only. So when my mother
had prayed with me and had kissed
me good night, I used to add silently
a prayer that I had composed for
myself for all living creatures. It ran
thus: "O heavenly Father, protect
and bless all things that have
breath; guard them from all evil,
and let them sleep in peace."
ALBERT SCHWEITZER

334 O God, my Master, should I gain
   the grace

To see thee face to face, when life is
ended,
Grant that a little dog, who once
pretended
That I was God, may see me face to
face!

B.C. COULTER,
from the French of Francis Jammes

335 A cat can be trusted to purr when
she is pleased, which is more than
can be said about human beings.

WILLIAM RALPH INGE

336 When an animal has nothing to do,
it goes to sleep. When a man has
nothing to do, he may ask questions.

BERNARD J.F. LONERGAN

337 When I play with my cat, who
knows whether I do not make her
more sport than she makes me?

MICHEL DE MONTAIGNE

338 When I carefully consider the curi-
ous habits of dogs,
I am compelled to conclude
That man is the superior animal.

When I consider the curious habits
of man,
I confess, my friend, I am puzzled.

EZRA POUND

339 Animals are such agreeable friends
—they ask no questions, they pass
no criticisms.

GEORGE ELIOT

340 Our expressions and our words
never coincide, which is why the
animals don't understand us.

MALCOLM DE CHAZAL

341 If modern civilized man had to kill
the animals he eats, the number of
vegetarians would rise astronomically.

CHRISTIAN MORGENSTERN

342 I once had a sparrow alight upon
my shoulder, while hoeing in a village garden, and I felt I was more
distinguished by that circumstance
than I should have been by any
epaulet I could have worn.

HENRY DAVID THOREAU

BEAUTY

343 He hath made everything beautiful
in his time.

Ecclesiastes 3:11

344 The being of all things is derived
from the Divine Beauty.

THOMAS AQUINAS

345 I pray thee, O God, that I may be
beautiful within.

SOCRATES

346 How goodness heightens beauty!

HANNAH MORE

347 Beauty is the mark God sets upon
virtue. Every natural action is grace-
ful. Every heroic act is also decent,
and causes the place and the bystanders to shine.

RALPH WALDO EMERSON

348 This is the spirit that Beauty must
ever induce, wonderment and a delicious trouble, longing and love and
a trembling that is all delight.

PLOTINUS

349 There is no excellent beauty that

hath not some strangeness in the proportion.

FRANCIS BACON

350 God's fingers can touch nothing but to mold it into loveliness.

GEORGE MAC DONALD

351 The saying that beauty is but skin deep is but a skin-deep saying.

HERBERT SPENCER

352 If you want a golden rule that will fit everybody, this is it: Have nothing in your houses that you do not know to be useful, or believe to be beautiful.

WILLIAM MORRIS

353 The spirit and the sense so easily grow dead to the impressions of the beautiful and the perfect that one ought every day to hear a little song, read a good poem, see a good picture, and, if it were possible, speak a few reasonable words.

JOHANN WOLFGANG VON GOETHE

354 I used to like to hear him admire the beauty of a flower; it was a kind of gratitude to the flower itself, and a personal love for its delicate form and color. I seem to remember him gently touching a flower he delighted in; it was the same simple admiration that a child might have.

FRANCIS DARWIN, *speaking of his father Charles Darwin*

BLESSINGS

(See *God's Goodness, God's Providence*)

355 Blessings we enjoy daily, and for the most of them, because they be so common, men forget to pay their praises. But let not us, because it is a sacrifice so pleasing to him who still protects us, and gives us flowers, and showers, and meat and content.

IZAAK WALTON

Our real blessings often appear to us 356 in the shape of pains, losses and disappointments; but let us have patience, and we soon shall see them in their proper figures.

JOSEPH ADDISON

The best things are nearest: breath 357 in your nostrils, light in your eyes, flowers at your feet, duties at your hand, the path of God just before you.

ROBERT LOUIS STEVENSON

We have forgotten the gracious 358 Hand which has preserved us in peace and multiplied and enriched and strengthened us, and have vainly imagined in the deceitfulness of our hearts that all these blessings were produced by some superior wisdom and virtue of our own.

ABRAHAM LINCOLN

Never undertake anything for which 359 you wouldn't have the courage to ask the blessings of heaven.

GEORG CHRISTIAN LICHTENBERG

Things worth remembering: 360
    The value of time,
    The success of perseverance,
    The pleasure of working,
    The dignity of simplicity,
    The worth of character,
    The improvement of talent,
    The influence of example,
    The obligation of duty,
    The wisdom of economy,
    The virtue of patience,

The joy of originating,
The power of kindness.

Anonymous

361 Let the beauty of the Lord our God
be upon us.

Psalms 90:17 (AV)

362 Seek ye first the kingdom of God,
and his righteousness; and all these
things shall be added unto you.

Matthew 6:33

363 Eye hath not seen, nor ear heard,
neither have entered into the heart
of man, the things which God hath
prepared for them that love him.

I Corinthians 2:9

BODY AND SOUL

364 The body is the socket of the soul.

Anonymous.

365 What soap is for the body, tears are
for the soul.

Jewish proverb

366 Man is a sun; and the senses are his
planets.

NOVALIS
(Friedrich von Hardenberg)

367 No one hates his body.

AUGUSTINE OF HIPPO

368 Grub first; then ethics.

BERTOLT BRECHT

369 Animals, we are told, are taught by
their organs. Yes, I would add, and
so are men, but men have this

further advantage that they can also
teach their organs in return.

JOHANN WOLFGANG VON GOETHE

Body and spirit are twins: God only   370
knows which is which.

CHARLES ALGERNON SWINBURNE

The soul, too, has her virginity and   371
must bleed a little before bearing
fruit.

GEORGE SANTAYANA

The soul is the wife of the body.   372
They do not have the same kind of
pleasure or, at least, they seldom
enjoy it at the same time.

PAUL VALÉRY

One can hardly think too little of   373
one's self. One can hardly think too
much of one's soul.

GILBERT KEITH CHESTERTON

The soul, like the body, lives by   374
what it feeds on.

JOSIAH GILBERT HOLLAND

We say we exchange words when we   375
meet. What we exchange is souls.

MINOT J. SAVAGE

As the flower turns to the sun, or the   376
dog to his master, so the soul turns
to God.

WILLIAM TEMPLE

Call the world if you please "the   377
vale of soul-making."

JOHN KEATS

Not believing in the glory of our   378
own soul is what the Vedanta calls
atheism.

SWAMI VIVEKANANDA

379 My soul looks like a seed.

                 BILLY, *age 8*

380 I think my soul is half full of gay colors and the other half filled with sad colors and the gay colors represent the good in life and the sad colors represent the bad.

                 LIZ, *age 10*

381 Joy, shipmate, joy!
(Pleas'd to my soul at death I cry,)
Our life is closed, our life begins,
The long, long anchorage we leave,
The ship is clear at last, she leaps!
She swiftly courses from the shore,
Joy, shipmate, joy.

            WALT WHITMAN

BROTHERHOOD

382 Men become what they are, sons of God, by becoming what they are, brothers of their brothers.

            MARTIN BUBER

383 No one can be perfectly free till all are free; no one can be perfectly moral till all are moral; no one can be perfectly happy till all are happy.

           HERBERT SPENCER

384 Until you have become really, in actual fact, the brother of everyone, brotherhood will not come to pass.

        FYODOR DOSTOEVSKY

385 If a man be gracious and courteous to strangers, it shows he is a citizen of the world, and that his heart is no island cut off from other lands, but a continent that joins them.

           FRANCIS BACON

The race of mankind would perish 386 did they cease to aid each other. We cannot exist without mutual help. All therefore that need aid have a right to ask it of their fellow-men; and no one who has the power of granting can refuse it without guilt.

           WALTER SCOTT

In all my travels the thing that has 387 impressed me most is the universal brotherhood of man—what there is of it.

           MARK TWAIN

Men are tattooed with their special 388 beliefs like so many South Sea Islanders; but a real human heart with divine love in it beats with the same glow under all the patterns of all earth's thousand tribes.

       OLIVER WENDELL HOLMES

Solitude and hunger and weariness 389 of spirit—these sharpened my perceptions so that I suffered not only my own sorrow but the sorrow of those around me. I was no longer myself. I was man. I was no longer a young girl . . . I was oppressed. I was that drug addict, screaming and tossing in her cell, beating her head against the wall. I was that shoplifter who for rebellion was sentenced to solitary. I was that woman who had killed her children, murdered her lover.

           DOROTHY DAY

Every man bears the whole stamp of 390 the human condition.

       MICHEL DE MONTAIGNE

Years ago I recognized my kinship 391 with all human beings, and I made up my mind I was not one whit better than the meanest on earth. I said then and I say now that while there is a lower class, I am of it; while there is a criminal class, I am of it; while there is a soul in prison, I am not free.

EUGENE V. DEBS

392 No man is an island, entire of itself; every man is a piece of the continent, a part of the main; if a clod be washed away by the sea, Europe is the less, as well as if a promontory were, as well as if a manor of thy friend's or thine own were; any man's death diminishes me, because I am involved in mankind; and therefore never send to know for whom the bell tolls; it tolls for thee.

JOHN DONNE

393 I understand now for the first time the mystery of the religion whence was born the civilization I claim as my own: "To bear the sin of man." Each man bears the sin of all men.

ANTOINE DE SAINT-EXUPÉRY

394 When the large-hearted William H. Taft was governor of the Philippine Islands he made public reference to "our Filipino brothers," and was answered in a derisive song by somebody who thought himself better than any Filipino:

He may be a brother of William H. Taft,
But he ain't no brother of mine.

All the same, he is; and whoever looks at the Orient in the aftermath of World War II is bound to see that whenever brotherhood is violated the blood of the victims will cry out from whatever ground the victor treads.

WALTER RUSSELL BOWIE

Thou shalt open thy hand wide unto   395
thy brother.
Deuteronomy 15:11

One is your Master, even Christ;   396
and all ye are brethren.
Matthew 23:8

Be kindly affectioned one to another   397
with brotherly love; in honor preferring one another.
Romans 12:10

CHANGE

All great changes are irksome to the human mind, especially those which are attended with great dangers and uncertain effects.   398

JOHN ADAMS

The more change, the more of the same old thing.
French proverb
399

He that will not apply new remedies must expect new evils.

FRANCIS BACON
400

We must all obey the great law of change. It is the most powerful law of nature.

EDMUND BURKE   401

There is danger in reckless change; but greater danger in blind conservatism.

HENRY GEORGE   402

Certainty generally is an illusion, and repose is not the destiny of man.

OLIVER WENDELL HOLMES, JR.   403

Progress is the mother of problems.   404
GILBERT KEITH CHESTERTON

405 The waters are out and no human force can turn them back, but I do not see why as we go with the stream we need sing Hallelujah to the river god.

JAMES FITZJAMES STEPHEN

406 All things flow; nothing abides.

HERACLITUS

407 One cannot step twice into the same river.

HERACLITUS

408 Earth changes, but thy soul and God stand sure.

ROBERT BROWNING

409 The spring is wearing into summer, and life is wearing into death; our friends are forsaking us, our hopes are declining; our riches are wasting; our mortifications are increasing, and is the question settled in our minds, what objects we pursue with undivided aim? Have we fixed ourselves by principles? Have we planted our stakes?

RALPH WALDO EMERSON

410 There is a certain relief in change, even though it be from bad to worse; as I have found in traveling in a stage coach, that it is often a comfort to shift one's position and be bruised in a new place.

WASHINGTON IRVING

CONSCIENCE

(See *Moral Law, Morality*)

411 And I will place within them as a guide
My Umpire Conscience, whom if they will hear,

Light after light well used they shall attain,
And to the end persisting, safe arrive.

JOHN MILTON

If conscience smite thee once, it is an admonition; if twice, it is a condemnation. 412

NATHANIEL HAWTHORNE

A good conscience is a continual Christmas. 413

BENJAMIN FRANKLIN

Conscience is God's presence in man. 414

EMMANUEL SWEDENBORG

The disease of an evil conscience is beyond the practice of all the physicians of all the countries in the world. 415

WILLIAM E. GLADSTONE

Wisdom entereth not into a malicious mind, and science without conscience is but the ruin of the soul. 416

FRANÇOIS RABELAIS

To sit alone with my conscience will be judgment enough for me. 417

CHARLES WILLIAM STUBBS

It is not history which teaches conscience to be honest; it is the conscience which educates history. Fact is corrupting, it is we who correct it by the persistence of our ideal. The soul moralizes the past in order not to be demoralized by it. Like the alchemists of the middle ages, she finds in the crucible of experience only the gold that she herself has poured into it. 418

HENRI FRÉDÉRIC AMIEL

419 Labor to keep alive in your breast that little spark of celestial fire called conscience.

GEORGE WASHINGTON

420 Conscience is the voice of the soul, as the passions are the voice of the body. No wonder they often contradict each other.

JEAN JACQUES ROUSSEAU

421 Conscience warns us as a friend before it punishes us as a judge.

KING STANISLAS I

422 It takes more than a soft pillow to insure sound sleep.

Anonymous

423 All too often a clear conscience is merely the result of a bad memory.

Ancient proverb

424 God breathes, not speaks, his verdicts.

ROBERT BROWNING

THE DEVIL

425 We are reminded of the old lady who rebuked someone for saying "What the devil!" on the ground that "she did not like to hear him speak so flippantly about a sacred personage."

DOROTHY L. SAYERS

426 The devil's boots don't creak.

Scottish proverb

427 The devil never tempts us with more success than when he tempts us with

a sight of our own good actions.

BISHOP THOMAS WILSON

Resist the devil, and he will flee   *428*
from you.

James 4:7

When I'm troubled by thoughts   *429*
which pertain to political questions or household affairs I take up a psalm or a text of Paul and fall asleep over it. But the thoughts which come from Satan demand more of me. Then I have to resort to more difficult maneuvers before I extricate myself, although I easily get the upper hand in thoughts of an economic or domestic character. However, when I'm angry with God and ask him whether it's he or I who's wrong, then it's more than I can handle.

MARTIN LUTHER

The heart of man is the place the   *430*
devils dwell in: I feel sometimes a hell within myself.

THOMAS BROWNE

At all times, all too many Christians   *431*
have behaved as though the devil were a First Principle, on the same footing as God. They have paid more attention to evil and the problem of its eradication than to good and the methods by which individual goodness may be deepened and the sum of goodness increased. The effects which follow too constant and intense a concentration upon evil are always disastrous. Those who crusade, not *for* God in themselves, but *against* the devil in others, never succeed in making the world better, but leave it either as it was, or sometimes even perceptibly

worse than it was before the crusade began. By thinking primarily of evil we tend, however excellent our intentions, to create occasions for evil to manifest itself.

ALDOUS HUXLEY

432 The Devil is a gentleman who never goes where he is not welcome.

JOHN A. LINCOLN

433 Say the truth and shame the Devil.

HUGH LATIMER

434 A religion can no more afford to degrade its Devil than to degrade its God.

HAVELOCK ELLIS

EVOLUTION

435 It is always worth while to inquire how far the doctrine of evolution has anything to do with any reasonable notion of progress. . . . If you take an unarmed saint and confront him with a hungry tiger, there will be a struggle for existence culminating in the survival of the fittest, which means, of course, the fittest to survive in those conditions; but it will not be a survival of the ethically best. There is no reason to suppose that the struggle for existence always favors what is ethically admirable.

WILLIAM TEMPLE

436 Man with all his noble qualities . . . still bears in his bodily frame the indelible stamp of his lowly origin.

CHARLES DARWIN

437 Unbroken Evolution under uniform conditions pleased every one—

except curates and bishops; it was the very best substitute for religion; a safe, conservative, practical, thoroughly Common-Law deity.

HENRY ADAMS

A creation of evolutionary type 438 (God *making things make themselves*) has for long seemed to some very great minds the most beautiful form imaginable in which God could act in the universe. Was it not St. Thomas who, comparing the viewpoint (fixist as we should call it today) of the Latin Fathers like St. Gregory, to the evolutionary viewpoint of the Greek Fathers and St. Augustine, said of the latter, *Magis placet*—it is more *acceptable*—"let us be glad to strengthen our minds by contact with this great thought!"

PIERRE TEILHARD DE CHARDIN

There are no shortcuts in evolution. 439

LOUIS D. BRANDEIS

Three ideas stand out above all 440 others in the influence they have exerted and are destined to exert upon the development of the human race: the idea of the Golden Rule, the idea of natural law, and the idea of age-long growth, or evolution.

ROBERT A. MILLIKAN

FAMILY

(See *Home, Parenthood*)

All happy families resemble one 441 another; every unhappy family is unhappy in its own fashion.

LEO TOLSTOY

442 He that hath no fools, knaves, or beggars in his family was begot by a flash of lightning.

Anonymous

443 Wife and children are a kind of discipline of humanity.

FRANCIS BACON

444 The family, grounded on marriage freely contracted, monogamous and indissoluble, is and must be considered the first and essential cell of human society.

POPE JOHN XXIII

445 The family is a good institution because it is uncongenial.

GILBERT KEITH CHESTERTON

446 Nobody's family can hang out the sign "Nothing the matter here."

Chinese proverb

447 There are no praises and no blessings for those who are ashamed of their families.

Jewish proverb

448 What a father says to his children is not heard by the world, but it will be heard by posterity.

JEAN PAUL RICHTER

449 The ties of family and of country were never intended to circumscribe the soul. If allowed to become exclusive, engrossing, clannish, so as to shut out the general claims of the human race, the highest end of Providence is frustrated, and home, instead of being the nursery, becomes the grave of the heart.

WILLIAM ELLERY CHANNING

GOOD AND EVIL

450 Woe unto them that call evil good, and good evil; that put darkness for light, and light for darkness; that put bitter for sweet, and sweet for bitter!

Isaiah 5:20

451 There are in every man, at every hour, two simultaneous postulations, one towards God, the other towards Satan.

CHARLES BAUDELAIRE

452 Dirt is matter out of place.

OLIVER LODGE

453 The germs of all things are in every heart, and the greatest criminals as well as the greatest heroes are but different modes of ourselves. Only evil grows of itself, while for goodness we want effort and courage.

HENRI FRÉDÉRIC AMIEL

454 The first prison I ever saw had inscribed on it *Cease to do evil: learn to do well;* but as the inscription was on the outside, the prisoners could not read it. It should have been addressed to the self-righteous free spectator in the street, and should have run *All have sinned, and fallen short of the glory of God.*

GEORGE BERNARD SHAW

455 Every criminal was once an infant love.

WILLIAM BLAKE

456 The roaring of lions, the howling of wolves, the raging of the stormy sea,

and the destructive sword, are portions of eternity too great for the eye of man.

WILLIAM BLAKE

457 There are people within whom the good traits of Cain's soul have their habitation, and these are very great.

RABBI URI OF STRELISK

458 Good is that which makes for unity; evil is that which makes for separateness.

ALDOUS HUXLEY

459 What is a weed? A plant whose virtues have not yet been discovered.

RALPH WALDO EMERSON

460 The only thing necessary for the triumph of evil is for good men to do nothing.

EDMUND BURKE

461 There is some soul of goodness in things evil,
Would men observingly distill it out.

WILLIAM SHAKESPEARE

462 Vice cannot know virtue too, but a virtuous nature, educated by time, will acquire a knowledge both of virtue and vice: the virtuous and not the vicious man has wisdom—in my opinion.

SOCRATES

463 There is nothing evil except that which perverts the mind and shackles the conscience.

AMBROSE OF MILAN

464 Hatred of evil destroys the spiritual world of man just as much as hatred

of the good, which does not mean that our attitude towards evil must not be ruthless, nor that there can be any question of a truce with it. Our attitude to evil must be twofold: we must be tolerant of it, as the Creator is tolerant, and we must mercilessly struggle against it. True spirituality consists in believing in the power of good rather than that of ill, in God rather than Satan.

NICOLAS BERDYAEV

HISTORY

History is God's roaring loom.   465

J.S. WHALE

The lessons of history summarized: 466
1. Whom the gods would destroy, they first make mad with power. 2. The mills of God grind slowly, but they grind exceeding small. 3. The bee fertilizes the flower it robs. 4. When it is dark enough, you can see the stars.

CHARLES A. BEARD

There is no history; only biography.   467

RALPH WALDO EMERSON

Every reminiscence is colored by   468
today's being what it is, and therefore by a deceptive point of view.

ALBERT EINSTEIN

The historian cannot choose his villains like the poet, nor invent them.   469
At a particular time they are "given." Given, as it were, perfectly clearly, by a higher power.

THEODOR HAECKER

470 What are all histories but God manifesting himself?
> OLIVER CROMWELL

471 Men make history and not the other way 'round. In periods when there is no leadership, society stands still. Progress occurs when courageous, skillful leaders seize the opportunity to change things for the better.
> HARRY S. TRUMAN

472 All the historical books which contain no lies are extremely tedious.
> ANATOLE FRANCE

473 History is the unfolding of miscalculations.
> BARBARA TUCHMAN

474 History is about the most cruel of all goddesses.
> FRIEDRICH ENGELS

475 There is no inevitability in history except as men make it.
> FELIX FRANKFURTER

476 History is little more than the register of the crimes, follies, and misfortunes of mankind.
> EDWARD GIBBON

477 Men make their own history, but they do not make it just as they please; they do not make it under circumstances chosen by themselves, but under circumstances directly found, given, and transmitted from the past.
> KARL MARX

478 Human history becomes more and more a race between education and catastrophe.
> H.G. WELLS

479 History is philosophy teaching by examples.
> DIONYSIUS OF HALICARNASSUS

HUMANITY

480 Humanity to me is not a mob. A mob is a degeneration of humanity. A mob is humanity going the wrong way.
> FRANK LLOYD WRIGHT

481 It is easier to love humanity as a whole than to love one's neighbor.
> ERIC HOFFER

482 Every so often, we pass laws repealing human nature.
> HOWARD LINDSAY

483 It will be very generally found that those who will sneer habitually at human nature, and affect to despise it, are among its worst and least pleasant samples.
> CHARLES DICKENS

484 Human nature is like a drunk peasant. Lift him into the saddle on one side, over he topples on the other side.
> MARTIN LUTHER

485 I do and I must reverence human nature . . . I know how it is despised, how it has been oppressed, how civil and religious establishments have for ages conspired to crush it. I know its history. I shut my eyes on none of its weaknesses and crimes. But injured, trampled on, and scorned as our nature is, I still turn to it with intense sympathy and strong hope. I bless it for its

kind affections, for its strong and tender love. I honor it for its struggles against oppression, for its growth and progress under the weight of so many chains and prejudices, for its achievements in science and art, and still more for its examples of heroic and saintly virtue. These are marks of a divine origin and the pledges of a celestial inheritance; and I thank God that my own lot is bound up with that of the human race.

WILLIAM ELLERY CHANNING

486 I know of no rights of race superior to the rights of humanity.

FREDERICK DOUGLASS

487 All that is human must retrograde if it does not advance.

EDWARD GIBBON

488 Be ashamed to die until you have won some victory for humanity.

HORACE MANN

JEWS

489 Thus saith the Lord of hosts: In those days it shall come to pass, that ten men shall take hold out of all languages of the nations, even shall take hold of the skirt of him that is a Jew, saying, We will go with you: for we have heard that God is with you.

Zechariah 8:23

490 I am a Jew. Hath not a Jew eyes? hath not a Jew hands, organs, dimensions, senses, affections, passions? fed with the same food, hurt with the same weapons, subject to the same diseases, healed by the same means, warmed and cooled by the same summer, as a Christian is? If you prick us, do we not bleed? If you tickle us, do we not laugh? If you poison us, do we not die? and if you wrong us, shall we not revenge? If we are like you in the rest, we will resemble you in that.

Shylock, in WILLIAM SHAKESPEARE'S The Merchant of Venice

The Hebrews have done more to 491 civilize men than any other nation. If I were an atheist, and believed in blind eternal fate, I should still believe that fate had ordained the Jews to be the most essential instrument for civilizing the nations.

JOHN ADAMS

The pursuit of knowledge for its 492 own sake, an almost fanatical love of justice, and a desire for personal independence—these are features of the Jewish tradition which make me thank my stars that I belong to it.

ALBERT EINSTEIN

The Jew's home has rarely been his 493 "castle"; throughout the ages it has been something far higher—his sanctuary.

JOSEPH H. HERTZ

Not long ago I was reading the 494 Sermon on the Mount with a rabbi. At nearly every verse he showed me very similar passages in the Hebrew Bible and Talmud. When he reached the words "Resist not evil" he did not say "This too is in the Talmud" but asked, with a smile, "Do the Christians obey this command?" I had nothing to say in reply, especially as at that particular time Christians, far from turning the other cheek, were smiting the Jews on both cheeks.

LEO TOLSTOY

495 In the sight of the anti-Semite, Jews can do nothing right. If they are rich, they are birds of prey. If they are poor, they are vermin. If they are in favor of war, they are exploiters of bloody feuds for their own profit. If they are anxious for peace, they are either instinctive cowards or traitors. If they give generously, they are doing it for some selfish purpose of their own. If they don't give, then what would one expect from a Jew?

DAVID LLOYD GEORGE

496 Even in that remote epoch, the Semite shepherd bore upon his forehead the seal of the absolute God, upon which was written, "This race will rid the earth of superstition."

ERNEST RENAN

MEN AND WOMEN

497 When men and women agree, it is only in their conclusions; their reasons are always different.

GEORGE SANTAYANA

498 Man and woman are one body and soul.

The Talmud

499 Who can tell how many of the most original thoughts put forth by male writers belong to a woman by suggestion? If I may judge by my own case, a very large proportion indeed.

JOHN STUART MILL

The woman who is known only 500 through a man is known wrong.

HENRY ADAMS

Women are supposed to be very 501 calm generally: but women feel just as men feel; they need exercise for their faculties, and a field for their efforts as much as their brothers do; they suffer from too rigid a constraint, too absolute a stagnation, precisely as men would suffer; and it is narrow-minded in their more privileged fellow-creatures to say that they ought to confine themselves to making puddings and knitting stockings, to playing on the piano and embroidering bags. It is thoughtless to condemn them, or laugh at them, if they seek to do more or learn more than custom has pronounced necessary for their sex.

CHARLOTTE BRONTË

No one knows like a woman how to 502 say things that are at once gentle and deep.

VICTOR HUGO

Women are not altogether in the 503 wrong when they refuse the rules of life prescribed to the world, for men only have established them and without their consent.

MICHEL DE MONTAIGNE

I would have woman lay aside all 504 thought, such as she habitually cherishes, of being taught and led by men. I would have her free from compromise, from complaisance, from helplessness, because I would have her good enough and strong enough to love one and all beings, from the fullness, not the poverty of being.

MARGARET FULLER

505 Being a woman is a terribly difficult task since it consists principally in dealing with men.

JOSEPH CONRAD

506 Probably no man ever got so much out of a surgical operation as Adam did.

The Arkansas Gazette

507 I had rather live with the woman I love in a world full of trouble than to live in heaven with nobody but men.

ROBERT G. INGERSOLL

MIRACLES

508 The miracles of Jesus were the ordinary works of his Father, wrought small and swift that we might take them in.

GEORGE MAC DONALD

509 When Moses threw the wand into the Red Sea, the sea, quite contrary to the expected miracle, did not divide itself to leave a dry passage for the Jews. Not until the first man had jumped into the sea did the promised miracle happen and the waves recede.

Jewish legend

510 If God willed it, brooms would shoot.

Jewish proverb

511 God raises the level of the impossible.

CORRIE TEN BOOM

512 We must first make up our minds about Christ before coming to conclusions about the miracles attributed to him.

F.F. BRUCE

Miracles are the swaddling clothes 513
of infant churches.

THOMAS FULLER

What is a miracle? The natural law 514
of a unique event.

EUGEN ROSENSTOCK-HUESSY

We know that the devil can work 515
miracles. Pharaoh's magicians did many of the things Moses did.

JACQUES ELLUL

All miracles are simply feeble lights 516
like beacons on our way to the port where shines the light, the total light of the resurrection.

JACQUES ELLUL

Miracles are not contrary to nature, 517
but only contrary to what we know about nature.

AUGUSTINE OF HIPPO

Miracles happen to those who be- 518
lieve in them.

BERNARD BERENSON

God will work a miracle rather than 519
break his word; he can do that—he cannot do this.

JEREMY TAYLOR

MORAL LAW

**(See *Conscience, Morality,
Goodness, Justice, Obedience*)**

In vain we call old notions fudge, 520
    And bend our conscience to
our dealing;

The Ten Commandments will not
budge
 And stealing will continue
stealing.
     JAMES RUSSELL LOWELL

521 Be not deceived; God is not
mocked: for whatsoever a man soweth, that shall he reap.
     Galatians 6:7

522 The laws are the secret avengers,
 And they rule above all lands:
They come on wool-soft sandals,
 But they strike with iron hands.
     EDWIN MARKHAM

523 All originality is an eaglet which
breaks through its shell only in the
sublime and fulminating atmosphere of Sinai.
     LOUIS BERTRAND

524 People need to be reminded more
often than they need to be instructed.
     SAMUEL JOHNSON

525 No man can break any of the Ten
Commandments. He can only break
himself against them.
     GILBERT KEITH CHESTERTON

526 We must never forget that Hitler
was able to crush the moralists, but
he was not able to crush thousands
of men who thought the First Commandment was really first.
     ELTON TRUEBLOOD

527 The Ten Commandments, completed by the evangelical precepts of
justice and charity, constitute the
framework of individual and collec-
tive survival.
     POPE JOHN XXIII

There is but one morality, as there is 528
but one geometry.
   VOLTAIRE (François Marie Arouet)

The stars in their courses fought 529
against Sisera.
     Judges 5:20

MYSTERY

I like things you don't have to 530
explain because you can't.
     HOWARD NEMEROV

The more unintelligent a man is, the 531
less mysterious existence seems to
him.
     ARTHUR SCHOPENHAUER

We are hemmed round with mys- 532
tery, and the greatest mysteries are
contained in what we see and do
every day.
     HENRI FRÉDÉRIC AMIEL

I love to lose myself in a mystery; to 533
pursue my reason to an *O altitudo!*
     THOMAS BROWNE

The eternal silence of these infinite 534
spaces frightens me.
     BLAISE PASCAL

The awful shadow of some unseen 535
Power
Floats, tho' unseen, amongst us.
     PERCY BYSSHE SHELLEY

All is mystery; but he is a slave who 536
will not struggle to penetrate the
dark veil.
     BENJAMIN DISRAELI

It is hard to say whether the doctors 537

of law or divinity have made the greater advances in the lucrative business of mystery.

EDMUND BURKE

538 A mystery is something of which we know that it is, though we do not know what it is.

JOSEPH COOK

539 A religion without mystery must be a religion without God.

JEREMY TAYLOR

540 The most beautiful experience we can have is the mysterious. It is the fundamental emotion which stands at the cradle of true art and true science.

ALBERT EINSTEIN

541 Here we are, you and I, and the millions of men and animals about us: the innumerable atoms which make our bodies, blown as it were by mysterious processes together, so that there has happened, just now, for every one of us, the wonder of wonders, we have come to life. And here we stand, with our senses, our keen intellects, our infinite devices, our nerves quivering to the touch of joy or pain; beacons of brief fire, burning between two unexplored eternities. What are we to make of this wonder while it is still ours?

GEORGE MEREDITH

NATURE

(See *God and His Creation*)

542 Every flower of the field, every fiber of a plant, every particle of an insect, carries with it the impress of its Maker, and can—if duly considered—read us lectures of ethics or divinity.

THOMAS POPE BLOUNT

It is the modest, not the presumptu- 543 ous, inquirer who makes a real and safe progress in the discovery of divine truths. One follows Nature and Nature's God; that is, he follows God in his works and in his word.

HENRY ST. JOHN,
Viscount Bolingbroke

An undevout astronomer is mad. 544

EDWARD YOUNG

Nature, the vicar of th' Almightie 545 Lord.

GEOFFREY CHAUCER

Nature gives us life like a mother, 546 but loves us like a step-mother.

GIACOMO LEOPARDI

Nature is a hanging judge. 547

Anonymous

Nature loves to hide. 548

HERACLITUS

All things are artificial, for nature is 549 the art of God.

THOMAS BROWNE

Nature, with equal mind, 550
Sees all her sons at play,
Sees man control the wind,
The wind sweep man away.

MATTHEW ARNOLD

There is no nature at an instant. 551

ALFRED NORTH WHITEHEAD

In nature there are neither rewards 552

nor punishments; there are consequences.

ROBERT G. INGERSOLL

553 The sky is the daily bread of the eyes.

RALPH WALDO EMERSON

554 Nature, to be commanded, must be obeyed.

FRANCIS BACON

555 Looked at in the wrong way, nature can be a substitute for God. This is because relative beauty can be jealous of absolute beauty.

HUBERT VAN ZELLER

556 Speak to the earth, and it shall teach thee.

Job 12:8

557 The firmament showeth his handiwork.

Psalm 19:1

558 Praise ye him, sun and moon: praise him, all ye stars of light.

Psalm 148:3

559 Do not I fill heaven and earth? saith the Lord.

Jeremiah 23:24

560 That was not first which is spiritual, but that which is natural; and afterward that which is spiritual.

I Corinthians 15:46

ORDER

561 Good order is the foundation of all good things.

EDMUND BURKE

Let all things be done decently and 562 in order.

I Corinthians 14:40

Order the beauty even of beauty is, 563
    It is the rule of bliss,
The very life and form and cause of
    pleasure;
    Which if we do not understand,
Ten thousand heaps of vain confused treasure
    Will but oppress the land.
In blessedness itself we that shall
    miss,
    Being blind, which is the cause
of bliss.

THOMAS TRAHERNE

The art of progress is to preserve 564 order amid change, and to preserve change amid order. Life refuses to be embalmed alive.

ALFRED NORTH WHITEHEAD

He who has no taste for order will 565 be often wrong in his judgment, and seldom considerate or conscientious in his actions.

JOHANN KASPAR LAVATER

Once you have missed the first but- 566 ton-hole, you'll never manage to button up.

JOHANN WOLFGANG VON GOETHE

Two dangers constantly threaten the 567 world: order and disorder.

PAUL VALÉRY

PARENTHOOD

(See *Home, Family*)

Some of you write and ask us why 568 we don't make more of your boys. I will tell you the main reason—because they are your boys.

WOODROW WILSON
when president of Princeton,
to alumni

569 Could I climb to the highest place in Athens, I would lift up my voice and proclaim: "Fellow citizens, why do you turn and scrape every stone to gather wealth and take so little care of your children, to whom one day you must relinquish it all?"

SOCRATES

570 The joys of parents are secret; and so are their griefs and fears. They cannot utter the one; they will not utter the other. Children sweeten labors; but they make misfortunes more bitter. They increase the cares of life; but they mitigate the remembrance of death.

FRANCIS BACON

571 A child tells in the street what its father and mother say at home.

The Talmud.

572 The best brought-up children are those who have seen their parents as they are. Hypocrisy is not the parents' first duty.

GEORGE BERNARD SHAW

573 Nobody can misunderstand a boy like his own mother.

NORMAN DOUGLAS

574 The religion of a child depends upon what its mother and its father are, and not on what they say.

HENRI FRÉDÉRIC AMIEL

575 Men are generally more careful of the breed of their horses and dogs than of their children.

WILLIAM PENN

He that will have his son have a 576 respect for him and his orders, must himself have a great reverence for his son.

JOHN LOCKE

We never know the love of the 577 parent until we become parents ourselves.

HENRY WARD BEECHER

The most important thing a father 578 can do for his children is to love their mother.

THEODORE M. HESBURGH

Few parents nowadays pay any re- 579 gard to what their children say to them; the old-fashioned respect for the young is fast dying out.

OSCAR WILDE

Pride is one of the seven deadly 580 sins; but it cannot be the pride of a mother in her children, for that is a compound of two cardinal virtues— faith and hope.

CHARLES DICKENS

PAST, PRESENT, AND FUTURE

We can only pay our debt to the 581 past by putting the future in debt to ourselves.

JOHN BUCHAN

Hats off to the past; coats off to the 582 future.

American proverb

What will be, is.   583
AUSTIN O'MALLEY

The future has a habit of suddenly 584

and dramatically becoming the present.

ROGER W. BABSON

585 That sign of old age, extolling the past at the expense of the present.

SYDNEY SMITH

586 Speak of the moderns without contempt, and of the ancients without idolatry.

LORD CHESTERFIELD
(Philip Dormer Stanhope)

587 Do not be like those people who think they are inaugurating a new era: as if before they came along there had been nothing but emptiness or chaos. Before we came there were our parents, and they were the latest link of a long and sacred chain. The generations which went before us left such wonderful proofs of their noble victories in the cause of truth and goodness that we fear we may never equal them in merit and glory. It would be a meritorious thing for us all frankly to admit that we should still be very wretched indeed, and hardly out of the phase of barbarism, if the civilization of past centuries had not seen to our baptism.

POPE JOHN XXIII

588 The mind needs room to turn around in, and when the future doesn't provide this dimension one chooses of necessity whatever spaciousness the remembered past affords.

JESSAMYN WEST

589 Neither a wise man nor a brave man lies down on the tracks of history to wait for the train of the future to run over him.

DWIGHT D. EISENHOWER

590 I try to be as philosophical as the old lady who said that the best thing - about the future is that it only comes one day at a time.

DEAN ACHESON

591 No man ever sank under the burden of the day. It is when tomorrow's burden is added to the burden of today that the weight is more than a man can bear. Never load yourself so. If you find yourself so loaded, at least remember this: it is your own doing, not God's. He begs you to leave the future to him, and mind the present.

GEORGE MAC DONALD

592 Those who cannot remember the past are doomed to repeat it.

GEORGE SANTAYANA

593 The past always looks better than it was; it's only pleasant because it isn't here.

PETER FINLEY DUNNE

594 My interest is in the future because I am going to spend the rest of my life there.

CHARLES F. KETTERING

595 Since Time is not a person we can overtake when he is gone, let us honor him with mirth and cheerfulness of heart while he is passing.

JOHANN WOLFGANG VON GOETHE

POWER

596 Power is never a good, except he be good that has it.

KING ALFRED

597 Power gradually extirpates from the mind every humane and gentle virtue.

EDMUND BURKE

598 Power tends to corrupt, and absolute power corrupts absolutely.

LORD ACTON (John Dalberg)

599 Power always thinks it has a great soul and vast views beyond the comprehension of the weak; and that it is doing God's work when it is violating all his laws. Our passions, ambitions, avarice, love and resentment, etc., possess so much metaphysical subtlety and so much overpowering eloquence that they insinuate themselves into the understanding and the conscience and convert both to their party.

JOHN ADAMS

600 Force is not a remedy.

JOHN BRIGHT

601 Power is not revealed by striking hard or often, but by striking true.

HONORÉ DE BALZAC

602 The effect of power and publicity on all men is the aggravation of self, a sort of tumor that ends by killing the victim's sympathies.

HENRY ADAMS

603 The enjoyment of power is fatal to the subtleties of life. Ruling classes degenerate by reason of their lazy indulgence in obvious gratifications.

ALFRED NORTH WHITEHEAD

604 You shall have joy, or you shall have power, said God; you shall not have both.

RALPH WALDO EMERSON

We cannot live by power, and a *605* culture that seeks to live by it becomes brutal and sterile. But we can die without it.

MAX LERNER

Power does not corrupt man; fools, *606* however, if they get into a position of power, corrupt power.

GEORGE BERNARD SHAW

In order to obtain and hold power a *607* man must love it. Thus the effort to get it is not likely to be coupled with goodness, but with the opposite qualities of pride, craft, and cruelty.

LEO TOLSTOY

SEX

About sex especially men are born *608* unbalanced; we might almost say men are born mad. They scarcely reach sanity till they reach sanctity.

GILBERT KEITH CHESTERTON

In its essence, the delight of sexual *609* love, the genetic spasm, is a sensation of resurrection, of renewing our life in another, for only in others can we renew our life and so perpetuate ourselves.

MIGUEL DE UNAMUNO

Sexuality throws no light upon love, *610* but only through love can we learn to understand sexuality.

EUGEN ROSENSTOCK-HUESSY

If you think you love your mistress *611* for her own sake, you are quite mistaken.

FRANÇOIS DE LA ROCHEFOUCAULD

612   It is to be recognized that sex is holy as well as wholesome . . . It is the means by which we may cooperate with God in bringing into the world children of his own destined for eternal life. Anyone, who has once understood that, will be quite as careful as any Puritan to avoid making jokes about sex; not because it is nasty, but because it is sacred. He would no more joke about sex than he would joke about the Holy Communion—and for exactly the same reason. To joke about it is to treat with lightness something that deserves reverence.

WILLIAM TEMPLE

613   You can get a large audience together for a striptease act—that is, to watch a girl undress on the stage. Now suppose you came to a country where you could fill a theater by simply bringing a covered plate on the stage and then slowly lifting the cover so as to let every one see, just before the lights went out, that it contained a mutton chop or a bit of bacon, would you not think that in that country something had gone wrong with the appetite for food? And would not anyone who had grown up in a different world think there was something equally queer about the state of the sex instinct among us?

C.S. LEWIS

614   Sex has become one of the most discussed subjects of modern times. The Victorians pretended it did not exist: the moderns pretend that nothing else exists.

FULTON J. SHEEN

615   Some things are better than sex, and some are worse, but there's nothing exactly like it.

W.C. FIELDS

Sex lies at the root of life, and we   616
can never learn to reverence life until we know how to understand sex.

HAVELOCK ELLIS

In the day that God created man, in   617
the likeness of God made he him; male and female created he them. . . .

Genesis 5:1–2

SLEEP

He giveth his beloved sleep.   618
Psalm 127:3

To sleep is to strain and purify the   619
emotions, to deposit the mud of life, to calm the fever of the soul, to return into the bosom of maternal nature, thence to re-issue, healed and strong. Sleep is a sort of innocence and purification. Blessed be he who gave it to the poor sons of men as the sure and faithful companion of life, our daily healer and consoler.

HENRI FRÉDÉRIC AMIEL

The sleep of a laboring man is   620
sweet, whether he eat little or much: but the abundance of the rich will not suffer him to sleep.

Ecclesiastes 5:12

A sleeping child gives me the im-   621
pression of a travelor in a very far country.

RALPH WALDO EMERSON

622 For what else is sleep but a daily death which does not completely remove man hence nor detain him too long? And what else is death, but a very long and very deep sleep from which God arouses man?
AUGUSTINE OF HIPPO

623 Sleep is, in fine, so like death I dare not trust it without my prayers.
THOMAS FULLER

624 It is a delicious moment, certainly, that of being well-nestled in bed and feeling that you shall drop gently to sleep. The good is to come, not past; the limbs are tired enough to render the remaining in one posture delightful; the labor of the day is gone.
LEIGH HUNT

625 In sleep, what difference is there between Solomon and a fool?
HENRY GEORGE BOHN

626 It is no small art to sleep; to achieve it one must keep awake all day.
FRIEDRICH WILHELM NIETZSCHE

TIME AND ETERNITY

627 Jacob served seven years for Rachel; and they seemed unto him but a few days, for the love he had to her.
Genesis 29:20

628 Every hour has its morning, noon, and night.
RALPH WALDO EMERSON

629 There is no mortar that time will not loose.
French proverb

630 Time and love are both wasted so long as time remains working hours and love without song.
EUGEN ROSENSTOCK-HUESSY

631 As if you could kill time without injuring eternity.
HENRY DAVID THOREAU

632 Life is too short to be little.
BENJAMIN DISRAELI

633 Life is short and we have not too much time for gladdening the hearts of those who are traveling the dark way with us. Oh, be swift to love! Make haste to be kind.
HENRI FRÉDÉRIC AMIEL

634 I still find each day too short for all the thoughts I want to think, all the walks I want to take, all the books I want to read, and all the friends I want to see.
JOHN BURROUGHS

635 When one has much to put into them, a day has a hundred pockets.
FRIEDRICH WILHELM NIETZSCHE

636 The created world is but a small parenthesis in eternity.
THOMAS BROWNE

637 The One remains, the many change and pass;
Heaven's light forever shines, Earth's shadows fly;
Life, like a dome of many-colored glass,
Stains the white radiance of Eternity.
PERCY BYSSHE SHELLEY

638 The months and days are the travelers of eternity. The years that come and go are also voyagers. I too for years past have been stirred by the

sight of a solitary cloud drifting with the wind to ceaseless thoughts of roaming.
MATSUO BASHO

639 Eternity is in love with the productions of time.
WILLIAM BLAKE

640 Eternity has no gray hairs! The flowers fade, the heart withers, man grows old and dies, the world lies down in the sepulchre of ages, but time writes no wrinkles on the brow of eternity.
REGINALD HEBER

641 Those who live in the Lord never see each other for the last time.
German proverb

TRUTH AND FALSEHOOD

642 It takes two to speak the truth—one to speak, another to hear.
HENRY DAVID THOREAU

643 The great truths are too important to be new.
W. SOMERSET MAUGHAM

644 Tell the truth and run.
Jugoslav proverb

645 Truths turn into dogmas the moment they are disputed.
GILBERT KEITH CHESTERTON

646 The truth is cruel, but it can be loved, and it makes free those who have loved it.
GEORGE SANTAYANA

Let us rejoice in the Truth, wherever 647 we find its lamp burning.
ALBERT SCHWEITZER

Truth exists, only falsehood has to 648 be invented.
GEORGES BRAQUE

Give me a good fruitful error every 649 time, full of seeds, bursting with its own corrections. You can keep your sterile truth for yourself.
VILFREDO PARETO

Truth lies within a little and certain 650 compass, but error is immense.
HENRY ST. JOHN,
Viscount Bolingbroke

I will be as harsh as truth and as 651 uncompromising as justice.
WILLIAM LLOYD GARRISON

Sir, don't tell me of deception; a lie, 652 Sir, is a lie, whether it be a lie to the eye or a lie to the ear.
SAMUEL JOHNSON

I speak truth, not as much as I 653 would, but as much as I dare; and I dare a little the more, as I grow older.
MICHEL DE MONTAIGNE

Truth is not only violated by false- 654 hood; it may be equally outraged by silence.
HENRI FRÉDÉRIC AMIEL

Truth never yet fell dead in the 655 streets; it has such affinity with the soul of man, the seed however broadcast will catch somewhere and produce its hundredfold.
THEODORE PARKER

Truth often suffers more by the heat 656

of its defenders than from the arguments of its opposers.

WILLIAM PENN

657 When you want to fool the world, tell the truth.

OTTO VON BISMARCK

658 If you are out to tell the truth, leave elegance to the tailor.

ALBERT EINSTEIN

659 The truth is more important than the facts.

FRANK LLOYD WRIGHT

660 Ye shall know the truth, and the truth shall make you free.

John 8:32

661 Ye shall know the truth, and the truth shall make you mad.

ALDOUS HUXLEY

662 What is intended as a little white lie often ends up as a double feature in technicolor.

MADENA R. WALLINGFORD

663 We must not satisfy ourselves with specious delusions that the truth must prevail; ultimately it is not to be doubted that it will; but, meanwhile, we must help it.

FRANK H. HALLOCK

664 I do not gladly utter any deep conviction of the soul in any company where I think it will be contested, no, nor unless I think it will be welcome. Truth has already ceased to be itself if polemically said.

RALPH WALDO EMERSON

665   I thirst for truth,

But shall not reach it till I reach the source.

ROBERT BROWNING

WONDER

The world will never starve for wonders; only for want of wonder.   666

GILBERT KEITH CHESTERTON

The most beautiful thing we can experience is the mysterious. It is the source of all true art and science.   667

ALBERT EINSTEIN

In wonder all philosophy began: in wonder it ends. But the first wonder is the offspring of ignorance; the last is the parent of adoration.   668

SAMUEL TAYLOR COLERIDGE

Two things fill the mind with ever increasing wonder and awe, the more often and the more intensely the mind is drawn to them: the starry heavens above me and the moral law within me.   669

IMMANUEL KANT

Wonder is the basis of worship.   670

THOMAS CARLYLE

As knowledge increases, wonder deepens.   671

CHARLES MORGAN

The greatest insights happen to us in moments of awe.   672

ABRAHAM JOSHUA HESCHEL

We have loved the stars too deeply to be fearful of the night.   673

Inscription in crypt of Allegheny Observatory,   University of Pittsburgh

WORLD

674 I believe that our great Maker is preparing the world, in his own good time, to become one nation, speaking one language.

GROVER CLEVELAND

675 I look upon the world as my parish.

JOHN WESLEY

676 It is not a world out of joint that makes our problem, but the shipwrecked soul in it. It is Hamlet, not his world, that is wrong.

P.T. FORSYTH

677 The world has become a global village.

MARSHALL MC LUHAN

678 I wonder, Flask, whether the world is anchored anywhere; if she is, she swings with an uncommon long cable, though.

HERMAN MELVILLE

679 The world is the best of all possible worlds, and *everything* in it is a necessary evil.

F.H. BRADLEY

680 The world's a book, writ by the eternal art
Of the great author; printed in man's heart,
'Tis falsely printed, though divinely penned,
And all the *errata* will appear at the end.

FRANCIS QUARLES

681 Don't call the world dirty because you have forgotten to clean your glasses.

Anonymous

682 We are told that when Jehovah created the world he saw that it was good. What would he say now?

GEORGE BERNARD SHAW

683 All the world's a stage, but most of us are stagehands.

Anonymous

684 Don't believe the world owes you a living; the world owes you nothing —it was here first.

ROBERT JONES BURDETTE

685 We can have both heaven and hell in this world.

Jewish proverb

686 The world is a tempestuous sea, immense in its depth and its breadth, and time is a frail bridge built over it—its beginning fastened with those cords of chaos that preceded existence, but the end is eternal bliss, lighted by God's countenance.

JEDAIA BEN BEDERSI

687 And I saw a new heaven and a new earth: for the first heaven and the first earth were passed away; and there was no more sea.

Revelation 21:1

III

Man

Lo, this only have I found, that God hath made man upright; but they have sought out many inventions.

Ecclesiastes 7:29

Know then thyself, presume not God to scan;
The proper study of mankind is man.
Plac'd on this isthmus of a middle state,
A being darkly wise, and rudely great:
With too much knowledge for the sceptic side,
With too much weakness for the stoic's pride,
He hangs between; in doubt to act, or rest,
In doubt to deem himself a God, or beast;
In doubt his mind or body to prefer;
Born but to die, and reas'ning but to err;
Alike in ignorance, his reason such,
Whether he thinks too little, or too much:
Chaos of thought and passion, all confus'd;
Still by himself abus'd, or disabus'd;
Created half to rise, and half to fall;
Great lord of all things, yet a prey to all;
Sole judge of truth, in endless error hurl'd:
The glory, jest, and riddle of the world!

Alexander Pope

AGES OF MAN

688   When, as a child, I laughed and
      wept,
          Time crept.
      When, as a youth, I dreamed and
      talked,
          Time walked.
      When I became a full-grown man,
          Time ran.
      And later, as I older grew,
          Time flew.
      Soon I shall find, while travelling
      on,
          Time gone.
      Will Christ have saved my soul by
      then?
          Amen.
                    Inscription on a clock
                    in Chester Cathedral

689   No wise man ever wished to be
      younger.
                    JONATHAN SWIFT

690   The man who is too old to learn was
      probably always too old to learn.
                    HENRY S. HASKINS

691   In seed time learn, in harvest teach,
      in winter enjoy.
                    WILLIAM BLAKE

692   No one is so old that he cannot live
      yet another year, nor so young that
      he cannot die today.
                    FERNANDO DE ROJAS

693   At twenty a man is full of fight and
      hope. He wants to reform the world.
      When a man is seventy he still
      wants to reform the world but he
      knows he can't.
                    CLARENCE DARROW

694   Lord, thou knowest better than I
      know myself that I am growing
      older. Keep me from getting too
      talkative, and thinking I must say
      something on every subject and on
      every occasion. Release me from
      craving to straighten out every-
      body's affairs. Teach me the glori-
      ous lesson that occasionally it is
      possible that I may be mistaken.
      Make me thoughtful, but not
      moody; helpful, but not bossy;
      thou knowest, Lord, that what I
      want most is a few friends at the
      end.
                    Anonymous

695   Infancy is the perpetual messiah,
      which comes into the arms of fallen
      men, and pleads with them to return
      to Paradise.
                    RALPH WALDO EMERSON

696   In ancient shadows and twilights
          Where childhood had strayed,
      The world's great sorrows were born
          And its heroes were made.
      In the lost boyhood of Judas
          Christ was betrayed.
                    Æ (George William Russell)

697   The barb in the arrow of childhood
      suffering is this: its intense loneli-
      ness, its intense ignorance.
                    OLIVE SCHREINER

698   Train your child in the way in which
      you know you should have gone
      yourself.
                    CHARLES H. SPURGEON

699   Nothing offends children more than
      to play down to them. All the great
      children's books—the *Pilgrim's Prog-*
      ress, Robinson Crusoe, Grimm's Fairy

Tales and *Gulliver's Travels*—were written for adults.

GEORGE BERNARD SHAW

700 For God's sake give me the young man who has brains enough to make a fool of himself.

ROBERT LOUIS STEVENSON

701 Youth, though it may lack knowledge, is certainly not devoid of intelligence; it sees through shams with sharp and terrible eyes.

HENRY L. MENCKEN

702 There is more felicity on the far side of baldness than young men can possibly imagine.

LOGAN PEARSALL SMITH

703 Live as long as you may, the first twenty years are the longest half of your life.

ROBERT SOUTHEY

704 There is a feeling of eternity in youth.

WILLIAM HAZLITT

705 Young men have a passion for regarding their elders as senile.

HENRY ADAMS

706 God help us if the younger generation ever stops being the despair of its grandparents.

DEEMS TAYLOR

707 I am not young enough to know everything.

JAMES M. BARRIE

708 One of the nice things about middle age is that nobody tells you what a nice change it is from being young.

DOROTHY CANFIELD FISHER

709 I have never yet heard any middle-aged man or woman who worked with his or her brains express any regret for the passing of youth.

DOROTHY L. SAYERS

710 Middle age is when you've met so many people that every new person you meet reminds you of someone else.

OGDEN NASH

711 The youth gets together materials for a bridge to the moon, and at length the middle-aged man decides to make a woodshed with them.

HENRY DAVID THOREAU

712 Middle age: when you begin to exchange your emotions for symptoms.

IRVIN S. COBB

713 To grow old is to pass from passion to compassion.

ALBERT CAMUS

714 Even in America, the Indian summer of life should be a little sunny and a little sad, like the season, and infinite in wealth and depth of tone —but never hustled.

HENRY ADAMS

715 The young man who has not wept is a savage; the old man who will not laugh is a fool.

GEORGE SANTAYANA

716 The older the fiddle the sweeter the tune.

English proverb

717 Age is not all decay; it is the ripening, the swelling, of the fresh life within, that withers and bursts the husk.

GEORGE MAC DONALD

718 The evening of a well spent life brings its lamps with it.

> JOSEPH JOUBERT

719 I observe that old men seldom have any advantage of new discoveries, because these are beside a way of thinking they have been long used to. Resolved, if ever I live to years, that I will be impartial to hear the reasons of all pretended discoveries, and receive them, if rational, how long so ever I have been used to another way of thinking.

> JONATHAN EDWARDS

720 If you live long enough, the venerability factor creeps in; you get accused of things you never did and praised for virtues you never had.

> I.F. STONE

721 All would live long, but none would be old.

> BENJAMIN FRANKLIN

722 The first forty years of life give us the text; the next thirty supply the commentary.

> ARTHUR SCHOPENHAUER

723 Methusaleh lived to be 969 years old, but what of that? There was nothing doing.

> MARK TWAIN

AMBITION

724 All ambitions are lawful except those which climb upward on the miseries or credulities of mankind.

> JOSEPH CONRAD

725 To be ambitious of true honor and of real glory and perfection of our nature is the very principle and incentive of virtue; but to be ambitious of titles, place, ceremonial respects, and civil pageantry, is as vain and little as the things are that we court.

> PHILIP SIDNEY

You cannot be anything if you want   *726* to be everything.

> SOLOMON SCHECHTER

Well is it known that ambition can   *727* creep as well as soar.

> EDMUND BURKE

The slave has but one master; the   *728* ambitious man has as many as can help in making his fortune.

> JEAN DE LA BRUYÈRE

'Tis a common proof   *729*
That lowliness is young ambition's
  ladder,
Whereto the climber-upward turns
  his face;
But when he once attains the up-
  most round,
He then unto the ladder turns his
  back,
Looks in the clouds, scorning the
  base degrees
By which he did ascend.

> WILLIAM SHAKESPEARE

He that seeketh to be eminent   *730* amongst able men hath a great task; but that is ever good for the public. But he that plots to be the only figure among ciphers is the decay of a whole age.

> FRANCIS BACON

Put personal ambition away from   *731* you, and then you will find consolation in living or in dying, whatever may happen to you.

HENRI FRÉDÉRIC AMIEL

732   Every eel hopes to become a whale.
German proverb

733   Everybody wants to *be* somebody; nobody wants to *grow*.

JOHANN WOLFGANG VON GOETHE

734   A noble man compares and estimates himself by an idea which is higher than himself; and a mean man, by one lower than himself. The one produces aspiration; the other ambition, which is the way in which a vulgar man aspires.

HENRY WARD BEECHER

ANGER

735   And the spirit of God came upon Saul when he heard these things, and his anger was kindled greatly.
I Samuel 11:6

736   Anger is one of the sinews of the soul. He who lacks it hath a maimed mind.

THOMAS FULLER

737   To seek to extinguish anger utterly is but a bravery of the Stoics. We have better oracles: "Be angry, but sin not." "Let not the sun go down upon your wrath."

FRANCIS BACON

738   People who fly into a rage always make a bad landing.

WILL ROGERS

Moral indignation is jealousy with a   739
halo.

H.G. WELLS

I was angry with my friend;   740
I told my wrath, my wrath did end.
I was angry with my foe;
I told it not, my wrath did grow.

WILLIAM BLAKE

Anger is never without an argu-   741
ment, but seldom with a good one.
GEORGE SAVILE, Marquis of Halifax

When angry, count ten before you   742
speak; when very angry, count a
hundred.

THOMAS JEFFERSON

To be angry is to revenge the fault   743
of others upon ourselves.

ALEXANDER POPE

Anybody can become angry—that   744
is easy; but to be angry with the
right person, and to the right degree,
and at the right time, and for the
right purpose, and in the right way
—that is not within everybody's
power and it is not easy.

ARISTOTLE

Think, when you are enraged at   745
anyone, what would probably become your sentiments should he die
during the dispute.

WILLIAM SHENSTONE

ART

Artistry's haunting curse, the In-   746
complete!

ROBERT BROWNING

747 Art is limitation; the essence of every picture is the frame.

GILBERT KEITH CHESTERTON

748 The fine arts once divorcing themselves from *truth* are quite certain to fall mad, if they do not die.

THOMAS CARLYLE

749 Art is the imposing of a pattern on experience, and our esthetic enjoyment in recognition of the pattern.

ALFRED NORTH WHITEHEAD

750 Artistic growth is, more than it is anything else, a refining of the sense of truthfulness. The stupid believe that to be truthful is easy; only the artist, the great artist, knows how difficult it is.

WILLA CATHER

751 Literature decays only as men become more and more corrupt.

JOHANN WOLFGANG VON GOETHE

752 There is no patriotic art and no patriotic science.

JOHANN WOLFGANG VON GOETHE

753 Art is I; Science is We.

CLAUDE BERNARD

754 The artist doesn't see things as they are, but as he is.

Anonymous

755 A good spectator also creates.

Swiss proverb

756 All great art and literature is propaganda.

GEORGE BERNARD SHAW

757 Art is a collaboration between God and the artist, and the less the artist does the better.

ANDRÉ GIDE

All great art is the expression of 758 man's delight in God's work, not his own.

JOHN RUSKIN

BIGOTRY

When, oh when, shall we learn that 759 loyalty to Christ is tested far more by the strength of our sympathy with truth than by the intensity of our hatred of error?

FREDERICK W. ROBERTSON

There is no bigotry like that of "free 760 thought" run to seed.

HORACE GREELEY

BIGOT, *n.* One who is obstinately 761 and zealously attached to an opinion that you do not entertain.

AMBROSE BIERCE,
The Devil's Dictionary

Waiting on God is a bore; but what 762 fun to argue, to score off opponents, to lose one's temper and call it "righteous indignation," and at last to pass from controversy to blows, from words to what St. Augustine so deliciously described as the "benignant asperity" of persecution and punishment!

ALDOUS HUXLEY

The experience of many ages proves 763 that men may be ready to fight to the death, and to persecute without pity, for a religion whose creed they do not understand, and whose precepts they habitually disobey.

THOMAS BABINGTON MACAULAY

The mind of a bigot is like the pupil 764

of the eye; the more light you pour upon it, the more it will contract.

OLIVER WENDELL HOLMES, JR.

765 Remember that zeal, being an excrescence of divine love, must in no sense contradict any action of love. Love to God includes love to our neighbor; and therefore no pretense of zeal for God's glory must make us uncharitable to our brother; for that is just so pleasing to God as hatred is an act of love.

JEREMY TAYLOR

766 Wisdom never has made a bigot, but learning has.

JOSH BILLINGS

767 A bigot delights in public ridicule, for he begins to think he is a martyr.

SYDNEY SMITH

768 They shall put you out of the synagogues: yea, the time cometh, that whosoever killeth you will think that he doeth God service. And these things will they do unto you, because they have not known the Father, nor me.

John 16:2–3

BOREDOM

769 A yawn may be defined as a silent yell.

GILBERT KEITH CHESTERTON

770 BORE, *n.* A person who talks when you wish him to listen.

AMBROSE BIERCE,
The Devil's Dictionary

The mass of men lead lives of quiet desperation.   771

HENRY DAVID THOREAU

The secret of being a bore is to tell everything.   772

VOLTAIRE (François Marie Arouet)

We are seldom tiresome to ourselves.   773

SAMUEL JOHNSON

There is no bore like a clever bore.   774

SAMUEL BUTLER

We often forgive those who bore us, but we cannot forgive those whom we bore.   775

FRANÇOIS DE LA ROCHEFOUCAULD

CHARACTER

Do men gather grapes of thorns, or figs of thistles?   776

Matthew 7:16

You cannot carve rotten wood.   777

Chinese proverb

Character is what you are in the dark.   778

DWIGHT L. MOODY

You can mold a mannerism, but you must chisel a character.   779

Anonymous

Sow a thought, and you reap an act;   780
    Sow an act, and you reap a habit;
Sow a habit, and you reap a character;
Sow a character, and you reap a destiny.

Anonymous

781 Men best show their character in trifles, where they are not on their guard. It is in insignificant matters, and in the simplest habits, that we often see the boundless egotism which pays no regard to the feelings of others, and denies nothing to itself.

ARTHUR SCHOPENHAUER

782 Reputation is what men and women think of us; character is what God and the angels know of us.

THOMAS PAINE

783 I have often thought that the best way to define a man's character would be to seek out the particular mental or moral attitude in which, when it came upon him, he felt himself most deeply and intensely active and alive. At such moments there is a voice inside which speaks and says: "This is the real me!"

WILLIAM JAMES

784 Talent without character is friskiness.

RALPH WALDO EMERSON

785 The reputation of a thousand years may be determined by the conduct of one hour.

Japanese proverb

786 A man never shows his own character so plainly as by the way he portrays another's.

JEAN PAUL RICHTER

787 Everyone is a moon, and has a dark side which he never shows to anybody.

MARK TWAIN

788 Character is a by-product; it is pro-

duced in the great manufacture of daily duty.

WOODROW WILSON

CIVILIZATION

The test of every civilization is the point below which the weakest and most unfortunate are not allowed to fall.

789

HERBERT HENRY ASQUITH

Civilization consists in the multiplication and refinement of human wants.

790

ROBERT A. MILLIKAN

A general definition of civilization: a civilized society is exhibiting the five qualities of truth, beauty, adventure, art, peace.

791

ALFRED NORTH WHITEHEAD

Civilized man's brain is a museum of contradictory truths.

792

REMY DE GOURMONT

The temptations of the wilderness are those of the flesh; the temptations of civilization are those of the mind.

793

EUGEN ROSENSTOCK-HUESSY

The longing to be primitive is a disease of culture; it is archaism in morals. To be so preoccupied with vitality is a symptom of anemia.

794

GEORGE SANTAYANA

Civilization is the slow process of learning to be kind.

795

Anonymous

CLEVERNESS

796 Many writers, especially of an aca-
demic or aesthetic kind (and never
more than today) seem to me to
stultify themselves because they are
neither clever enough to be brilliant,
nor honest enough to be simple.
F.L. LUCAS

797 Clever people never listen and stupid people never talk.
OSCAR WILDE

798 Cleverness is serviceable for everything, sufficient for nothing.
HENRI FRÉDÉRIC AMIEL

799 I have always thought it rather interesting to follow the involuntary
movements of fear in clever people.
Fools coarsely display their coward-
ice in all its nakedness, but the
others are able to cover it with a veil
so delicate, so daintily woven with
small plausible lies, that there is
some pleasure to be found in contemplating this ingenious work of
the human intelligence.
ALEXIS DE TOCQUEVILLE

800 Clever men are the tools with which
bad men work.
WILLIAM HAZLITT

801 What makes us so bitter against
people who outwit us is that they
think themselves cleverer than we
are.
FRANÇOIS DE LA ROCHEFOUCAULD

802 Too clever is dumb.
OGDEN NASH

COMMON SENSE

Common sense is not so common. 803
VOLTAIRE (François Marie Arouet)

Nothing astonishes men so much as 804
common sense and plain dealing.
RALPH WALDO EMERSON

Common sense is in medicine the 805
master workman.
PETER MERE LATHAM

I don't know why it is that the 806
religious never ascribe common
sense to God.
W. SOMERSET MAUGHAM

I think that common sense, in a 807
rough dogged way, is technically
sounder than the special schools of
philosophy, each of which squints
and overlooks half the facts and half
the difficulties in its eagerness to
find in some detail the key to the
whole.
GEORGE SANTAYANA

COMPROMISE

Compromise is odious to passionate 808
natures because it seems a surrender, and to intellectual natures because it seems a confusion; but to
the inner man, to the profound
Psyche within us, whose life is
warm, nebulous and plastic, compromise seems the path of profit and
justice.
GEORGE SANTAYANA

Life cannot subsist in society but by 809
reciprocal concessions.
SAMUEL JOHNSON

810 A lean compromise is better than a fat lawsuit.

Anonymous

811 Better bend than break.

Scottish proverb

812 An appeaser is one who feeds a crocodile—hoping it will eat him last.

WINSTON CHURCHILL

813 People talk about the middle of the road as though it were unacceptable. Actually, all human problems, excepting morals, come into the gray areas. Things are not all black and white. There have to be compromises. The middle of the road is all of the usable surface. The extremes, right and left, are in the gutters.

DWIGHT D. EISENHOWER

814 What are facts but compromises? A fact merely marks the point where we have agreed to let investigation cease.

BLISS CARMAN

CONCEIT

(See *Pride*)

815 Conceit is God's gift to little men.

BRUCE BARTON

816 The world tolerates conceit from those who are successful, but not from anybody else.

JOHN BLAKE

817 I've never any pity for conceited people, because I think they carry their comfort about with them.

GEORGE ELIOT

And so we plow along, as the fly *818* said to the ox.

HENRY WADSWORTH LONGFELLOW

Has God forgotten all I have done *819* for him?

LOUIS XIV, *upon hearing the news of the French defeat at Malplaquet*

Talk to a man about himself and he *820* will listen for hours.

BENJAMIN DISRAELI

Every man has a right to be conceited until he is successful. *821*

BENJAMIN DISRAELI

I strive automatically to bring the *822* world into harmony with my own nature.

GEORGE BERNARD SHAW

EGOTIST, *n.* A person of low taste, *823* more interested in himself than in me.

AMBROSE BIERCE,
The Devil's Dictionary

CRITICISM

A true critic ought to dwell rather *824* upon excellencies than imperfections, to discover the concealed beauties of a writer, and communicate to the world such things as are worth their observation.

JOSEPH ADDISON

Never forget what a man says to *825* you when he is angry.

HENRY WARD BEECHER

826 We must remember that every new creation has been greeted with the words with which the poetry of Keats was greeted, in the massive judgment of the *Edinburgh Review,* "This will never do."

HALFORD E. LUCCOCK

827 To criticize is to appreciate, to appropriate, to take intellectual possession, to establish, in fine, a relation with the criticized thing and to make it one's own.

HENRY JAMES

828 The good critic is one who tells of his mind's adventures among masterpieces.

ANATOLE FRANCE

829 Criticism is properly the rod of divination: a hazel switch for the discovery of buried treasure, not a birch twig for the castigation of offenders.

ARTHUR SYMONS

830 A fly may sting a stately horse and make him wince, but one is but an insect, and the other is a horse still.

SAMUEL JOHNSON

831 You will never be an inwardly religious and devout man unless you pass over in silence the shortcomings of your fellow men, and diligently examine your own weaknesses.

THOMAS À KEMPIS

832 To avoid criticism, do nothing, say nothing, be nothing.

ELBERT HUBBARD

833 If I tried to read, much less answer all the criticism made of me and all the attacks leveled against me, this office would be closed for all other business. I do the best I know how, the very best I can. I mean to keep on doing this, down to the very end. If the end brings me out all wrong, then ten angels swearing I had been right would make no difference. If the end brings me out all right, then what is said against me now will not amount to anything.

ABRAHAM LINCOLN

CUSTOM

The old order changeth, yielding 834 place to new,
And God fulfils himself in many ways,
Lest one good custom should corrupt the world.

ALFRED, LORD TENNYSON

Custom reconciles us to everything. 835

EDMUND BURKE

Without the aid of prejudice and 836 custom I should not be able to find my way across the room.

WILLIAM HAZLITT

Where it is customary, the cow is 837 put to bed.

Swiss proverb

The difference between law and cus- 838 tom is that it takes a lot of nerve to violate a custom.

Anonymous

839 Some of the roads most used lead nowhere.

Jewish proverb

840 Custom has furnished the only basis that ethics have ever had.

JOSEPH WOOD KRUTCH

CYNICISM

841 A cynic is just a man who found out when he was about ten that there wasn't any Santa Claus, and he's still upset.

JAMES GOULD COZZENS

842 A cynic is a man who knows the price of everything and the value of nothing.

OSCAR WILDE

843 Cynicism in literary works usually signifies a certain element of disappointed ambition. When one no longer knows what to do in order to astonish and survive, one offers one's *pudenda* to the public gaze. Everyone knows perfectly well what he will see; but it is sufficient to make the gesture.

PAUL VALÉRY

844 The habit of thinking ill of everything and everyone is tiresome to ourselves and to all around us.

POPE JOHN XXIII

845 By letting themselves be cynical, unhappy people aggravate their melancholy. They are like a dog which tears at its wounded paw so as to hurt the pain.

HUBERT VAN ZELLER

DEMOCRACY

Democracy assumes that there are *846* extraordinary possibilities in ordinary people.

HARRY EMERSON FOSDICK

You can never have a revolution in *847* order to establish a democracy. You must have a democracy in order to have a revolution.

GILBERT KEITH CHESTERTON

Man's capacity for justice makes *848* democracy possible. His inclination to injustice makes democracy necessary.

REINHOLD NIEBUHR

Men, as well as women, do not need *849* political rights in order that they may govern, but in order that they may not be misgoverned.

JOHN STUART MILL

A fanatical belief in democracy *850* makes democratic institutions impossible.

BERTRAND RUSSELL

Democracy is good. I say this be- *851* cause other systems are worse.

JAWAHARLAL NEHRU

Democracy is a condition where *852* people believe that other people are as good as they are.

STUART CHASE

Democracy becomes a government *853* of bullies tempered by editors.

RALPH WALDO EMERSON

It is a besetting vice of democracies *854* to substitute public opinion for law.

This is the usual form in which masses of men exhibit their tyranny.

JAMES FENIMORE COOPER

855 Democracy means not "I am as good as you are" but "You are as good as I am."

THEODORE PARKER

DESPAIR

856 Remember that despair belongs only to passionate fools or villains, such as were Ahitophel and Judas, or else to devils and damned persons; and as the hope of salvation is a good disposition towards it, so is despair a certain consignment to eternal ruin. A man may be damned for despairing to be saved. Despair is the proper passion of damnation.

JEREMY TAYLOR

857 We need not despair of any man as long as he lives.

AUGUSTINE OF HIPPO

858 Despair is the conclusion of fools.

BENJAMIN DISRAELI

859 I have plumbed the depths of despair and have found them not bottomless.

THOMAS HARDY

EDUCATION

(See *Civilization, Knowledge*)

860 The test of every religious, political, or educational system, is the man it forms. If a system injured the intelligence it is bad. If it injures the character it is vicious. If it injures the conscience it is criminal.

HENRI FRÉDÉRIC AMIEL

Education—whether its object be 861 children or adults, individuals or an entire people, or even oneself—consists in creating motives. To show what is beneficial, what is obligatory, what is good—that is the task of education.

SIMONE WEIL

A man who has never gone to 862 school may steal from a freight car; but if he has a university education, he may steal the whole railroad.

THEODORE ROOSEVELT

An education which is not religious 863 is atheistic; there is no middle way. If you give to children an account of the world from which God is left out, you are teaching them to understand the world without reference to God. If he is then introduced, he is an excrescence. He becomes an appendix to his own creation.

WILLIAM TEMPLE

Perhaps the most valuable result of 864 all education is the ability to make yourself do the thing you have to do, when it ought to be done, whether you like it or not; it is the first lesson that ought to be learned; and however early a man's training begins, it is probably the last lesson that he learns thoroughly.

THOMAS HENRY HUXLEY

A teacher affects eternity; he can 865 never tell where his influence stops.

HENRY ADAMS

866 Our colleges ought to have lit up in us a lasting relish for the better kind of man, a loss of appetite for mediocrities.

WILLIAM JAMES

867 I have never let my schooling interfere with my education.

MARK TWAIN

868 A good education is not so much one which prepares a man to succeed in the world, as one which enables him to sustain failure.

BERNARD IDDINGS BELL

869 Education is a weapon, whose effect depends upon who holds it in his hands and at whom it is aimed.

JOSEF STALIN

870 Every method of education founded, wholly or in part, on the denial or forgetfulness of original sin and grace, and relying solely on the powers of human nature, is unsound.

POPE PIUS XI

ENDS AND MEANS

871 To do evil that good may come of it is for bunglers in politics as well as morals.

WILLIAM PENN

872 As soon as men decide that all means are permitted to fight an evil, then their good becomes indistinguishable from the evil that they set out to destroy.

CHRISTOPHER DAWSON

873 I have spent my days stringing and unstringing my instrument, while the song I came to sing remains unsung.

RABINDRANATH TAGORE

The church [in the Inquisition] committed herself, on the highest possible principles, to a breach of the highest possible principles.   874

CHARLES WILLIAMS

I remember a young theological student of my own day who was on the point of writing his thesis. He had a card index of his material; it was beautifully arranged with red ink, black ink, tabs, and notches. He was so absorbed in it that days slipped by, and every day there was added improvement. After a while he stopped thinking of his thesis and could think of nothing but the index. The last I heard of it, it was a better index than ever! That will happen to anybody who lets it!   875

PAUL SCHERER

FALL OF MAN

A man is a god in ruins.   876

RALPH WALDO EMERSON

It is said: It was because Adam ate the apple that he was lost and fell. I say: It was because of his arrogating something to himself, because of his I, Mine, Me, and the like. Had he eaten seven apples, and yet never arrogated anything to himself, he would not have fallen: but as soon as he arrogated something to himself, he fell, and would have fallen if he had never bitten into the apple.   877

Theologia Germania

878 The man without a navel still lives in me.

THOMAS BROWNE

879 Adam ate the apple, and our teeth still ache.

Hungarian proverb

880 The desire of power in excess caused the angels to fall; the desire of knowledge in excess caused man to fall.

FRANCIS BACON

881 I do not doubt that if the Paradisal man could now appear among us, we should regard him as an utter savage, a creature to be exploited, or, at best, patronized. Only one or two, and those the holiest among us, would glance a second time at the naked, shaggy-bearded, slow-spoken creature: but they, after a few minutes, would fall at his feet.

C.S. LEWIS

882 We find ourselves out of sympathy with God from the start.

E.J. BICKNELL

883 In nature a repulsive caterpillar turns into a lovely butterfly. But with human beings it is the other way 'round: a lovely butterfly turns into a repulsive caterpillar.

ANTON CHEKHOV

884 Over and over again, as we break some rule which seems rather arbitrary and meaningless, we discover the principle which had dictated it. We set in motion the causes and effects from which we understand, for the first time, why there had ever been that prohibition; then it is too late. The discovery is called the Fall of Man.

WILLIAM TEMPLE

885 Each new person born into the human race is involved in all its accumulated error.

E.F. SCOTT

886 Certain new theologians dispute original sin, which is the only part of Christian theology which can really be proved.

GILBERT KEITH CHESTERTON

887 Everything is good when it leaves the hands of the Creator; everything degenerates in the hands of man.

JEAN JACQUES ROUSSEAU

888 The ox knoweth his owner, and the ass his master's crib: but Israel doth not know, my people doth not consider.

Isaiah 1:3

889 Eden is on no map, and Adam's fall fits no historical calendar. Moses is not nearer the Fall than we are, because he lived three thousand years before our time. The Fall refers not to some datable aboriginal calamity in the historic past of humanity, but to a dimension of human experience which is always present—namely, that we who have been created for fellowship with God repudiate it continually; and that the whole of mankind does this along with us. Every man is his own "Adam," and all men are solidarily "Adam." Thus, Paradise before the Fall is . . . our "memory" of a divinely intended quality of life, given to us along with our consciousness of guilt.

J.S. WHALE

FANATICISM

(See *Bigotry*)

890 But when a man's religion becomes really frantic; when it is a positive torment to him; and, in fine, makes this earth of ours an uncomfortable inn to lodge in; then I think it high time to take that individual aside and argue the point with him.

HERMAN MELVILLE

891 Fanaticism consists in redoubling your efforts when you have forgotten your aim.

GEORGE SANTAYANA

892 A fanatic is one who can't change his mind and won't change the subject.

WINSTON CHURCHILL

893 But Faith, fanatic Faith, once wedded fast
To some dear falsehood, hugs it to the last.

THOMAS MOORE

894 Fanaticism, the false fire of an overheated mind.

WILLIAM COWPER

895 A fanatic is a man who does what he thinks the Lord would do if he knew the facts of the case.

FINLEY PETER DUNNE

FEAR

896 He that fears you present will hate you absent.

THOMAS FULLER

897 Fear is sharp-sighted, and can see things underground, and much more in the skies.

MIGUEL DE CERVANTES

898 Cruelty and fear shake hands together.

HONORÉ DE BALZAC

899 If you have a fearful thought, share it not with a weakling, whisper it to your saddle-bow, and ride forth singing.

KING ALFRED

900 The free man is he who does not fear to go to the end of his thought.

LÉON BLUM

901 The first and great commandment is, Don't let them scare you.

ELMER DAVIS

902 There is only one man I fear, and his name is James Garfield.

JAMES A. GARFIELD

903 A great fear, when it is ill managed, is the parent of superstition; but a discreet and well guided fear produces religion.

JEREMY TAYLOR

904 Fear is one of the passions of human nature of which it is impossible to divest it. You remember the Emperor Charles V, when he read upon the tombstone of a Spanish nobleman, "Here lies one who never knew fear," wittily said, "Then he never snuffed a candle with his fingers."

SAMUEL JOHNSON

905 Let me assert my firm belief that the only thing we have to fear is fear itself—nameless, unreasoning terror

which paralyzes needed efforts to convert retreat into advance.

FRANKLIN D. ROOSEVELT

906 "I will have no man in my boat," said Starbuck, "who is not afraid of a whale." By this, he seemed to mean, not only that the most reliable and useful courage was that which arises from the fair estimation of the encountered peril, but that an utterly fearless man is a far more dangerous comrade than a coward.

HERMAN MELVILLE

907 Those who love to be feared fear to be loved; they themselves are of all people most abject; some fear them, but they fear everyone.

FRANCIS DE SALES

FLATTERY

908 Flattery corrupts both the receiver and giver.

EDMUND BURKE

909 For I know not how to give flattering titles; in so doing my maker would soon take me away.

Job 32:22

910 A man's body is remarkably sensitive. Pat him on the back and his head swells.

Anonymous

911 He who cannot love must learn to flatter.

JOHANN WOLFGANG VON GOETHE

912 Baloney is the unvarnished lie laid on so thick you hate it. Blarney is flattery laid on so thin you love it.

FULTON J. SHEEN

Flattery is like cologne water, to be 913 smelled of, not swallowed.

JOSH BILLINGS

FOOLISHNESS

To laugh at men of sense is the 914 privilege of fools.

JEAN DE LA BRUYERE

When a new idea gets into an unfur- 915 nished mind it has the time of its life. There is nothing to oppose its autocratic rule.

SAMUEL MC CHORD CROTHERS

There are more fools than knaves in 916 the world, else the knaves would not have enough to live upon.

SAMUEL BUTLER

No one is a fool always, everyone 917 sometimes.

Anonymous

Unless a man knows Latin he is 918 never a great fool.

Anonymous

It is an honor for a man to cease 919 from strife: but every fool will be meddling.

Proverbs 20:3

Nobody can describe a fool to the 920 life without much patient self-inspection.

FRANK MOORE COLBY

He that is giddy thinks the world 921 turns round.

WILLIAM SHAKESPEARE

922 Fools and wise folk are alike harmless. It is the half-wise, and the half-foolish, who are most dangerous.

JOHANN WOLFGANG VON GOETHE

923 Suffer fools gladly. They may be right.

HOLBROOK JACKSON

FRIENDSHIP

924 A friend loveth at all times, and a brother is born for adversity.

Proverbs 17:17

925 Persons are fine things, but they cost too much! for *thee* I must pay *me*.

RALPH WALDO EMERSON

926 It is one of the blessings of old friends that you can afford to be stupid with them.

RALPH WALDO EMERSON

927 A friend is the one who comes in when the whole world has gone out.

Anonymous

928 To know someone here or there with whom you feel there is understanding in spite of distances or thoughts unexpressed—that can make of this earth a garden.

JOHANN WOLFGANG VON GOETHE

929 We have fewer friends than we imagine, but more than we know.

HUGO VON HOFMANNSTHAL

930 Every man should keep a fair-sized cemetery in which to bury the faults of his friends.

HENRY WARD BEECHER

931 A friend is one who warns you.

Jewish proverb

932 If a man does not make new acquaintances as he advances through life, he will soon find himself left alone. A man, Sir, should keep his friendship in constant repair.

SAMUEL JOHNSON

933 The older I grow in years, the more I wonder and my joy increases when I see the power of these words of Jesus—"I have called you friends" —to move the human heart. The one word "friend" breaks down each barrier of reserve, and we have boldness in his presence. Our hearts go out in love to meet his love.

CHARLES F. ANDREWS

934 Faithful are the wounds of a friend, but the kisses of an enemy are deceitful.

Proverbs 27:6

935 The language of friendship is not words but meanings.

HENRY DAVID THOREAU

936 A man cannot speak to his son but as a father; to his wife but as a husband; to his enemy but upon terms: whereas a friend may speak as the case requires, and not as it sorteth with the person.

FRANCIS BACON

937 Friendship is always a sweet responsibility, never an opportunity.

KAHLIL GIBRAN

GLUTTONY

938 Gluttons dig their graves with their teeth.

Jewish proverb

939 More people die from overeating than from undernourishment.

The Talmud

940 There are more gluttons than drunkards in hell.

Anonymous

941 In general, mankind, since the improvement of cookery, eats twice as much as nature requires.

BENJAMIN FRANKLIN

942 Most people eat as though they were fattening themselves for the market.

EDGAR W. HOWE

GOSSIP

943 Gossip is vice enjoyed vicariously.

ELBERT HUBBARD

944 Whether it be to friend or foe, talk not of other men's lives.

Ecclesiasticus 19:8

945 I lay it down as a fact that if all men knew what others say of them, there would not be four friends in the world.

BLAISE PASCAL

946 Gossip is a low form of the communion of saints.

Anonymous

947 Gossip is a sort of smoke that comes from the dirty tobacco-pipes of those who diffuse it; it proves nothing but the bad taste of the smoker.

GEORGE ELIOT

948 Never listen to accounts of the frailties of others; and if anyone should complain to you of another, humbly ask him not to speak of him at all.

JOHN OF THE CROSS

949 Whoever gossips to you will gossip of you.

Spanish proverb

950 The only time people dislike gossip is when you gossip about them.

WILL ROGERS

GOVERNMENT

(See *Politics*)

951 The real science of political economy, which has yet to be distinguished from the bastard science, as medicine from witchcraft, and astronomy from astrology, is that which teaches nations to desire and labor for the things that lead to life.

JOHN RUSKIN

952 Injustice cannot reign if the community does not furnish a due supply of unjust agents.

HERBERT SPENCER

953 The triumph of demagogues is short-lived. But the ruins are eternal.

CHARLES PÉGUY

954 Tyranny is always better organized than freedom.
CHARLES PÉGUY

955 Everything begins in mysticism and ends in politics.
CHARLES PÉGUY

956 No matter how noble the objectives of a government, if it blurs decency and kindness, cheapens human life, and breeds ill will and suspicion—it is an evil government.
ERIC HOFFER

957 Government, like dress, is the badge of lost innocence.
THOMAS PAINE

958 Bad laws are the worst sort of tyranny.
EDMUND BURKE

959 A good government remains the greatest of human blessings, and no nation has ever enjoyed it.
WILLIAM RALPH INGE

960 The basis of effective government is public confidence.
JOHN F. KENNEDY

961 No man is good enough to govern another man without that other's consent.
ABRAHAM LINCOLN

962 The firm basis of government is justice, not pity.
WOODROW WILSON

963 Almost any system of government will work if the people will.
Anonymous

964 There is no government without mumbo-jumbo.
HILAIRE BELLOC

When a man assumes a public trust, 965 he should consider himself as public property.
THOMAS JEFFERSON

Public officers are the servants and 966 agents of the people, to execute the laws which the people have made.
GROVER CLEVELAND

There is no worse heresy than that 967 the office sanctifies the holder of it. That is the point at which the negation of Catholicism and the negation of Liberalism meet and keep high festival, and the end learns to justify the means.
LORD ACTON (John Dalberg)

An oppressive government is more 968 to be feared than a tiger.
CONFUCIUS

All free governments are managed 969 by the combined wisdom and folly of the people.
JAMES A. GARFIELD

The more perfect civilization is, the 970 less occasion has it for government.
JAMES OTIS

GRIEF

(See *Bereavement*)

To weep is to make less the depth of 971 grief.
WILLIAM SHAKESPEARE

You cannot prevent the birds of 972 sorrow from flying over your head, but you can prevent them from building nests in your hair.
Chinese proverb

973 Ah, why should we wear black for the guests of God?

JOHN RUSKIN

974 Sorrow makes us all children again, —destroys all differences on intellect. The wisest knows nothing.

RALPH WALDO EMERSON

975 Grief is the agony of an instant; the indulgence of grief, the blunder of a life.

BENJAMIN DISRAELI

976 There are wounds of the spirit which never close, and are intended in God's mercy to bring us ever nearer to him, and to prevent us leaving him, by their very perpetuity. Such wounds, then, may almost be taken as a pledge, or at least as a ground for the humble trust, that God will give us the great gift of perseverance to the end. . . . This is how I comfort myself in my own great bereavements.

JOHN HENRY NEWMAN

977 I would maintain the sanctity of human joy and human grief. I bow in reverence before the emotions of every melted heart. We have a human right to our sorrow. To blame the deep grief which bereavement awakens, is to censure all strong human attachments. The more intense the delight in their presence, the more poignant the impression of their absence; and you cannot destroy the anguish unless you forbid the joy. A morality which rebukes sorrow rebukes love. When the tears of bereavement have had their natural flow, they lead us again to life and love's generous joy.

JAMES MARTINEAU

It is with sorrows, as with countries, 978 each man has his own.

FRANÇOIS RENÉ DE CHATEAUBRIAND

Only when grief finds its work done 979 can God dispense us from it.

HENRI FRÉDÉRIC AMIEL

Without grief, which is the string of 980 this venturesome kite, man would soar too quickly and too high, and the chosen souls would be lost for the race, like balloons which, save for gravitation, would never return from the empyrean.

HENRI FRÉDÉRIC AMIEL

Grief knits two hearts in closer 981 bonds than happiness ever can, and common suffering is a far stronger link than common joy.

ALPHONSE DE LAMARTINE

Grievances are a form of impa- 982 tience. Griefs are a form of patience.

ROBERT FROST

If we could read the secret history of 983 the world, we should find in each man's life sorrow and suffering enough to disarm all hostility.

HENRY WADSWORTH LONGFELLOW

GUILT

(See *Sin*)

All have sinned, and come short of 984 the glory of God.

Romans 3:23

This is the excellent foppery of the 985 world, that, when we are sick in fortune—often the surfeit of our own behavior—we make guilty of our disasters the sun, the moon, and the stars: as if we were villains by necessity; fools by heavenly compulsion, knaves, thieves, and teachers by spherical predominance, drunkards, liars, and adulterers by an enforced obedience of planetary influence.

WILLIAM SHAKESPEARE

986 What we call real estate—the solid ground to build a house on—is the broad foundation on which nearly all the guilt of this world rests.

NATHANIEL HAWTHORNE

987 It is better that ten guilty persons escape than one innocent suffer.

WILLIAM BLACKSTONE

988 Guilt matters. Guilt must always matter.
Unless guilt matters the whole world is meaningless.

ARCHIBALD MAC LEISH

989 Every man is guilty of all the good he didn't do.

VOLTAIRE (François Marie Arouet)

990 To take upon oneself not punishment but *guilt*—that alone would be godlike.

FRIEDRICH WILHELM NIETZSCHE

HABIT

991 Habit is a shirt made of iron.
Czech proverb

992 We first make our habits, and then our habits make us.

JOHN DRYDEN

993 I never knew a man to overcome a bad habit gradually.

JOHN R. MOTT

994 Habit with him was all the test of truth:
"It must be right: I've done it from my youth."

GEORGE CRABBE

995 There is no more miserable human being than one in whom nothing is habitual but indecision.

WILLIAM JAMES

996 Two quite opposite qualities equally bias our minds—habit and novelty.

JEAN DE LA BRUYÈRE

997 Habit is everything—even in love.

MARQUIS DE VAUVENARGUES
(Luc de Clapiers)

998 The strength of a man's virtue should not be measured by his special exertions, but by his habitual acts.

BLAISE PASCAL

HATE

999 Better a dish of vegetables if love go with it than a fat ox eaten in hatred.
Proverbs 15:17
(New English Bible)

1000 Think of the end that awaits you and have done with hate.
Ecclesiasticus 28:6
(New English Bible)

1001 Love blinds us to faults, but hatred blinds us to virtues.

MOSES IBN EZRA

1002 Men hate more steadily than they love.
SAMUEL JOHNSON

1003 The man who sows hatred reaps remorse.
SOLOMON IBN GABIROL

1004 Short is the road that leads from fear to hate.
Italian proverb

1005 The price of hating other human beings is loving oneself less.
ELDRIDGE CLEAVER

1006 Saul owed his conversion neither to true love, nor to true faith, nor to any other truth. It was solely his hatred of the Christians that set him upon the road to Damascus, and to that decisive experience which was to decide the whole course of his life. He was brought to this experience by following with conviction the course in which he was most completely mistaken.
CARL G. JUNG

1007 We fear something before we hate it; a child who fears noises becomes a man who hates noise.
CYRIL CONNOLLY

1008 Hatred is the madness of the heart.
LORD BYRON (George Gordon)

1009 A man who lives, not by what he loves but by what he hates, is a sick man.
ARCHIBALD MACLEISH

1010 Hatred is self-punishment.
HOSEA BALLOU

HOME

(See *Family*)

You can't appreciate home till 1011 you've left it, money till it's spent, your wife till she's joined a woman's club, or Old Glory till you see it hanging on a broomstick on the shanty of a consul in a foreign town.
O. HENRY
(William Sydney Porter)

Let a man behave in his own house 1012 as a guest.
RALPH WALDO EMERSON

Home is the place where, when you 1013 have to go there, they have to take you in.
ROBERT FROST

Home is where the heart is. 1014
PLINY THE ELDER

Home was quite a place when peo- 1015 ple stayed there.
E.B. WHITE

A house is no home unless it contain 1016 food and fire for the mind as well as for the body.
MARGARET FULLER

Pity the home where everyone is the 1017 head.
Jewish proverb

Dine on onions, but have a home; 1018 reduce your food, but add to your dwelling.
The Talmud

To build a house with borrowed 1019

money is like collecting stones for your own tomb.

Ecclesiasticus 21:8
(New English Bible)

1020 The worst feeling in the world is the homesickness that comes over a man occasionally when he is at home.

EDGAR W. HOWE

HONOR

1021 There are no perfectly honorable men; but every true man has one main point of honor and a few minor ones.

GEORGE BERNARD SHAW

1022 The louder he talked of his honor, the faster we counted our spoons.

RALPH WALDO EMERSON

1023 Honor lies in honest toil.

GROVER CLEVELAND

1024 Those only deserve a monument who do not need one.

WILLIAM HAZLITT

HYPOCRISY

1025 Hypocrisy is the homage that vice pays to virtue.

FRANÇOIS DE LA ROCHEFOUCAULD

1026 It is disconcerting to note that there has been a marked increase in hypocrisy in this century. Many a Victorian who broke the seventh commandment would have con-

demned any public attack on standards which he himself found too exacting. Hypocrisy begins not only when men fail to practice what they preach but also when they begin to preach what they practice. Victorian writers who went to bed with a mistress did not feel it necessary to persuade themselves and others that fornication was enlightened and adultery progressive.

ARNOLD LUNN and GARTH LEAN

A bad man is worse when he pre- 1027 tends to be a saint.

FRANCIS BACON

It is with pious fraud as with a bad 1028 action; it begets a calamitous necessity of going on.

THOMAS PAINE

No man, for any considerable pe- 1029 riod, can wear one face to himself and another to the multitude, without finally getting bewildered as to which may be the true.

NATHANIEL HAWTHORNE

A hypocrite is a person who—but 1030 who isn't?

DON MARQUIS

When the fox preaches, look to your 1031 geese.

German proverb

Where there is no religion, hypoc- 1032 risy becomes good taste.

GEORGE BERNARD SHAW

Not every one that saith unto me, 1033 Lord, Lord, shall enter into the kingdom of heaven; but he that doeth the will of my Father.

Matthew 7:21

IDOLATRY

1034   Whatever a man seeks, honors, or exalts more than God, this is the god of his idolatry.

WILLIAM B. ULLATHORNE

1035   When men have gone so far as to talk as though their idols have come to life, it is time that someone broke them.

RICHARD H. TAWNEY

1036   When modern man declares that he wants a practical religion, a religion that works, a religion that gets results, he is not usually aware of what he really wants—a god who will run errands for him. Our world—and, one must fear, our churches—are full of idolaters. These people believe in God after a fashion, but always after their own fashion. They believe about God whatever they think advantageous to themselves. They allow God to maintain heaven; they forbid him to maintain a hell. They require that God shall be what they want him to be and do what they want him to do; they insist that God *is* as they want him to be. The god of their belief is an idol.

CARROLL E. SIMCOX

1037   The calves of Jeroboam still remain in the world, and will remain to the last day; not that any man now makes calves like Jeroboam's, but upon whatsoever a man depends or trusts—God set aside—this is the calves of Jeroboam, that is, other and strange gods, honored and worshiped instead of the only, true, living and eternal God, who only can and will help and comfort in time of need. In like manner also, all such as rely and depend upon their art, wisdom, strength, sanctity, riches, honor, power, or anything else, under what title or name soever, on which the world builds, make and worship the calves of Jeroboam.

MARTIN LUTHER

IGNORANCE

Nothing has more retarded the advancement of learning than the disposition of vulgar minds to ridicule and vilify what they cannot comprehend.   1038

SAMUEL JOHNSON

To be ignorant of one's ignorance is the malady of the ignorant.   1039

BRONSON ALCOTT

There is nothing that makes a man suspect much, more than to know little.   1040

FRANCIS BACON

Ignorance is excusable when it is borne like a cross, but when it is wielded like an ax, and with moral indignation, then it becomes something else indeed.   1041

FLANNERY O'CONNOR

Ignorance is not so damnable as humbug, but when it prescribes pills it may happen to do more harm.   1042

GEORGE ELIOT

Most ignorance is vincible ignorance. We don't know because we don't want to know.   1043

ALDOUS HUXLEY

1044 A man must have a certain amount of intelligent ignorance to get anywhere.

CHARLES F. KETTERING,
on his 70th birthday

1045 He knows so little and knows it so fluently.

ELLEN GLASGOW

1046 Everybody is ignorant, only on different subjects.

WILL ROGERS

1047 There is nothing more frightful than ignorance in action.

JOHANN WOLFGANG VON GOETHE

1048 Herein is the evil of ignorance, that he who is neither good nor wise is nevertheless satisfied with himself: he has no desire for that of which he feels no want.

SOCRATES

1049 I believe in the forgiveness of sins and the redemption of ignorance.

ADLAI STEVENSON

JUDGING OTHERS

1050 How rarely we weigh our neighbor in the same balance in which we weigh ourselves!

THOMAS À KEMPIS

1051 It is well, when one is judging a friend, to remember that he is judging you with the same god-like and superior impartiality.

ARNOLD BENNETT

1052 To undertake executions for the master executioner (Heaven) is like hewing wood for the master carpenter. Whoever undertakes to do so rarely escapes injuring his own hands.

LAO TZU

1053 We all make mistakes, but everyone makes different mistakes.

LUDWIG VAN BEETHOVEN, *dying*

1054 Let not this weak, unknowing hand
        Presume thy bolts to throw,
      And deal damnation 'round the land
        On each I judge thy foe.

      If I am right, thy grace impart
        Still in the right to stay;
      If I am wrong, oh teach my heart
        To find that better way.

LUDWIG VAN BEETHOVEN, *dying*

ALEXANDER POPE

1055 Beware of the man of complete unquestionable virtue, the upstanding self-righteous citizen, who for all creatures of weakness has one general attitude: "Give them hell."

DAVID ABRAHAMSEN

1056 Thou to wax fierce
      In the cause of the Lord,
      To threat and to pierce
      With the heavenly sword!
      Anger and zeal
      And the joy of the brave,
      Who bade thee to feel,
      Sin's slave?
      The altar's pure flame
      Consumes as it soars,
      Faith meetly may blame
      For it serves and adores.
      Thou warnest and smitest,
      Yet Christ must atone
      For a soul that thou slightest—
      Thine own.

JOHN HENRY NEWMAN

1057 Judge not, that ye be not judged.
Matthew 7:1

1058 You will not become a saint through other people's sins.
ANTON CHEKHOV

1059 One must judge men, not by their opinions but by what their opinions have made of them.
GEORG CHRISTIAN LICHTENBERG

1060 Nobody would conclude another to be damned if he did not wish him to be so.
JOHN HALES

1061 My children, said my Grandfather, you will never see anything worse than yourselves.
RALPH WALDO EMERSON

1062 Looking [in other people] for the faults, which I had a secret consciousness were in myself, has more hindered my progress in love and gentleness than all things else.
FREDERICK DENISON MAURICE

KNOWLEDGE

1063 If a little knowledge is dangerous, where is the man who has so much as to be out of danger?
THOMAS HENRY HUXLEY

1064 If you have knowledge, let others light their candles at it.
MARGARET FULLER

1065 Knowledge is proud that he has learn'd so much;
Wisdom is humble that he knows no more.
WILLIAM COWPER

1066 This devil of a man (Poincaré) is the opposite of Briand: the latter knows nothing, and understands everything; the other knows everything, and understands nothing.
GEORGES CLEMENCEAU

1067 There's nothing you can't prove if your outlook is sufficiently limited.
DOROTHY L. SAYERS

1068 Learn everything you possibly can, and you will discover later that none of it was superfluous.
HUGH OF ST. VICTOR

1069 Quarry the granite rock with razors, or moor the vessel with a thread of silk; then may you hope with such keen and delicate instruments as human knowledge and human reason to contend against those giants, the passion and the pride of man.
JOHN HENRY NEWMAN

1070 Knowledge is the small part of ignorance that we arrange and classify.
AMBROSE BIERCE

1071 I keep six honest serving-men
(They taught me all I knew);
Their names are What and Why and When
And How and Where and Who.
RUDYARD KIPLING

1072 Knowledge and human power are synonymous.
FRANCIS BACON

1073 Knowledge without integrity is dangerous and dreadful.
SAMUEL JOHNSON

1074 All wish to know, but none want to pay the price.
JUVENAL

1075 The preservation of the means of knowledge among the lowest ranks is of more importance to the public than all the property of all the rich men in the country.

JOHN ADAMS

1076 It is in knowledge as in swimming; he who flounders and splashes on the surface, makes more noise, and attracts more attention than the pearl-diver who quietly dives in quest of treasures to the bottom.

WASHINGTON IRVING

LAUGHTER

(See *Cheerfulness, Happiness, Humor*)

1077 Sudden glory is the passion which maketh those grimaces called laughter.

THOMAS HOBBES

1078 We know the degree of refinement in men by the matter they laugh at and by the ring of the laugh.

GEORGE MEREDITH

1079 Man is the only animal that laughs and weeps; for he is the only animal that is struck by the difference between what things are and what they might have been.

WILLIAM HAZLITT

1080 The man who cannot laugh is not only fit for treasons, stratagems, and spoils; but his whole life is already a treason and a stratagem.

THOMAS CARLYLE

1081 Everything is funny as long as it is happening to somebody else.

WILL ROGERS

As the crackling of thorns under a pot, so is the laughter of the fool; this also is vanity.   1082

Ecclesiastes 7:6

He who laughs, lasts.   1083

MARY PETTIBONE POOLE

Laughing is the sensation of feeling   1084
good all over, and showing it principally in one spot.

JOSH BILLINGS

The fellow who laughs last may   1085
laugh best, but he gets the reputation of being a dumbbell.

Anonymous

LAW

Legalism is simply law growing can-   1086
cerously.

E.G. SELWYN

God is law, say the wise; O Soul,   1087
  and let us rejoice,
For if He thunder by law the thunder is yet His voice.

ALFRED, LORD TENNYSON

Men of most renowned virtue have   1088
sometimes by transgressing most truly kept the law.

JOHN MILTON

Probably all laws are useless; for   1089
good men do not need laws at all, and bad men are made no better by them.

DEMONAX THE CYNIC

Wherever law ends, tyranny begins.   1090

JOHN LOCKE

1091 Men are not hanged for stealing horses, but that horses may not be stolen.
GEORGE SAVILE, Marquis of Halifax

1092 Any government is free to the people under it where the laws rule and the people are a party to the laws.
WILLIAM PENN

1093 Laws are like cobwebs, which may catch small flies, but let wasps and hornets break through.
JONATHAN SWIFT

1094 To say "It is only a man-made law" is to miss the point. Only when civil laws are at variance with the laws of God are they strictly man-made.
HUBERT VAN ZELLER

1095 There is but one law for all, namely, that law which governs all law, the law of our Creator, the law of humanity, justice, equity—the law of nature, and of nations.
EDMUND BURKE

1096 Law will never be strong or respected unless it has the sentiment of the people behind it. If the people of a state make bad laws, they will suffer for it. They will be the first to suffer. Suffering, and nothing else, will implant that sentiment of responsibility which is the first step to reform.
JAMES BRYCE

1097 The law, in its majestic equality, forbids the rich as well as the poor to sleep under bridges, to beg in the streets, and to steal bread.
ANATOLE FRANCE

1098 Laws that do not embody public opinion can never be enforced.
ELBERT HUBBARD

Man is an able creature, but he has *1099* made 32,647,389 laws and hasn't yet improved on the Ten Commandments.
Anonymous

It is the spirit and not the form of *1100* law that keeps justice alive.
EARL WARREN

We cannot expect to breed respect *1101* for law and order among people who do not share the fruits of our freedom.
HUBERT H. HUMPHREY

Let reverence for the laws be *1102* breathed by every American mother to the lisping babe that prattles on her lap. Let it be taught in schools, in seminaries, and in colleges. Let it be written in primers, spelling-books, and almanacs. Let it be preached from the pulpit, proclaimed in legislative halls, and enforced in courts of justice. And, in short, let it become the political religion of the nation.
ABRAHAM LINCOLN

LEADERSHIP

(See *Power, Influence*)

Leadership is the power to evoke the *1103* right response in other people.
HUMPHREY MYNORS

In this world no one rules by mere *1104* love; if you are but amiable, you are no hero; to be powerful, you must be strong, and to have dominion you must have a genius for organizing.
JOHN HENRY NEWMAN

1105 It is no loss of liberty to subordinate ourselves to a natural leader.

GEORGE SANTAYANA

1106 The man most fit for high station is not the man who demands it.

MOSES IBN EZRA

1107 The question "Who ought to be the boss?" is like asking "Who ought to be the tenor in the quartet?" Obviously, the man who can sing tenor.

HENRY FORD

1108 A leader is best when he is neither seen nor heard,

Not so good when he is adored and glorified,

Worst when he is hated and despised.

"Fail to honor people, they will fail to honor you."

But of a good leader, when his work is done, his aim fulfilled,

The people will say, "We did this ourselves."

LAO TZU

1109 Beware of the chief seat, because it shifts.

Jewish proverb

1110 A man is led the way he wishes to follow.

The Talmud

1111 When a man is able to take abuse with a smile, he is worthy to become a leader.

NACHMAN OF BRATSLAV

1112 If the blind lead the blind, both shall fall into the ditch.

Matthew 15:14

1113 The final test of a leader is that he leaves behind him in other men the conviction and the will to carry on.

WALTER LIPPMANN

The nation will find it very hard to *1114* look up to the leaders who are keeping their ears to the ground.

WINSTON CHURCHILL

LONELINESS

(See *Solitude*)

Essentially loneliness is the knowl- *1115* edge that one's fellow human beings are incapable of understanding one's condition and therefore are incapable of bringing the help most needed. It is not a question of companionship—many are ready to offer this and companionship is certainly not to be despised—but rather one of strictly sharing, of identifying. No two human beings can manage this, so to a varying extent loneliness at times is the lot of all.

HUBERT VAN ZELLER

Language has created the word *lone-* *1116* *liness* to express the pain of being alone, and the word *solitude* to express the glory of being alone.

PAUL TILLICH

The whole conviction of my life now *1117* rests upon the belief that loneliness, far from being a rare and curious phenomenon, peculiar to myself and to a few other solitary men, is the central and inevitable fact of human existence.

THOMAS WOLFE

1118   People are lonely because they build
walls instead of bridges.
JOSEPH FORT NEWTON

1119   Yes: I am alone on earth: I have
always been alone. . . . Do not
think you can frighten me by telling
me that I am alone. France is alone;
and God is alone; and what is my
loneliness before the loneliness of
my country and my God? I see now
that the loneliness of God is His
strength: what would He be if He
listened to your jealous little counsels? Well, my loneliness shall be my
strength too: it is better to be alone
with God: His friendship will not
fail me, nor His counsel, nor His
love. In His strength I will dare, and
dare, and dare, until I die.
The Maid,
in G. B. SHAW's Saint Joan

1120   Columbus discovered no isle or key
so lonely as himself.
RALPH WALDO EMERSON

1121   Shakespeare, Leonardo da Vinci,
Benjamin Franklin, and Lincoln
. . . were not afraid of being lonely
because they knew that was when
the creative mood in them could
work.

CARL SANDBURG

1122   Loneliness is the first thing which
God's eye nam'd not good.
JOHN MILTON

MANNERS

(See *Courtesy*)

1123   A man's attire, and excessive laughter, and gait, show what he is.
Ecclesiasticus 19:30

1124   The test of good manners is being
able to put up pleasantly with bad
ones.
Anonymous

1125   Good manners are made up of petty
sacrifices.
RALPH WALDO EMERSON

1126   There is always a best way of doing
everything, if it be to boil an egg.
Manners are the happy ways of
doing things.
RALPH WALDO EMERSON

1127   Hail ye small sweet courtesies of
life!
LAURENCE STERNE

1128   It is superstitious to put one's faith
in conventions; but it is arrogance
not to submit to them.
BLAISE PASCAL

1129   Few are qualified to shine in company; but it is in most men's power
to be agreeable.
JONATHAN SWIFT

1130   Now as to politeness, I would ven-
ture to call it benevolence in trifles.
WILLIAM PITT

1131   There are bad manners everywhere,
but an aristocracy is bad manners
organized.
HENRY JAMES

1132   Manners maketh man.
WILLIAM OF WYKEHAM

1133   Manners easily and rapidly mature
into morals.
HORACE MANN

MARRIAGE

1134 Marriage must be a relation either of sympathy or of conquest.

GEORGE ELIOT

1135 What greater thing is there for two human souls than to feel that they are joined for life, to strengthen each other in all labor, to rest on each other in all sorrow, to minister to each other in all pain, to be one with each other in silent unspeakable memories of the moment of the last parting?

GEORGE ELIOT

1136 A good marriage is that in which each appoints the other guardian of his solitude.

RAINER MARIA RILKE

1137 Let there be spaces in your togetherness.

KAHLIL GIBRAN

1138 Certainly wife and children are a kind of discipline of humanity; and single men, though they may be many times more charitable, because their means are less exhaust, yet, on the other side, they are more cruel and hardhearted (good to make severe inquisitors), because their tenderness is not so often called upon.

FRANCIS BACON

1139 Success in marriage is more than finding the right person: it is a matter of being the right person.

RABBI B.R. BRICKNER

1140 A person's character is but half formed until after wedlock.

CHARLES SIMMONS

1141 Marriages are best made of dissimilar material.

THEODORE PARKER

1142 What God hath joined together no man shall ever put asunder: God will take care of that.

GEORGE BERNARD SHAW

1143 Marriage is a step so grave and decisive that it attracts light-hearted, variable men by its very awfulness.

ROBERT LOUIS STEVENSON

1144 "Adam knew Eve his wife and she conceived." It is a pity that this is still the only knowledge of their wives at which some men seem to arrive.

F.H. BRADLEY

1145 Marriage is a covered dish.

Swiss proverb

1146 The difficulty with marriage is that we fall in love with a personality, but must live with a character.

PETER DE VRIES

1147 Marriage is our last, best chance to grow up.

JOSEPH BARTH

1148 Where there's marriage without love, there will be love without marriage.

BENJAMIN FRANKLIN

1149 A successful marriage is an edifice that must be rebuilt every day.

ANDRÉ MAUROIS

1150 A good many things are easier said than done—including the marriage ritual.

Anonymous

1151　Many a man in love with a dimple makes the mistake of marrying the whole girl.

Anonymous

1152　Love-making is radical, while marriage is conservative.

ERIC HOFFER

1153　Love is an ideal thing, marriage a real thing; a confusion of the real with the ideal never goes unpunished.

JOHANN WOLFGANG VON GOETHE

1154　If you are afraid of loneliness, don't marry.

ANTON CHEKHOV

1155　A man too good for the world is no good for his wife.

Yiddish proverb

1156　The true index of a man's character is the health of his wife.

CYRIL CONNOLLY

MONEY

1157　Money is like muck, no good except it be spread.

FRANCIS BACON

1158　If you want to know what a man really is like, take note how he acts when he loses money.

New England proverb

1159　Money really adds no more to the wise than clothes can to the beautiful.

Jewish proverb

1160　Nothing that is God's is obtainable by money.

TERTULLIAN

The chief value of money lies in the fact that one lives in a world in which it is overestimated.　1161

HENRY L. MENCKEN

Money often asks too much.　1162

RALPH WALDO EMERSON

The moral problem of our age is concerned with the love of money, with the habitual appeal to the money motive in nine-tenths of the activities of life.　1163

JOHN MAYNARD KEYNES

Make all you can, save all you can, give all you can.　1164

JOHN WESLEY

If money is at the root of all evil, it is also at the root of all morality.　1165

Anonymous

I don't like money actually, but it quiets my nerves.　1166

JOE LOUIS

I have a hundred rubles which I don't know what to do with. This peasant peddler in her ragged sheepskin stands there and looks at me timidly. But what good would my money do her? Would it add the value of a single hair to her happiness or to her peace of mind?　1167

LEO TOLSTOY

But they that will be rich fall. into temptation and a snare, and into many foolish and hurtful lusts, which drown men in destruction and perdition. For the love of money is the root of all evil: which while some coveted after, they have erred from the faith, and pierced themselves through with many sorrows.　1168

I Timothy 6:9–10

MUSIC

1169 Music strikes in me a profound contemplation of the First Composer.

THOMAS BROWNE

1170 The man that hath no music in himself,
Nor is not mov'd with concord of sweet sounds,
Is fit for treasons, stratagems, and spoils;
The motions of his spirit are dull as night,
And his affections dark as Erebus.
Let no such man be trusted. Mark the music.

WILLIAM SHAKESPEARE

1171 Music is essentially useless, as life is.

GEORGE SANTAYANA

1172 Music is love in search of a word.

SIDNEY LANIER

1173 What is law doesn't make progress, but what is gospel does. God has preached the gospel through music, too, as may be seen in Josquin, all of whose compositions flow freely, gently, and cheerfully, are not forced or cramped by rules, and are like the song of the finch.

MARTIN LUTHER

1174 So is music an asylum. It takes us out of the actual and whispers to us dim secrets that startle our wonder as to who we are, and for what, whence, and whereto, all the great interrogatories, like questioning angels, float in on its waves of sound.

RALPH WALDO EMERSON

1175 I am inclined to think that a hunt for folk songs is better than a manhunt of the heroes who are so highly extolled.

LUDWIG VAN BEETHOVEN

Music is the only language in which 1176 you cannot say a mean or sarcastic thing.

JOHN ERSKINE

After silence that which comes nearest 1177 to expressing the inexpressible is music.

ALDOUS HUXLEY

OPTIMISM AND PESSIMISM

Optimism is a kind of heart stimulant—the digitalis of failure. 1178

ELBERT HUBBARD

The American people never carry 1179 an umbrella. They prefer to walk in eternal sunshine.

ALFRED E. SMITH

The place where optimism most 1180 flourishes is the lunatic asylum.

HAVELOCK ELLIS

A pessimist is what he is because of 1181 the taxes the optimists have put upon him.

Anonymous

Optimism supplies the basic energy 1182 of civilization. Optimism doesn't wait on facts. It deals with prospects. Pessimism is a waste of time.

NORMAN COUSINS

An optimist is a man who has never 1183 had much experience.

DON MARQUIS

1184   The optimist proclaims that we live in the best of all possible worlds; and the pessimist fears this is true.
JAMES BRANCH CABELL

1185   The only limit to our realization of tomorrow will be our doubts of today.
FRANKLIN D. ROOSEVELT

1186   Pessimism, when you get used to it, is as agreeable as optimism.
ARNOLD BENNETT

1187   I am an optimist. It doesn't seem too much use being anything else.
WINSTON CHURCHILL

1188   There is no sadder sight than a young pessimist, except an old optimist.
MARK TWAIN

ORIGINALITY

1189   Our Lord never thought of being original.
GEORGE MAC DONALD

1190   The more intelligent a man is, the more originality he discovers in men. Ordinary people see no difference between men.
BLAISE PASCAL

1191   Nothing is more original, more *oneself* than to be nourished by others; only one must be able to digest them.
PAUL VALÉRY

1192   Originality does not consist in saying what no one has ever said

before, but in saying exactly what you think yourself.
JAMES FITZJAMES STEPHEN

Originality is simply a pair of fresh   1193
eyes.
THOMAS WENTWORTH HIGGINSON

The merit of originality is not nov-   1194
elty, it is sincerity. The believing man is the original man; he believes for himself, not for another.
THOMAS CARLYLE

PATRIOTISM

That man is little to be envied   1195
whose patriotism would not gain force upon the plain of Marathon, or whose piety would not grow warmer among the ruins of Iona.
SAMUEL JOHNSON

Patriotism is the last refuge of a   1196
scoundrel.
SAMUEL JOHNSON

I love the University of Salamanca;   1197
for when the Spaniards were in doubt as to the lawfulness of their conquering America, the University of Salamanca gave it as their opinion that it was not lawful.
SAMUEL JOHNSON

A man's feet must be planted in his   1198
country, but his eyes should survey the world.
GEORGE SANTAYANA

Ethan Allen and Stark, with whom   1199
he may in some respects be com-

PHILOSOPHY

pared, were rangers in a lower and less important field. They could bravely face their country's foes, but he [John Brown] had the courage to face his country herself when she was wrong.

HENRY DAVID THOREAU

1200 Patriotism makes a man a gentleman; nationalism makes him a cad.

ERNEST FREMONT TITTLE

1201 What is patriotism but the love of the good things we ate in our childhood?

LIN YUTANG

1202 The last thing which the thought of the Empire inspires in me is a desire to boast—to wave a flag, or to shout "Rule Britannia!" When I think about it, I am more inclined to go into a corner by myself and pray.

LORD MILNER

1203 Indeed, I tremble for my country when I reflect that God is just.

THOMAS JEFFERSON

1204 A nation's life is about as long as its reverential memory.

WHITTAKER CHAMBERS

1205 The man who prefers his country before any other duty shows the same spirit as the man who surrenders every right to the state. They both deny that right is superior to authority.

LORD ACTON (John Dalberg)

1206 This is a beautiful country.

JOHN BROWN
on his way to the gallows

I have gained this by philosophy: 1207 that I do without being commanded what others do only from fear of the law.

ARISTOTLE

I have tried too in my time to be a 1208 philosopher; but I don't know how, cheerfulness was always breaking in.

OLIVER EDWARDS

Touchstone's question, "Hast any 1209 philosophy in thee, shepherd?" will never cease to be one of the tests of a well-born nature. It says, Is there space and air in your mind, or must your companions gasp for breath whenever they talk with you?

WILLIAM JAMES

The true philosopher, who is not 1210 one chiefly by profession, must be prepared to tread the wine-press alone. He may indeed flourish like the green-bay tree in a grateful environment, but more often he will rather resemble a reed shaken by the wind. Whether starved or fed by the accidents of fortune he must find his essential life in his own ideal.

GEORGE SANTAYANA

Any two philosophers can tell each 1211 other all they know in two hours.

OLIVER WENDELL HOLMES, JR.

The philosopher has to be the bad 1212 conscience of his age.

FRIEDRICH WILHELM NIETZSCHE

A philosophical fashion catches on 1213 like a gastronomical fashion: one can no more refute an idea than a sauce.

E. MICHEL CIORAN

1214 To be a philosopher is not merely to have subtle thoughts, nor even to found a school, but so to love wisdom as to live according to its dictates, a life of simplicity, independence, magnanimity, and trust.

HENRY DAVID THOREAU

1215 The first step toward philosophy is incredulity.

DENIS DIDEROT

1216 Philosophy asks the simple question: What is it all about?

ALFRED NORTH WHITEHEAD

1217 A peasant and a philosopher may be equally *satisfied,* but not equally *happy.* Happiness consists in the multiplicity of agreeable consciousness.

SAMUEL JOHNSON

1218 The primary assurances of religion are the ultimate questions of philosophy.

WILLIAM TEMPLE

1219 Women make us poets, children make us philosophers.

MALCOLM DE CHAZAL

PLEASURE

1220 Among the actions which count as prayer, I include visits of courtesy and kindness, also necessary recreation of body and mind, so long as these be innocent and kept within the bounds of Christian conduct.

JEAN NICOLAS GROU

Now our duty standeth on the 1221 sunny side. For so good a God do we serve, that he hath made it our duty to be happy, so that we cannot please him except we be infinitely pleased ourselves.

JEREMY TAYLOR

We tire of those pleasures we take, 1222 but never of those we give.

JOHN PETIT-SENN

Whenever you are sincerely pleased 1223 you are nourished.

RALPH WALDO EMERSON

In diving to the bottom of pleasure 1224 we bring up more gravel than pearls.

HONORÉ DE BALZAC

POLITICS

Magnanimity in politics is not sel- 1225 dom the truest wisdom; and a great empire and little minds go ill together.

EDMUND BURKE

Those who would treat politics and 1226 morality apart will never understand the one or the other.

JOHN, VISCOUNT MORLEY

Power politics is the diplomatic 1227 name for the law of the jungle.

ELY CULBERTSON

Politics is a profession; a serious, 1228 complicated and, in its true sense, a noble one.

DWIGHT D. EISENHOWER

A politician thinks of the next elec- 1229

tion, a statesman of the next generation.

J.F. CLARKE

1230 To let politics become a cesspool, and then avoid it because it is a cesspool, is a double crime.

HOWARD CROSBY

1231 Any party which takes credit for the rain must not be surprised if its opponents blame it for the drought.

DWIGHT R. MORROW

1232 Nothing doth more hurt in a state than that cunning men pass for wise.

FRANCIS BACON

1233 These are my politics: to change what we can; to better what we can; but still to bear in mind that man is but a devil weakly fettered by some generous beliefs and impositions; and for no word however sounding, and no cause however just or pious, to relax the strictures of these bonds.

ROBERT LOUIS STEVENSON

1234 Whenever a man has cast a longing eye on offices, a rottenness begins in his conduct.

THOMAS JEFFERSON

1235 Who is to guard the "guards" themselves?

JUVENAL

1236 Society in every state is a blessing, but government, even in its best state, is a necessary evil; in its worst state, an intolerable one.

THOMAS PAINE

1237 The penalty that good men pay for not being interested in politics is to be governed by men worse than themselves.

PLATO

The good of man must be the end of the science of politics.   1238

ARISTOTLE

Politics is not an exact science.   1239

OTTO VON BISMARCK

Politics is the science of the possible,   1240 the attainable.

OTTO VON BISMARCK

Politics are a part of morals.   1241

HENRY EDWARD MANNING

PREJUDICE

A good many people think they are   1242 thinking when they are merely rearranging their prejudices.

WILLIAM JAMES

Dogs bark at every one they do not   1243 know.

HERACLITUS

To prejudge other people's notions   1244 before we have looked into them is not to show their darkness but to put out our own eyes.

JOHN LOCKE

Prejudice is the child of ignorance.   1245

WILLIAM HAZLITT

It is never too late to give up your   1246 prejudices.

HENRY DAVID THOREAU

He who knows only his own side of   1247 the case knows little of that.

JOHN STUART MILL

1248 The man who never alters his opinion is like standing water, and breeds reptiles of the mind.

WILLIAM BLAKE

1249 He who begins by loving Christianity better than truth will proceed by loving his own sect or church better than Christianity and end in loving himself better than all.

SAMUEL TAYLOR COLERIDGE

PRIDE

(See *Conceit*)

1250 Pride is at the bottom of all great mistakes.

JOHN RUSKIN

1251 Man, whose joy consisteth in comparing himself with other men, can relish nothing but what is eminent.

THOMAS HOBBES

1252 It is only people of small moral stature who have to stand on their dignity.

ARNOLD BENNETT

1253 Most of the trouble in the world is caused by people wanting to be important.

T.S. ELIOT

1254 Of all the causes which conspire to blind
Man's erring judgment, and misguide the mind,
What the weak head with strongest bias rules,
Is pride, the never-failing vice of fools.

ALEXANDER POPE

1255 There are two states or conditions of pride. The first is one of self-approval, the second one of self-contempt. Pride is seen probably at its purest in the latter.

HENRI FRÉDÉRIC AMIEL

1256 If you harden your heart with pride, you soften your brain with it, too.

Jewish proverb

1257 The passions grafted on wounded pride are the most inveterate; they are green and vigorous in old age.

GEORGE SANTAYANA

1258 Haughtiness toward men is rebellion to God.

MOSES NAHMANIDES

1259 You can have no greater sign of a confirmed pride than when you think you are humble enough.

WILLIAM LAW

1260 God sends no one away empty except those who are full of themselves.

DWIGHT L. MOODY

1261 The earth is strewn with the exploded bladders of the puffed up.

CARL SANDBURG

1262 Be not proud of race, face, place, or grace.

CHARLES H. SPURGEON

1263 There are only two kinds of men: the righteous who believe themselves sinners, and the rest, sinners who believe themselves righteous.

BLAISE PASCAL

1264 Not much evil is done by evil people. Most of the evil is done by good people, who do not know that they are not good.

REINHOLD NIEBUHR

1265 Let him that thinketh he standeth beware lest he fall.

I Corinthians 10:12

RACE

1266 God that made the world and all things therein. . . . hath made of one blood all nations of men for to dwell on the face of the earth.

Acts 17:24, 26

1267 The real "white man's burden" is not insolently to dominate colored or black people under the guise of protection, it is to desist from the hypocrisy which is eating into them. It is time white men learned to treat every human being as their equal.

MOHANDAS GANDHI

1268 Minds broken in two. Hearts broken. Conscience torn from acts. A culture split in a thousand pieces. This is segregation.

LILIAN SMITH

1269 The essential corruption of racial segregation is not that it is supported by lies but that people believe the lies.

HARRY GOLDEN

1270 After all, there is but one race—humanity.

GEORGE MOORE

1271 The existence of any pure race with special endowments is a myth, as is the belief that there are races all of

whose members are foredoomed to eternal inferiority.

FRANZ BOAS

A heavy guilt rests upon us for what 1272 the whites of all nations have done to the colored peoples. When we do good to them, it is not benevolence —it is atonement.

ALBERT SCHWEITZER

Mere connection with what is 1273 known as a superior race will not permanently carry an individual forward unless the individual has worth.

BOOKER T. WASHINGTON

The future of mankind belongs to its 1274 mongrels and not to its handsome but brainless Borzois.

GEORGE BERNARD SHAW

REVENGE

Dearly beloved, avenge not your- 1275 selves, but rather give place unto wrath: for it is written, Vengeance is mine; I will repay, saith the Lord.

Romans 12:19

Revenge is barren: its delight is 1276 murder and its satiety, despair.

JEAN PAUL RICHTER

Vengeance is mine, saith the Lord; 1277 and that means that it is not the Lord Chief Justice's.

GEORGE BERNARD SHAW

Distrust all in whom the impulse to 1278 punish is powerful.

FRIEDRICH WILHELM NIETZSCHE

1279 The smallest revenge will poison the soul.
Jewish proverb

1280 Blood that has been shed does not rest.
Jewish proverb

1281 A man that studieth revenge keepeth his own wounds green.
FRANCIS BACON

1282 Revenge is the abject pleasure of an abject mind.
JUVENAL

1283 The conception of punishment as a moral duty to impose suffering in order to reform and regenerate the criminal is false and always has a touch of bigotry and hypocrisy about it.
NICOLAS BERDYAEV

1284 Revenge is often like biting a dog because the dog bit you.
AUSTIN O'MALLEY

REVOLUTION

1285 One hundred and eighty-one years ago, our forefathers started a revolution that still goes on.
DWIGHT D. EISENHOWER

1286 Every revolution was once a thought in one man's mind, and when the same thought occurs to another man it is the key to that era.
RALPH WALDO EMERSON

1287 It is not the insurrections of ignorance that are dangerous, but the revolts of intelligence.
JAMES RUSSELL LOWELL

Revolutions are ambiguous things. 1288 Their success is generally proportionate to their power of adaptation and to the reabsorption within them of what they rebelled against.
GEORGE SANTAYANA

Few revolutionists would be such if 1289 they were heirs to a baronetcy.
GEORGE SANTAYANA

Remember always that all of us, and 1290 you and I especially, are descended from immigrants and revolutionists.
FRANKLIN D. ROOSEVELT,
*speaking to Daughters
of the American Revolution*

Repression is the seed of revolution. 1291
DANIEL WEBSTER

Every revolutionary ends by becom- 1292 ing either an oppressor or a heretic.
ALBERT CAMUS

Most revolutionaries are potential 1293 Tories, because they imagine that everything can be put to rights by altering the *shape* of society.
GEORGE ORWELL

Revolutions are not made; they 1294 come. A revolution is as natural a growth as an oak. It comes out of the past. Its foundations are laid far back.
WENDELL PHILLIPS

There is nothing more difficult to 1295 take in hand, more perilous to conduct, or more uncertain in its success, than to take the lead in the introduction of a new order of things.
NICCOLÒ MACHIAVELLI

It is unfortunate, that the efforts of 1296

mankind to recover the freedom of which they have been so long deprived, will be accompanied with violence, with errors, and even with crimes. But while we weep for the means, we must pray for the end.

THOMAS JEFFERSON

1297 The scrupulous and the just, the noble, humane, and devoted natures; the unselfish and the intelligent may begin a movement—but it passes away from them. They are not the leaders of a revolution. They are its victims.

JOSEPH CONRAD

1298 Revolutions do not always establish freedom.

MILLARD FILLMORE

1299 Certainly no revolution that has ever taken place in society can be compared to that which has been produced by the words of Jesus Christ.

MARK HOPKINS

1300 This country, with its institutions, belongs to the people who inhabit it. Whenever they shall grow weary of the existing government they can exercise their constitutional right of amending it, or their revolutionary right to dismember or overthrow it.

ABRAHAM LINCOLN

1301 Revolutions have never lightened the burden of tyranny; they have only shifted it to another shoulder.

GEORGE BERNARD SHAW

1302 The purity of a revolution can last a fortnight.

JEAN COCTEAU

1303 Those who make peaceful revolu-

tion impossible will make violent revolution inevitable.

JOHN F. KENNEDY

RICH AND POOR

Satan now is wiser than of yore, *1304* And tempts by making rich, not making poor.

ALEXANDER POPE

Becky Sharp's acute remark that it *1305* is not difficult to be virtuous on ten thousand a year has its application to nations; and it is futile to expect a hungry and squalid population to be anything but violent and gross.

THOMAS HENRY HUXLEY

So long as all the increased wealth *1306* which modern progress brings goes but to build up great fortunes, to increase luxury and make sharper the contrast between the House of Have and the House of Want, progress is not real and cannot be permanent.

HENRY GEORGE

He hath filled the hungry with good *1307* things, and the rich he hath sent empty away.

Luke 1:53

Whoso mocketh the poor reproach- *1308* eth his maker.

Proverbs 17:5

He who knows how to be poor *1309* knows everything.

JULES MICHELET

Laws grind the poor, and rich men *1310* rule the law.

OLIVER GOLDSMITH

1311 The rich will do everything for the poor but get off their backs.

KARL MARX

1312 This must be put bluntly: every man who has more than is necessary for his livelihood and that of his family, and for the normal development of his intelligence, is a thief and a robber. If he has too much, it means that others have too little.

ROMAIN ROLLAND

1313 Only the rich preach content to the poor.

HOLBROOK JACKSON

1314 What is the matter with the poor is poverty; what is the matter with the rich is uselessness.

GEORGE BERNARD SHAW

1315 The accumulation of vast wealth while so many are languishing in misery is a grave transgression of God's law, with the consequence that the greedy, avaricious man is never at ease in his mind: he is in fact a most unhappy creature.

POPE JOHN XXIII

SELFISHNESS

1316 Let me have my own way exactly in everything, and a sunnier and pleasanter creature does not exist.

THOMAS CARLYLE

1317 Selfishness is the only real atheism.

ISRAEL ZANGWILL

1318 No indulgence of passion destroys the spiritual nature so much as respectable selfishness.

GEORGE MAC DONALD

Next to the very young, I suppose 1319 the very old are the most selfish.

WILLIAM MAKEPEACE THACKERAY

The best preserved thing in all his- 1320 tory is an Egyptian mummy. The surest way to make a mummy out of yourself is to give all your attention to preserving life.

HALFORD E. LUCCOCK

The least pain in our little finger 1321 gives us more concern than the destruction of millions of our fellow men.

WILLIAM HAZLITT

When a man is all wrapped up in 1322 himself he makes a pretty small package.

JOHN RUSKIN

I gave a little tea party   1323
This afternoon at three.
      'Twas very small,
         Three guests in all—
I, myself, and me.

Myself ate up the sandwiches
While I drank all the tea,
      'Twas also I
         Who ate the pie
And passed the cake to me.

JESSICA NELSON NORTH

Doing nothing for others is the 1324 undoing of one's self. We must be purposely kind and generous, or we miss the best part of existence. The heart that goes out of itself, gets large and full of joy. This is the great secret of the inner life. We do ourselves the most good doing something for others.

HORACE MANN

1325 The world is the glass through which we see our Maker. But what men do is this: They put the dull quicksilver of their own selfishness behind the glass, and so it becomes not the transparent medium through which God shines, but the dead opaque which reflects back themselves. So it gives back their own false feelings and nature.

FREDERICK W. ROBERTSON

1326 We have always known that heedless self-interest was bad morals; we know now that it is bad economics.

FRANKLIN D. ROOSEVELT

1327 He who lives only to benefit himself confers on the world a benefit when he dies.

TERTULLIAN

SIN

1328 There is only one calamity—sin.

JOHN CHRYSOSTOM

1329 Sin is not a monster to be mused on, but an impotence to be got rid of.

MATTHEW ARNOLD

1330 These six things doth the Lord hate: yea, seven are an abomination unto him: a proud look, a lying tongue, and hands that shed innocent blood, an heart that deviseth wicked imaginations, feet that be swift in running to mischief, a false witness that speaketh lies, and he that soweth discord among brethren.

Proverbs 6:16–19

1331 As Martin Luther put it, the "natural man" (i.e. man fallen from his true nature and unredeemed from his spoilt sinful nature) is *incurvatus in se*, "bent inwards upon himself," instead of looking away from himself towards God and his fellows in love. That is what sin is, and all our sins can be reduced to that, even what we call the sins of the flesh.

DONALD M. BAILLIE

Men are not punished for their sins, 1332 but by them.

ELBERT HUBBARD

The safest road to Hell is the grad- 1333 ual one—the gentle slope, soft underfoot, without sudden turnings, without milestones, without guideposts.

C.S. LEWIS

The worst sin towards our fellow 1334 creatures is not to hate them, but to be indifferent to them: that's the essence of inhumanity.

GEORGE BERNARD SHAW

Sin is energy in the wrong channel. 1335
AUGUSTINE OF HIPPO

No sin is small. No grain of sand is 1336 small in the mechanism of a watch.

JEREMY TAYLOR

"Thou shalt not get found out" is 1337 not one of God's commandments; and no man can be saved by trying to keep it.

LEONARD BACON

The sin ye do two by two ye must 1338 pay for one by one!

RUDYARD KIPLING

One reason sin flourishes is that it is 1339 treated like a cream puff instead of a rattlesnake.

BILLY SUNDAY

1340 God may forgive you your sins, but your nervous system won't.

ALFRED KORZYBSKI

1341 There is no man so good who, were he to submit all his thoughts and actions to the law, would not deserve hanging ten times in his life.

MICHEL DE MONTAIGNE

1342 For the religious man to do wrong is to defy his King; for the Christian, it is to wound his Friend.

WILLIAM TEMPLE

SOLITUDE

1343 I never found the companion that was so companionable as solitude.

HENRY DAVID THOREAU

1344 But little do men perceive what solitude is, and how far it extendeth. For a crowd is not company; and faces are but a gallery of pictures; and talk but a tinkling cymbal, where there is no love.

FRANCIS BACON

1345 Society is like the air, necessary to breathe, but insufficient to live on.

GEORGE SANTAYANA

1346 He who does not enjoy solitude will not love freedom.

ARTHUR SCHOPENHAUER

1347 Solitude, though it be silent as light, is like light, the mightiest of agencies; for solitude is essential to man. All men come into this world *alone;* all leave it *alone.*

THOMAS DE QUINCEY

1348 It is easy in the world to live after the world's opinion; it is easy in solitude to live after your own; but the great man is he who in the midst of the crowd keeps with perfect sweetness the independence of solitude.

RALPH WALDO EMERSON

1349 All men's misfortunes spring from their hatred of being alone.

JEAN DE LA BRUYÈRE

1350 To go up alone into the mountain and come back as an ambassador to the world, has ever been the method of humanity's best friends.

EVELYN UNDERHILL

1351 I live in that solitude which is painful in youth, but delicious in the years of maturity.

ALBERT EINSTEIN

1352 Come now, little man! Flee for a while from your tasks, hide yourself for a little space from the turmoil of your thoughts. Come, cast aside your burdensome cares, and put aside your laborious pursuits. For a little while give your time to God, and rest in him for a little while. Enter into the inner chamber of your mind, shut out all things save God and whatever may aid you in seeking God; and having barred the door of your chamber, seek him.

ANSELM OF CANTERBURY

SUCCESS AND FAILURE

1353 The figure of the Crucified invalidates all thought which takes success for its standard.

DIETRICH BONHOEFFER

1354 'Tis not in mortals to command
     success,
     But we'll do more, Sempronius—
     we'll deserve it.
                    JOSEPH ADDISON

1355 Nothing recedes like success.
                    WALTER WINCHELL

1356 The life of every man is a diary in
     which he means to write one story
     and writes another, and his hum-
     blest hour is when he compares the
     volume as it is with what he vowed
     to make it.
                    JAMES M. BARRIE

1357 It is often the failure who is the
     pioneer in new lands, new undertak-
     ings, and new forms of expression.
                    ERIC HOFFER

1358 Any coward can fight a battle when
     he's sure of winning; but give me
     the man who has pluck to fight
     when he's sure of losing. That's my
     way, sir; and there are many vic-
     tories worse than a defeat.
                    GEORGE ELIOT

1359 There is only one success—to spend
     your life in your own way.
                    CHRISTOPHER MORLEY

1360 Try not to become a man of success
     but rather try to become a man of
     value.
                    ALBERT EINSTEIN

1361 He's no failure. He's not dead yet.
                    DAVID LLOYD GEORGE

1362 A man can fail many times, but he
     isn't a failure until he begins to
     blame somebody else.
                    JOHN BURROUGHS

1363 A failure is a man who has blun-
     dered but is not able to cash in on
     the experience.
                    ELBERT HUBBARD

1364 From the Taoist point of view, an
     educated man is one who believes
     he has not succeeded when he has,
     but is not so sure he has failed when
     he fails.
                    LIN YUTANG

TEMPTATION

(See *Sin*)

1365 God is better served in resisting a
     temptation to evil than in many
     formal prayers. This is but twice or
     thrice a day; but that every hour
     and moment of the day. So much
     more is our continual watch than
     our evening and morning devotion.
                    WILLIAM PENN

1366 Let no man think himself to be holy
     because he is not tempted, for the
     holiest and highest in life have the
     most temptations. How much higher
     the hill is, so much is the wind there
     greater; so, how much higher the life
     is, so much the stronger is the temp-
     tation of the enemy.
                    JOHN WYCLIFFE

1367 The beginning of all temptations to
     evil is instability of temper and want
     of trust in God; for even as a ship
     without a helm is tossed about by
     the waves, so is a man who is
     careless and infirm of purpose
     tempted, now on this side, now on
     that. As fire testeth iron, so doth
     temptation the upright man. Often-
     times we know not what strength we

have; but temptation revealeth to us what we are.

THOMAS A KEMPIS

1368 There hath no temptation taken you but such as is common to man: but God is faithful, who will not suffer you to be tempted above that ye are able; but will with the temptation also make a way to escape, that ye may be able to bear it.

I Corinthians 10:13

1369 It is good to be without vices, but it is not good to be without temptations.

WALTER BAGEHOT

1370 O cunning enemy, that, to catch a saint,
With saints dost bait thy hook!
Most dangerous
Is that temptation that doth goad us on
To sin in loving virtue.

WILLIAM SHAKESPEARE

1371 Honest bread is all very well—it's the butter that makes the temptation.

DOUGLAS JERROLD

1372 Blessed is the man that endureth temptation: for when he is tried, he shall receive the crown of life.

James 1:12

1373 As the Sandwich-Islander believes that the strength and valor of the enemy he kills passes into himself, so we gain the strength of the temptations we resist.

RALPH WALDO EMERSON

1374 When we do ill, the devil tempteth us; when we do nothing, we tempt him.

THOMAS FULLER

VIOLENCE

(See *Hate, Power, War and Peace*)

The practice of violence, like all 1375 action, changes the world, but the most probable change is to a more violent world.

HANNAH ARENDT

Through violence you may murder 1376 the hater, but you do not murder hate. In fact, violence only increases hate. So it goes. Returning violence for violence multiplies violence, adding deeper darkness to a night already devoid of stars.

MARTIN LUTHER KING, JR.

Degeneracy follows every autocratic 1377 system of violence, for violence inevitably attracts moral inferiors. Time has proven that illustrious tyrants are succeeded by scoundrels.

ALBERT EINSTEIN

Violence does even justice unjustly. 1378

THOMAS CARLYLE

A good portion of the evils that 1379 afflict mankind is due to the erroneous belief that life can be made secure by violence.

LEO TOLSTOY

All they that take the sword shall 1380 perish with the sword.

Matthew 26:52

WAR AND PEACE

There's many a boy here today who 1381 looks on war as all glory, but, boys, it's all hell.

GENERAL WILLIAM T. SHERMAN

1382 It is well that war is so terrible, or
we should get too fond of it.
GENERAL ROBERT E. LEE

1383 War is much too serious a matter to
be entrusted to the military.
GEORGES CLEMENCEAU

1384 Older men declare war. But it is
youth that must fight and die. And
it is youth who must inherit the
tribulation, the sorrow, and the
triumphs that are the aftermath of
war.
HERBERT HOOVER

1385 War is not an instinct but an invention.
JOSÉ ORTEGA Y GASSET

1386 Wars are not "acts of God." They
are caused by man, by man-made
institutions, by the way in which
man has organized his society. What
man has made, man can change.
FRED M. VINSON

1387 We [Christians in war] are called to
the hardest of all tasks; to fight
without hatred, to resist without
bitterness, and in the end, if God
grant it so, to triumph without vin-
dictiveness.
WILLIAM TEMPLE

1388 In War: Resolution. In Defeat:
Defiance. In Victory: Magnanimity.
In Peace: Good Will.
WINSTON CHURCHILL

1389 Atomic warfare is bad enough; biological warfare would be worse; but
there is something that is worse than
either. The French can tell you what
it is; or the Czechs, or the Greeks, or
the Norwegians, or the Filipinos; it
is subjection to an alien oppressor.
ELMER DAVIS

1390 How good bad music and bad reasons sound when we march against
an enemy!
FRIEDRICH WILHELM NIETZSCHE

1391 War hath no fury like a noncomba-
tant.
CHARLES E. MONTAGUE

1392 For a war to be just, three conditions are necessary—public authority, just cause, right motive.
THOMAS AQUINAS

1393 Never was so much false arithmetic
employed on any subject, as that
which has been employed to persuade nations that it is their interest
to go to war. Were the money which
it has cost to gain, at the close of a
long war, a little town, or a little
territory, the right to cut wood here,
or to catch fish there, expended in
improving what they already possess, in making roads, opening rivers, building ports, improving the
arts, and finding employment for
their idle poor, it would render them
much stronger, much wealthier and
happier.
THOMAS JEFFERSON

1394 War is one of the constants of
history, and has not diminished with
civilization or democracy. In the last
3,421 years of recorded history only
268 have seen no war. We have
acknowledged war as at present the
ultimate form of competition and
natural selection in the human species. *Polemos pater panton*, said Heraclitus; war, or competition, is the
father of all things, the potent
source of ideas, inventions, institutions, and states. Peace is an unstable equilibrium, which can be pre-

served only by acknowledged supremacy or equal power.

WILL AND ARIEL DURANT

1395 War is an ugly thing, but not the ugliest of things: the decayed and degraded state of moral and patriotic feeling which thinks nothing is worth a war is worse.

JOHN STUART MILL

1396 I hate war as only a soldier who has lived it can, only as one who has seen its brutality, its futility, its *stupidity*.

DWIGHT D. EISENHOWER

1397 In modern warfare there are no victors; there are only survivors.

LYNDON B. JOHNSON

1398 What we need to discover in the social realm is the moral equivalent of war: something heroic that will speak to men as universally as war does, and yet will be compatible with their spiritual selves as war has proved itself to be incompatible.

WILLIAM JAMES

WEAKNESS

1399 My strength is made perfect in weakness.

II Corinthians 12:9

1400 Weakness, not vice, is virtue's worst enemy.

FRANÇOIS DE LA ROCHEFOUCAULD

1401 Like all weak men he laid an exaggerated stress on not changing one's mind.

W. SOMERSET MAUGHAM

There are two kinds of weakness, 1402 that which breaks and that which bends.

JAMES RUSSELL LOWELL

The greatest weakness of all is the 1403 fear of appearing weak.

JEAN JACQUES ROUSSEAU

We must have a weak spot or two in 1404 our character before we can love it much.

OLIVER WENDELL HOLMES

When God delivered Israel out of 1405 Egypt, he didn't send an army. We would have sent an army or an orator! But God sent a man who had been in the desert for forty years, and had an impediment in his speech. It is weakness that God wants! Nothing is small when God handles it.

DWIGHT L. MOODY

WEALTH

(See *Money*)

Few of us can stand prosperity. 1406 Another man's, I mean.

MARK TWAIN

Mr. Money is a good Catholic. 1407

Spanish proverb

I cannot call riches better than the 1408 baggage of virtue; the Roman word is better, *impedimenta*. For as the baggage is to an army, so is riches to virtue. It cannot be spared, or left behind, but it hindreth the march; yea, and the care of it sometimes loseth or disturbeth the victory. Of great riches there is no real use, except it be in the distribution; the rest is but conceit.

FRANCIS BACON

1409 As the partridge sitteth on eggs, and hatcheth them not; so he that getteth riches, and not by right, shall leave them in the midst of his days, and at his end shall be a fool.

Jeremiah 17:11

1410 It is easier for a camel to go through the eye of a needle, than for a rich man to enter into the kingdom of God.

Matthew 19:24

1411 There is a time when a man distinguishes the idea of felicity from the idea of wealth; it is the beginning of wisdom.

RALPH WALDO EMERSON

1412 Prosperity is only an instrument to be used; not a deity to be worshipped.

CALVIN COOLIDGE

1413 Rich men without convictions are more dangerous in modern society than poor women without chastity.

GEORGE BERNARD SHAW

1414 Many years ago Rudyard Kipling made a commencement address at McGill University in Montreal. He said one striking thing which deserves to be kept in remembrance. He was warning the students against an overconcern for money, or position, or glory. He said: "Some day you will meet a man who cares for none of these things. Then you will know how poor you are." That has happened on a grand scale. Jesus cared for none of these things. And

for nineteen centuries he has led many people to see how poor they are with only a collection of *things* to show for their journey through life, and no spiritual resources.

HALFORD E. LUCCOCK

Since all the riches of this world   *1415*
May be gifts from the Devil and
    earthly kings,
I should suspect that I worship'd the
    Devil
If I thanked God for worldly things.

The countless gold of a merry heart,
The rubies and pearls of a loving
    eye,
The indolent never can bring to the
    mart,
Nor the cunning hoard up in his
    treasury.

WILLIAM BLAKE

WICKEDNESS

(See *Sin, Good and Evil*)

There are bad people who would be   *1416*
less dangerous if they had no good
in them.

FRANÇOIS DE LA ROCHEFOUCAULD

The belief in a supernatural source   *1417*
of evil is not necessary: men alone
are quite capable of every wickedness.

JOSEPH CONRAD

Corruption never has been compul-   *1418*
sory.

ANTHONY EDEN

Those who admire strength in a   *1419*
rascal do not live in his town.

Anonymous

1420 The wicked flee, when no man pursueth; but the righteous are bold as a lion.

Proverbs 28:1

1421 It requires great abilities to have the *power* of being very wicked; but not to *be* very wicked. It requires great abilities to conquer an army, but none to massacre it after it is conquered.

SAMUEL JOHNSON

1422 None of us feels the true love of God till we realize how wicked we are. But you can't teach people that—they have to learn by experience.

DOROTHY L. SAYERS

1423 Wickedness sucks in the greater part of its own venom, and poisons itself therewith.

MICHEL DE MONTAIGNE

WIT

1424 Wit has truth in it; wisecracking is simply calisthenics with words.

DOROTHY PARKER

1425 Satire is a kind of glass, wherein beholders do generally discover everybody's face but their own.

JONATHAN SWIFT

1426 If you want to be witty, work on your character and say what you think on every occasion.

STENDHAL (Henri Beyle)

1427 Many get the name for being witty, only to lose the credit for being sensible.

GRACIAN

The man who sees the consistency in things is a wit; the man who sees the inconsistency in things is a humorist.   1428

GILBERT KEITH CHESTERTON

I prefer cheerful people to witty ones; wit is cheerfulness painfully intellectualized.   1429

Anonymous

Many that are wits in jest are fools in earnest.   1430

Anonymous

Wit ought to be a glorious treat, like caviar; never spread it about like marmalade.   1431

NOEL COWARD

Wit is a treacherous dart. It is perhaps the only weapon with which it is possible to stab oneself in one's own back.   1432

GEOFFREY BOCCA

Wit sometimes enables us to act rudely with impunity.   1433

FRANÇOIS DE LA ROCHEFOUCAULD

Blows are sarcasms turned stupid; wit is a form of force that leaves the limbs at rest.   1434

GEORGE ELIOT

WORDS

A word fitly spoken is like apples of gold in pictures of silver.   1435

Proverbs 25:11

In love and divinity what is most worth saying cannot be said.   1436

COVENTRY PATMORE

1437 I am not so lost in lexicography as to forget that *words are the daughters of earth, and that things are the sons of heaven.*

SAMUEL JOHNSON

1438 It is a sad but sure truth that every time you speak of a fine purpose, especially if with eloquence and to the admiration of bystanders, there is the less chance of your ever making a fact of it in your own poor life.

THOMAS CARLYLE

1439 Nothing, surely, is more alive than a word.

J. DONALD ADAMS

1440 Words are what hold society together.

STUART CHASE

1441 Our words are a faithful index of the state of our souls.

FRANCIS DE SALES

1442 Eating words has never given me indigestion.

WINSTON CHURCHILL

1443 The pipe and the psaltery make sweet melody: but a pleasant tongue is above them both.

Ecclesiasticus 40:21

1444 Words are tools which automatically carve concepts out of experience.

JULIAN S. HUXLEY

1445 The difference between the right word and the almost right word is the difference between the lightning and the lightning bug.

MARK TWAIN

1446 He that talketh what he knoweth will also talk what he *knoweth not.*

FRANCIS BACON

1447 "Those Macedonians," said Philip, "are a rude and clownish people, they call a spade a spade."

PLUTARCH

1448 I say unto you, That every idle word that men shall speak, they shall give account thereof in the day of judgment. For by thy words thou shalt be justified, and by thy words thou shalt be condemned.

Matthew 12:36–37

WORLDLINESS

1449 More people are kept from a true sense and state of religion by a regular kind of sensuality and indulgence than by gross drunkenness. More men live regardless of the great duties of piety through too great a concern for worldly goods than through direct injustice.

WILLIAM LAW

1450 The first common mistake to get rid of is that mankind consists of a great mass of religious people and a few eccentric atheists. It consists of a huge mass of worldly people, and a small percentage of people deeply interested in religion and concerned about their own souls and other peoples'. . . . The passionately religious are a people apart; and if they were not hopelessly outnumbered by the worldly, they would turn the world upside down, as St. Paul was reproached, quite justly, for wanting to do. Few people can number among their personal acquaintances a single atheist or a single Plymouth Brother.

GEORGE BERNARD SHAW

1451   One belongs to the world as long as one is more ashamed of a *faux pas,* a display of ignorance, a wrong turn of phrase, than of an unloving action.

THEODOR HAECKER

1452   The unalterable law of "the world" is that evil is fought with evil, and that the devil is driven out by Beelzebub. And so long as that remains unaltered, Christianity is not victorious.

THEODOR HAECKER

WORRY

1453   The freedom now desired by many is not freedom to do and dare but freedom from care and worry.

JAMES TRUSLOW ADAMS

1454   Worry is the interest paid by those who borrow trouble.

GEORGE LYON

1455   There is nothing that wastes the body like worry, and one who has any faith in God should be ashamed to worry about anything whatsoever.

MOHANDAS GANDHI

1456   Worry affects the circulation, the heart, the glands, the whole nervous system. I have never known a man who died from overwork, but many who died from doubt.

CHARLES H. MAYO

1457   The reason why worry kills more people than work is that more people worry than work.

ROBERT FROST

1458   I have never yet met a healthy person who worried very much about his health, or a really good person who worried much about his soul.

J.B.S. HALDANE

IV

Christic and
His Church

In him was life; and the life was the light of men.

John 1:4

O loving wisdom of our God!
When all was sin and shame,
A second Adam to the fight
And to the rescue came.

O wisest love! that flesh and blood,
Which did in Adam fail,
Should strive afresh against the foe,
Should strive, and should prevail.

John Henry Newman

The Father is begetting his Son unceasingly, and
furthermore he begets me his Son, his very own
Son.

Meister Eckhart

ADOPTION AND BAPTISM

(See *Sacraments*)

1459 Christians are made, not born.

ST. JEROME

1460 In German the word *sein* signifies two things, to be and to belong to him.

FRANZ KAFKA

1461 At baptism we are regenerated into the fellowship of the ever blessed and glorious Trinity.

FREDERICK DENISON MAURICE

1462 He gives the right to become sons of God to those who receive him, that is, to those who "believe on his Name." The Name is the manifested nature; to baptize into the Name of the Father, the Son, and the Holy Ghost is to plunge or bathe the person in the manifested love of God.

WILLIAM TEMPLE

1463 According to the New Testament, all men have in principle received baptism long ago, namely on Golgotha, at Good Friday and Easter.

OSCAR CULLMANN

1464 Baptism signifies that the old Adam in us is to be drowned by daily sorrow and repentance, and perish with all sins and evil lusts; and that the new man should daily come forth again and rise, who shall live before God in righteousness and purity forever.

MARTIN LUTHER

1465 Our adoptive sonship is in its supernatural reality a reflection of the sonship of the Word. God has not communicated to us the whole of his nature but a participation of it.

R. GARRIGOU-LAGRANGE

1466 When Luther was most afflicted with temptations and doubts he would write two words on his table with a piece of chalk: *Baptizatus sum* (I have been baptized). He meant that baptism was the foundation of his Christian certainty. In the fact that he was baptized before he had any knowledge of salvation or desire for it, God teaches him that the divine mercy sought him independently of his attitude towards God.

J.S. WHALE

1467 I was at Rome on Christmas Eve.
Festive bells—everywhere the Feast o' the Babe,
Joy upon earth, peace and good will to man!
I am baptized. I started and let drop The dagger.

Count Guido, in
ROBERT BROWNING'S
The Ring and the Book

1468 Ye have not received the spirit of bondage again to fear; but ye have received the Spirit of adoption, whereby we cry, Abba, Father.

Romans 8:15

1469 As many of you as have been baptized into Christ have put on Christ.

Galatians 3:27

1470 Is this a sombre thought on the happy day of baptism—that one is thereby dedicated to death? But is there anything more consoling? We are reminded that our mortal life is to be, along with Jesus, not absurd but fruitful.

A New Catechism

APOSTLES AND APOSTOLICITY

1471   And the wall of the city had twelve foundations, and in them the names of the twelve apostles of the Lamb.
Revelation 21:14

1472   The Apostles received the Gospel for us from the Lord Jesus Christ; Jesus Christ was sent from God. Christ, then, is from God and the Apostles are from Christ.
CLEMENT OF ROME

1473   The Church is . . . Apostolic; because it continues stedfastly in the Apostles' teaching and fellowship.
Book of Common Prayer

1474   When pilgrims on the road of God meet one another, they have something to say. A man may be of value to another man, not because he wishes to be important, not because he possesses some inner wealth of soul, not because of something he is, but because of what he is—not. His importance may consist in his poverty, in his hopes and fears, in his waiting and hurrying, in the direction of his whole being towards what lies beyond his horizon and his power. The importance of an apostle is negative rather than positive. In him a void becomes visible. And for this reason he is something to others: he is able to share grace with them, to focus their attention, and to establish them in waiting and in adoration. The Spirit gives grace through him. Possessing nothing, he has nothing of his own to offer, and so, the more he imparts, the more he receives; and the more he receives, the more he imparts. There is therefore no question of Christians saying to one another—"Did you receive from me?" or "Did I receive from you?" Since neither is, or possesses, anything, nothing passes from the one to the other. It is sufficient that what is, is—above us and behind us and beyond us.
KARL BARTH

ASCENSION OF CHRIST

The early church's belief in the   1475
Ascension can be read as its refusal to allows its Lord to be localized or spatially restricted. The Ascension in its simplest terms means that Jesus is mobile. He is not a baal, but the Lord of all history.
HARVEY COX

Yea, and the Resurrection and   1476
    Uprise
To the right hand of the throne—
    what is it beside,
When such truth, breaking bounds,
    o'erfloods my soul,
And as I saw the sin and death, even
    so
See I the need yet transiency of
    both,
The good and glory consummated
    thence?
I saw the power; I see the Love,
    once weak,
Resume the power. . . .
ROBERT BROWNING

1477 He exhibited the actuality of his body, carrying the lovely and adorable matter, with which all souls are everlastingly conjoined, into his eternity.

CHARLES WILLIAMS

1478 The Flesh and Blood of the Ascended Son of Man are plainly not mere matter; if they were, the resultant astronomical problems would be overwhelming—for where in the universe are they? "By the right hand of the Father" where the Ascended Son is seated is not a far-off place; it is here; wherever a man be, for him it is here. The Flesh and Blood of the Ascended Son of man are Spirit and Life.

WILLIAM TEMPLE

1479 We are not to think of him disappearing into the blue sky like a skylark: still less as "soaring through tracts unknown" to some astronomically remote place. The Ascension is much more wonderful and mysterious than that. He passed out of time and space altogether. He did not go up, as one ascends in an airplane; he went up, as an heir to the throne becomes king, as a boy goes up from the fourth form into the fifth form, as a soldier rises when he becomes a general. He is not "in the bright place far away" for he is "not far from each one of us" (Acts 18:27).

C.B. MOSS

1480 The heaven that hides him from our sight
　　Knows neither near nor far:
An altar candle sheds its light
　　As surely as a star;

And where his loving people meet
　　To share the gift divine,

There stands he with unhurrying feet;
　　There heavenly splendors shine.

HOWARD CHANDLER ROBBINS

ATONEMENT

I give up every plea beside— *1481*
Lord, I am damn'd; but thou hast died.

JOHN WESLEY

Since Christ accepted the thief on *1482* the cross just as he was and received Paul after all his blasphemies and persecutions, we have no reason to despair. Good God, what do you think it means that he has given his only Son? It means that he also offers whatever else he possesses.

MARTIN LUTHER

For the sake of each of us he laid *1483* down his life—worth no less than the universe. He demands of us in return our lives for the sake of each other.

CLEMENT OF ALEXANDRIA

Faith is the spiritual appropriation *1484* of Christ's saving deed. In consequence, atonement is both accomplished *for us* and wrought *in us*.

VINCENT TAYLOR

I, if I be lifted up from the earth, *1485* will draw all men unto me.

John 12:32

If, when we were enemies, we were *1486* reconciled to God by the death of

his Son, much more, being reconciled, we shall be saved by his life.
Romans 5:10

1487 It is one of the great principles of Christianity, that all that happened to Jesus Christ must fulfil itself in the spirit and body of every Christian.

BLAISE PASCAL

1488 The death of Christ justifies us inasmuch as through it charity is excited in our hearts.

PETER THE LOMBARD

1489 You can say that Christ died for your sins. You may say that the Father has forgiven us because Christ has done for us what we ought to have done. You may say that we are washed in the blood of the Lamb. You may say that Christ has defeated death. They are all true. If any of them does not appeal to you, leave it alone and get on with the formula that does. And, whatever you do, do not start quarreling with other people because they use a different formula from yours.

C.S. LEWIS

1490 The man who takes the risks of believing in a universe ruled over by a Christ-like God finds all the fountains of faith and joy playing in his spirit. Laughter is his heritage while he can see the face of God in the face of Jesus. And the deepest and most beautiful mystery of the Christian faith is found at Calvary. For if you can be sure that there is a cross in the heart of God you can be sure of laughter in the heart of man.

LYNN HAROLD HOUGH

BETHLEHEM

Since we are not yet ready for the 1491 banquet of our Father, let us grow familiar with the manger of our Lord Jesus Christ.

AUGUSTINE OF HIPPO

Let us not flutter too high, but 1492 remain by the manger and the swaddling clothes of Christ, "in whom dwelleth all the fullness of the Godhead bodily." There a man cannot fail of God, but finds him most certainly.

MARTIN LUTHER

Trumpets! Lightnings! The earth 1493 trembles! but into the Virgin's womb thou didst descend with noiseless tread.
The Greek Anthology

The manger is heaven, yea, greater 1494 than heaven. Heaven is the handiwork of this child.
The Greek Anthology

One dance, one song for shepherds 1495 and angels, for man and God are become one.
The Greek Anthology

No longer do the Magi bring pres- 1496 ents to Fire and the Sun; for this child made Sun and Fire.
The Greek Anthology

They all were looking for a king 1497
    To slay their foes and lift them high;
Thou cam'st, a little baby thing
    That made a woman cry.

GEORGE MAC DONALD

1498 Of "the Word made flesh" I add yet farther: what flesh? The flesh of an infant. What, *Verbum infans,* the Word an infant? The Word, and not be able to speak a word? How evil agreeth this! This he put up. How born, how entertained? In a stately palace, cradle of ivory, robes of estate? No; but a stable for his palace, a manger for his cradle, poor clouts for his array.

LANCELOT ANDREWES

1499 The Christ-child stood at Mary's knee,
    His hair was like a crown,
And all the flowers looked up at him,
    And all the stars looked down.

GILBERT KEITH CHESTERTON

1500 The whole life of Christ was a continual Passion; others die martyrs but Christ was born a martyr. He found a Golgotha even in Bethlehem, where he was born; for to his tenderness then the straws were almost as sharp as the thorns after, and the manger as uneasy at first as his cross at last. His birth and his death were but one continual act, and his Christmas day and his Good Friday are but the evening and morning of one and the same day. And as even his birth is his death, so every action and passage that manifests Christ to us is his birth, for *Ephiphany* is *manifestation.*

JOHN DONNE

CHRISTIANITY

1501 We may be suspicious of the clergy, and refuse to have anything to do with catechisms, and yet love the Holy and the Just, who came to save and not to curse. Jesus will always supply us with the best criticisms of Christianity, and when Christianity has passed away the religion of Jesus will in all probability survive. After Jesus as God we shall come back to faith in the God of Jesus.

HENRI FRÉDÉRIC AMIEL

The primary declaration of Christianity is not "This do!" but "This happened!"   *1502*

EVELYN UNDERHILL

National Christianity is impossible without a nation of Christs.   *1503*

GEORGE BERNARD SHAW

Christianity is completed Judaism, or it is nothing.   *1504*

BENJAMIN DISRAELI

Life for the Christian is a dialogue with God.   *1505*

J.H. OLDHAM

To be a Christian is to be a man. To be a Christian does not mean to be religious in a particular way, to cultivate some particular form of asceticism, but to be a man. It is not some religious act which makes a Christian what he is but participation in the suffering of God in the life of the world.   *1506*

DIETRICH BONHOEFFER

Christianity is dogmatical, devotional, practical all at once; it is esoteric and exoteric; it is indulgent and strict; it is light and dark; it is love, and it is fear.   *1507*

JOHN HENRY NEWMAN

One person is a king and rules,   *1508*

another is a subject and obeys; but if both are Christians, both have in common a gift so great that in the sight of it the difference between ruling and obeying is as nothing.

JOHN HENRY NEWMAN

1509 Christian life is the life of Christ in man and man in Christ.

ROMANO GUARDINI

1510 The essence of Christianity is simply and solely belief in the unification of the world in God through the Incarnation.

PIERRE TEILHARD DE CHARDIN

1511 In a word, what the soul is to the body, Christians are to the world. The soul is locked up in the body, yet it holds the body together.

Epistle to Diognetus

1512 Rightly understood, there are no Christians: there is only the eternal opportunity of becoming Christians —an opportunity at once accessible and inaccessible to all men.

KARL BARTH

1513 You are Christians; somehow, no one ever plucked
A rag, even, from the body of the Lord,
To wear and mock with, but, despite himself,
He looked the greater and was the better.

ROBERT BROWNING

1514 On the ancient minster at Basle are two sculptured groups: St. Martin, cutting his cloak in two with his sword to clothe a beggar, and St. George, spurring his horse against the dragon that devastated the country. Every Christian should em-

body both kinds of sainthood in his life.

WALTER RAUSCHENBUSCH

A Christian is nothing but a sinful   1515 man who has put himself to school to Christ for the honest purpose of becoming better.

HENRY WARD BEECHER

CHURCH

The church of Christ is not an   1516 institution; it is a new life with Christ and in Christ, guided by the Holy Spirit.

SERGIUS BULGAKOV

The church is in Christ as Eve was   1517 in Adam.

RICHARD HOOKER

In the primitive church the chalices   1518 were of wood, the prelates of gold. In these days the church hath chalices of gold and prelates of wood.

GIROLAMO SAVONAROLA

Sire, it belongs in truth to the   1519 church of God, in the name of which I speak, to receive blows and to give them; but it will please your majesty to take notice that it is an anvil that has worn out many hammers.

THEODORE BEZA,
to the King of Navarre

The church, like the ark of Noah, is   1520 worth saving; not for the sake of the unclean beasts and vermin that almost filled it, and probably made most noise and clamor in it, but for the little corner of rationality, that was as much distressed by the stink within as by the tempest without.

WILLIAM WARBURTON,
onetime Bishop of Gloucester

1521 What matters in the church is not religion but the form of Christ, and its taking form amidst a band of men.

DIETRICH BONHOEFFER

1522 It is said of the true church, the King's daughter is all glorious within. Let our care therefore be of our minds more than of our bodies, if we would be of her communion.

WILLIAM PENN

1523 Let us have no more talk of the church not having the answers. It has. The answers are our Lord's answers.

HARRY BLAMIRES

1524 No man can have God for his father who has not the church for his mother.

CYPRIAN, *Bishop of Carthage*

1525 We don't *go* to church, we *are* the church.

ERNEST SOUTHCOTT

1526 Where the Scripture is silent, the church is my text.

THOMAS BROWNE

1527 The church is not possession of the kingdom, it is the struggle for it. But it is a struggle consoled by the promise that the gates of hell will not prevail against it.

A New Catechism

1528 The church and the sacraments exist to rescue character and bring out the best in it. Christ did this during

his lifetime and has been doing it ever since.

HUBERT VAN ZELLER

There are many sheep without, 1529 many wolves within.

AUGUSTINE OF HIPPO

It may take a crucified church to 1530 bring a crucified Christ before the eyes of the world.

WILLIAM E. ORCHARD

O Lord, we beseech thee, let thy 1531 continual pity cleanse and defend thy church; and, because it cannot continue in safety without thy succor, preserve it evermore by thy help and goodness; through Christ our Lord.

Book of Common Prayer

CONVERSION

Paul was transformed in Christ as 1532 nature becomes charming in spring.

NORIMOTO IINO

If the "once-born" temperament 1533 constitutes the ballast of the church, the "twice-born" is, under God, its motive power.

N.P. WILLIAMS

While I silently ponder on that 1534 change wrought in me, I find no language equal to it, nor any means to convey to another a clear idea of it. I looked on the works of God in this visible creation, and an awfulness covered me; my heart was tender and often contrite, and universal love to my fellow-creatures increased in me. This will be understood by such as have trodden the same path.

JOHN WOOLMAN

1535 A miner once interrupted John Hutton when he was preaching, by leaping to his feet and leading the whole congregation in the doxology. Later he explained that he had been a Christian only for some months, and that it was all so gloriously different that he could not sit still in his place. For, said he, "I was a bad lot; I drank; I pawned the furniture; I knocked my wife about; and now life is real life, and splendidly worth while." Asked how he fared among his fellows down in the pit, he laughed and replied, "Today they asked me, 'You don't seriously credit that old yarn about Jesus turning the water into wine?' " To which, it appeared, he had made the devastating answer, "I know nothing about water and wine, but I know this, that in my house Christ has turned beer into furniture; and that is a good enough miracle for me!"

ARTHUR J. GOSSIP

1536 Turn yourselves, and live ye.
Ezekiel 18:32

1537 Except ye be converted, and become as little children, ye shall not enter into the kingdom of heaven.
Matthew 18:3

1538 I thought on my ways, and turned my feet unto thy testimonies.
Psalm 119:59 (AV)

1539 When thou art converted, strengthen thy brethren.
Luke 22:32

CROSS

The West begins at Golgotha.   1540
JACQUES MARITAIN

Jesus was crucified not in a cathe-   1541
dral between two candles, but on a cross between two thieves.
GEORGE F. MAC LEOD

There are some sciences that may be   1542
learned by the head, but the science of Christ crucified can only be learned by heart.
CHARLES H. SPURGEON

The poet Heine once had a vision of   1543
the gods holding banquet on high Olympus. To that feast came a wan Figure bearing a cross which he laid down amongst the flowers, whereupon every god sunk shamefacedly away.

ROBERT NELSON SPENCER

Jesus will be in agony even to the   1544
end of the world. We must not sleep during that time.

BLAISE PASCAL

. . . that terrible tree, which is the   1545
death of God and the life of man.
GILBERT KEITH CHESTERTON

I see his blood upon the rose   1546
And in the stars the glory of his eyes,
His body gleams amid eternal snows,
His tears fall from the skies.

I see his face in every flower;
The thunder and the singing of the birds
Are but his voice—and carven by his power

Rocks are his written words.

All pathways by his feet are worn,
His strong heart stirs the ever-
    beating sea,
His crown of thorns is twined with
    every thorn,
His cross is every tree.

JOSEPH MARY PLUNKETT

1547 Who is he who hath the happiest
lot? Even he who is strong to suffer
somewhat for God.

THOMAS À KEMPIS

1548 Jesus now has many lovers of his
heavenly kingdom, but few bearers
of his cross.

THOMAS À KEMPIS

1549 We may not know, we cannot tell,
    What pains he had to bear,
But we believe it was for us
    He hung and suffered there.

He died that we might be forgiv'n,
    He died to make us good,
That we might go at last to heav'n,
    Saved by his precious blood.

CECIL FRANCES ALEXANDER

1550 Almighty God, whose most dear
Son went not up to joy but first he
suffered pain, and entered not into
glory before he was crucified; mercifully grant that we, walking in the
way of the cross, may find it none
other than the way of life and
peace; through the same Jesus
Christ our Lord.

Book of Common Prayer

DESCENT INTO HELL

1551 Christ also hath once suffered for
our sins, the just for the unjust, that
he might bring us to God, being put
to death in the flesh, but quickened
by the Spirit: by which also he went
and preached unto the souls in
prison, which sometimes were dis-
obedient. . . .

I Peter 3:18–20

"He *descended into Hell.*" Mighty 1552
words! which I do not pretend I can
penetrate, or reduce under any
forms of the intellect. If I could, I
think they would be of little worth
to me. But I accept them as news
that there is no corner of God's
universe of which his love has not
brooded, none over which the Son
of God and the Son of Man has not
asserted his dominion. I claim a
right to tell this news to every peasant and beggar of the land. I may
bid him rejoice, and give thanks,
and sing merry songs to the God
who made him, because there is
nothing created which his Lord and
Master has not redeemed, of which
he is not the King; I may bid him
fear nothing around him or beneath
him while he trusts in him.

FREDERICK DENISON MAURICE

We want to remember that "hell" in 1553
the Bible means a number of things.
It isn't just the place of everlasting
punishment. It is also the experience
of being separated from God, or of
feeling forsaken by him. Hell is the
grave of death. Christ descended
into the dreadful God-forsakenness
of paying the death penalty for
sinners, and into the grave. As one
of the biblical writers put it, he
tasted death for every man. So,
when we declare that he descended
into hell we are affirming that there
is no hell of guilt, of God-forsaken-

ness, of pain, of dying, which we can possibly undergo, that he has not undergone before us—and hallowed for us by his experiencing it. When we descend into any of our hells, before or after death, he has been there before us—and he is there now. Because he descended into hell we who believe in him can say, quite literally, with the Psalmist: "If I go down to hell, thou art there also."

CARROLL E. SIMCOX

ECCLESIASTICISM
(See *Church*)

1554 If you wish to sail comfortably in the barque of Peter, stay away from the engine room.

RONALD KNOX

1555 The true meaning of the church has given way to the manipulations of the organization. In place of the sacraments, we have the committee meeting; in place of confession, the bazaar; in place of pilgrimage, the dull drive to hear the deadly speaker; in place of community, a collection of functions. This trivialization of religious life has made the middle-class search for religious meaning even more desperate. One begins to wonder after a time whether the search itself isn't pointless, since every church activity seems to lead further into a maze of superficiality which is stultifying the middle-class community.

GIBSON WINTER

1556 And of all plagues with which mankind are cursed,

Ecclesiastical tyranny's the worst.

DANIEL DEFOE

ECUMENISM

Nothing is so false to the spirit of ecumenism as a false irenicism.   1557

Second Vatican Council

Some of us worked long enough in a shipbuilding district to know that welding is impossible except the materials to be joined are at white heat temperature; and none of our denominational convictions is at white heat. When you try to weld them they only fall apart.   1558

GEORGE F. MAC LEOD

Putting all the ecclesiastical corpses into one graveyard will not bring about a resurrection.   1559

DAVID M. LLOYD-JONES

The unity of the church is something much more than unity of ecclesiastical structure, though it cannot be complete without this. It is the love of God in Christ possessing the hearts of men so as to unite them in itself—as the Father and the Son are united in that love of Each for Each which is the Holy Spirit.   1560

WILLIAM TEMPLE

EUCHARIST
(See *Sacraments*)

Love is that liquor sweet and most divine   1561

Which my God feels as blood, and I
as wine.

GEORGE HERBERT

1562 This is the food that appeases the
hunger of the devoted heart. Faith is
its seasoning, and devotion and fra-
ternal charity its relish. The teeth of
the body may break this food, but
only an unfaltering faith can savor
it.

THOMAS AQUINAS

1563 The Christian metaphysics is—that
he eats God.

THEODOR HAECKER

1564 The effect of our communion in the
Body and Blood of Christ is that we
are transformed into what we con-
sume, and that he in whom we have
died and in whom we have risen
from the dead lives and is manifested in every movement of our
body and of our spirit.

POPE LEO I

1565 If you have received worthily, you
are what you have received.

AUGUSTINE OF HIPPO

1566 One Sunday it happened that St.
John could not be at church with his
friends, for like Elisha, like Jesus, he
was taken by the armed men, and
held in prison. But God consoled
him with a vision: he saw the Christian sacrament that morning not as
men see it, but as it is seen in
heaven. His spirit went up; he saw
the throne of Glory, and the four
cherubim full of eyes in every part,
who sleep not, saying Holy, Holy,
Holy. And he saw the sacrifice, the
Lamb of God: a Lamb standing as
though slaughtered; a Lamb alone

worthy to open for mankind the
blessed promises of God. He saw
the Lamb, and then the angels. I
saw, he says, and heard the voice of
many angels round about the
Throne, the number of them ten
thousand times ten thousand, and
thousands of thousands: saying with
a loud voice, Worthy is the Lamb
who was slain to receive the power
and riches and wisdom and might
and honor and glory and blessing.
That is the Christian eucharist. Certainly when we gather here, those
that are with us are more than those
who stand upon the opposing side.
For all heaven is one with us, when
once we lift our hearts up to the
Lord, and praise the everlasting
Love, the One God in three Persons,
Father, Son, and Holy Ghost; to
whom be ascribed, as is most justly
due, all might, dominion, majesty
and power, henceforth and for ever.

AUSTIN FARRER

1567 To those who know a little of Christian history probably the most moving of all the reflections it brings is
not the thought of the great events
and the well-remembered saints, but
of those innumerable millions of
entirely obscure faithful men and
women, every one with his or her
own individual hopes and fears and
joys and sorrows and loves—and
sins and temptations and prayers—
once every whit as vivid and alive as
mine are now. They have left not
the slightest trace in this world, not
even a name, but have passed to
God utterly forgotten by men. Yet
each one of them once believed and
prayed as I believe and pray, and
found it hard and grew slack and
sinned and repented and fell again.

Each of them worshipped at the eucharist, and found their thoughts wandering and tried again, and felt heavy and unresponsive and yet knew—just as really and pathetically as I do these things. There is a little ill-spelled ill-carved rustic epitaph of the fourth century from Asia Minor:—"Here sleeps the blessed Chione, who has found Jerusalem for she prayed much." Not another word is known of Chione, some peasant woman who lived in that vanished world of Christian Anatolia. But how lovely if all that should survive after sixteen centuries were that one had prayed much, so that the neighbors who saw all one's life were sure one must have found Jerusalem! What did the Sunday eucharist in her village church every week for a life-time mean to the blessed Chione—and to the millions like her then, and every year since? The sheer stupendous *quantity* of the love of God which this ever repeated action has drawn from the obscure Christian multitudes is in itself an overwhelming thought. (All that going with one to the altar every morning!)

GREGORY DIX

EVANGELISM

1568 There is no expeditious road
To pack and label men for God,
And save them by the barrel-load.
FRANCIS THOMPSON

1569 The church has nothing to do but to save souls; therefore spend and be spent in this work. It is not your business to speak so many times, but to save souls as you can; to bring as many sinners as you possibly can to repentance.
JOHN WESLEY

1570 When a man genuinely and humbly feels he has discovered the buried treasure of the gospel he naturally wants to spread the good news to others and so to bring them closer to God. He must be on guard, however, not to let them stop short at himself.
HUBERT VAN ZELLER

1571 People of zeal and forceful character can do harm by wanting to impose their zeal and character on others. God wants people formed in his own image, not in mine. I may not put my signature to a masterpiece of God's.
HUBERT VAN ZELLER

1572 Evangelism is a sharing of gladness.
Anonymous

1573 Social problems exist wherever men exist. The evangelical is not teacher's pet; he has no privileged corner in the universe. Our Lord pointed out that the rain falls on the just and unjust. Nor does the evangelical have a vest-pocket solution to every towering issue that comes along. He does have Jesus; he believes that Jesus is adequate to meet human need at every level; and he believes that to know Christ is to have a head start in grappling with the dilemmas that society poses. He does not, however, confuse dilemma-grappling with the process of coming to know Christ; that is, he does not consider social action to be the same thing as evangelism. Evangelism is presenting Christ to men in the power of the Holy Spirit. Social action is an effort to apply Christ in finding solutions to human problems. When social action is mistaken for evangelism the church has ceased to manufacture its own blood cells and is dying of leukemia. When social action becomes more important than evangelism the church has forgotten to breathe and is already dead of heart failure.

SHERWOOD WIRT

1574 O merciful God, who hast made all men, and hatest nothing that thou hast made, nor desirest the death of a sinner, but rather that he should be converted and live; have mercy upon all who know thee not as thou art revealed in the Gospel of thy Son. Take from them all ignorance, hardness of heart, and contempt of thy Word; and so fetch them home, blessed Lord, to thy fold, that they may be made one flock under one shepherd, Jesus Christ our Lord, who liveth and reigneth with thee and the Holy Spirit, one God, world without end.

Book of Common Prayer

FOLLOWING CHRIST

1575 Be ye followers of me, even as I also am of Christ.

I Corinthians 11:1

1576 Christ does not really teach one anything, but by being brought into his presence one becomes something. And everybody is predestined

to his presence. Once at least in his life each man walks with Christ to Emmaus.

OSCAR WILDE

Day by day, dear Lord, of thee three 1577
  things I pray:
To see thee more clearly,
Love thee more dearly,
Follow thee more nearly,
Day by day.

RICHARD OF CHICHESTER

On account of him there have come 1578
to be many Christs in the world, even all who, like him, loved righteousness and hated iniquity.

ORIGEN OF ALEXANDRIA

Happy are they who know that 1579
discipleship simply means the life which springs from grace, and that grace simply means discipleship.

DIETRICH BONHOEFFER

You can't be the salt of the earth 1580
without smarting someone.

Anonymous

He comes to us as One unknown, 1581
without a name, as of old, by the lake-side, he came to those men who knew him not. He speaks to us the same word: "Follow thou me!" and sets us to the tasks which he has to fulfil for our time. He commands. And to those who obey him, whether they be wise or simple, he will reveal himself in the toils, the conflicts, the sufferings which they shall pass through in his fellowship, and, as an ineffable mystery, they shall learn in their own experience who he is.

ALBERT SCHWEITZER

1582 In the beginning was the Word, and
the Word was made flesh and dwelt
among us. God speaks to me not
through the thunder and the earth-
quake, not through the ocean and
the stars, but through the Son of
Man, and speaks in a language
adapted to my imperfect sight and
hearing. I want to follow the Best I
know, and here it is. If any one can
show me anything better, I will
follow that.

WILLIAM LYON PHELPS

1583 There are two words used a great
deal by Jesus in the Gospels. One is
"Come" and the other is "Go." It's
no use coming unless you go, and
it's no use going unless you come.
Anonymous

1584 The attempts of Christians to be
Christians now are almost as ridiculous as the attempts of the first men
to be human.

G.A. STUDDERT-KENNEDY

1585 The doctrine of Christ exceeds all
the doctrine of holy men; and he
who has the Spirit will find in it *the
hidden manna.* But it falls out that
many who often hear the Gospel of
Christ feel little desire for it because
they have not the Spirit of Christ.
But whoever wants fully to understand the words of Christ must try
to conform his life wholly to the life
of Christ.

THOMAS À KEMPIS

1586 As the Prophet says: "I am not
weary, following thee" (Jeremiah
17:16). Who can be weary following
Jesus? For he himself says: "Come
to me, all you who labor and are
burdened, and I will give you rest."
Let us, then, always follow Jesus

and never falter, for if we follow him
we never fail because he gives his
strength to his followers. The nearer
you are to this strength, the stronger
you will be.

AMBROSE OF MILAN

FORGIVENESS

We pardon to the extent that we   1587
love.

FRANÇOIS DE LA ROCHEFOUCAULD

"I can forgive, but I cannot forget"   1588
is only another way of saying "I
cannot forgive."

HENRY WARD BEECHER

To forgive all is as inhuman as to   1589
forgive none.

SENECA

Forgiveness of sins is the very heart   1590
of Christianity, and yet it is a
mighty dangerous thing to preach.

MARTIN LUTHER

The forgiveness of God is the foun-   1591
dation of every bridge from a hopeless past to a courageous present.

GEORGE ADAM SMITH

Nothing in this lost world bears the   1592
impress of the Son of God so surely
as forgiveness.

ALICE CARY

To err is human, to forgive divine.   1593
ALEXANDER POPE

Humanity is never so beautiful as   1594
when praying for forgiveness or else
forgiving another.

JEAN PAUL RICHTER

1595   It is surely better to pardon too
much than to condemn too much.
GEORGE ELIOT

1596   Praised be my Lord for all those
who pardon one another for his
love's sake, and who endure weakness and tribulation; blessed are
they who peaceably shall endure,
for thou, O most Highest, shalt give
them a crown.
FRANCIS OF ASSISI

1597   You who are letting miserable mis-
understandings run on from year to
year, meaning to clear them up
some day; you who are keeping
wretched quarrels alive because you
cannot quite make up your minds
that now is the day to sacrifice your
pride and kill them; you who are
letting your neighbor starve—until
you hear that he is dying of starva-
tion; or letting your friend's heart
ache for a word of appreciation or
sympathy, which you mean to give
him some day; if you could only
know and see and feel all of a
sudden that time is short, how it
would break the spell! How you
would go instantly and do the thing
which you might never have another
chance to do!
PHILLIPS BROOKS

1598   The discretion of a man deferreth
his anger; and it is his glory to pass
over a transgression.
Proverbs 19:11

1599   When ye stand praying, forgive, if
ye have ought against any: that your
Father also who is in heaven may
forgive you your trespasses.
Mark 11:25

GOSPEL

The Gospel was not good advice but   1600
good news.
WILLIAM RALPH INGE

Our reading of the Gospel story can   1601
be and should be an act of personal
communion with the living Lord.
WILLIAM TEMPLE

God writes the Gospel not in the   1602
Bible alone, but on trees, and
flowers, and clouds, and stars.
MARTIN LUTHER

How petty are the books of the   1603
philosophers with all their pomp,
compared with the gospels!
JEAN JACQUES ROUSSEAU

The Gospel is a declaration, not a   1604
debate.
JAMES S. STEWART

It [St. John's gospel] is God's love   1605
letter to the world.
HENRY WARD BEECHER

The church is said to be losing   1606
ground among educated Africans
because it does not procure for them
political reforms. But that is not
what the church is for. The church
exists primarily to preach the gospel
of the Lord Jesus Christ. Church-
men must do all they can to bring
about the reign of justice . . . but
the fact remains that the message of
the church is a message about God.
People are trying to use God as a
means to an end, to say that a man
should be a Christian because that
would make him moral, or would
make him free. It is as though Christ
had said, "Blessed are they that see

God for they shall be pure in heart."
But he didn't. You are to be pure in
heart in order that you may see
God.

GEOFFREY CLAYTON, *onetime Archbishop of Cape Town, South Africa.*

GRACE

1607 The law was given by Moses, but
grace and truth came by Jesus
Christ.

John 1:17

1608 Grace is the New Testament word
for the divine adequacy.

OSCAR F. BLACKWELDER

1609 A state of mind that sees God in
everything is evidence of growth in
grace and a thankful heart.

CHARLES G. FINNEY

1610 But for the grace of God there goes
John Bradford.

JOHN BRADFORD, *seeing some criminals taken to the gallows*

1611 God gives power only to men who
need it. He does not waste power.
He gives it to those who have
tackled something so big, so overwhelming, that their own resources
are quite insufficient. Such a tack-
ling of a task too big for human
power is the opening of the door
through which there comes the rush-
ing of a mighty wind of the spirit.

HALFORD E. LUCCOCK

1612 Grace does not destroy nature, it
perfects it.

THOMAS AQUINAS

Grace does not entirely change na- 1613
ture but uses nature as it finds it. So
if somebody is kind when converted
through faith, he becomes a gentle
preacher like Master Hausmann. If
he is by nature irascible and severe,
like Cordatus, he preaches after this
fashion. On the other hand, if he is
fitted by nature with some slyness,
intelligence, and power of reason,
like Philip, he uses these qualities
for the benefit of mankind.

MARTIN LUTHER

These things are beautiful beyond 1614
belief:
The pleasant weakness that comes
after pain,
The radiant greenness that comes
after rain,
The deepened faith that follows
after grief,
And the awakening to love again.

Anonymous

They travel lightly whom God's 1615
grace carries.

THOMAS À KEMPIS

Many Christians seem to under- 1616
stand the concept of being saved by
grace, but they have missed the
concept of being sustained by grace.

JAMES D. MALLORY, JR.

When I want to move my hand, it 1617
moves. I don't have to stop and
think, "How shall I move it?" It
happens. But if I find myself to be a
selfish kind of person and want to
be unselfish, it doesn't happen.
Therefore, something has got to take
hold of us from outside.

WILLIAM TEMPLE

Grace is God himself, his loving 1618

energy at work within his church and within our souls.

EVELYN UNDERHILL

1619 Through the golden moments of musical communion with God, Mother's words still remind me of what should come first: "Grace must always come before greatness."

MARIAN ANDERSON

1620 There is no such way to attain to a greater measure of grace as for a man to live up to the little grace he has.

PHILLIPS BROOKS

1621 If grace perfects nature it must expand all our natures into the full richness of the diversity which God intended when he made them, and heaven will display far more variety than hell. "One fold" doesn't mean "one pool." Cultivated roses and daffodils are no more alike than wild roses and daffodils.

C.S. LEWIS

1622 What the New Testament is telling us, in mysterious images and dark metaphors, is that in our life as members of Christ's body, we already are given a real but partial participation in the good things of God of which the full enjoyment awaits us in heaven. In the words of a great Christian theologian, "Grace is nothing else than a kind of beginning of glory in us."

E.L. MASCALL

1623 Give us grace and strength to persevere. Give us courage and gaiety and the quiet mind. Spare to us our friends and soften to us our enemies. Give us the strength to en-counter that which is to come, that we may be brave in peril, constant in tribulation, temperate in wrath and in all changes of fortune, and down to the gates of death loyal and loving to one another.

ROBERT LOUIS STEVENSON

INCARNATION

I think that the purpose and cause 1624 of the Incarnation was that God might illuminate the world by his wisdom and excite it to the love of himself.

PETER ABÉLARD

Jesus marks the point in history at 1625 which it becomes possible for man to adopt consciously as his own purpose the purpose which is already inherent in his own nature.

JOHN MACMURRAY

Poor creature though I be, I am the 1626 hand and foot of Christ. I move my hand and my hand is wholly Christ's hand, for deity is become inseparably one with me. I move my foot, and it is aglow with God.

SYMEON THE NEW THEOLOGIAN

He became what we are that he 1627 might make us what he is.

ATHANASIUS OF ALEXANDRIA

Every Christian must be Christ him- 1628 self.

ANGELUS SILESIUS

I once talked to a continental pastor 1629 who had seen Hitler, and had, by all human standards, good cause to hate him. "What did he look like?" I asked. "Like all men," he replied. "That is, like Christ."

C.S. LEWIS

1630 He *gave* a vision of God where others could only *speak* of it.

KENNETH E. KIRK

1631 In his moral sonship to God Jesus Christ is not a median figure, half God, half man; he is a single person wholly directed as man toward God and wholly directed in his unity with the Father toward men. He is mediatorial, not median.

RICHARD NIEBUHR

1632 Jesus Christ is a God whom we approach without pride, and before whom we humble ourselves without despair.

BLAISE PASCAL

1633 Humanity seeks the ideal, but it seeks it in a person, not in an abstraction. A man, the incarnation of the ideal, whose biography might serve as a frame for all the aspirations of the time is what the religious mind sought.

ERNEST RENAN

1634 He is what God means by man. He is what man means by God.

J.S. WHALE

1635 The biography of Jesus in the New Testament is a "White House to log cabin" story. All depends upon the identification of the chief actor. Is the "hero" a man or is he God? Classical Christianity identifies him as God. The biographical drama is then a kind of hero-story in reverse.

THEODORE O. WEDEL

1636 The beauty of the world is Christ's tender smile for us coming through matter.

SIMONE WEIL

1637 There is a sense in which the earthly incarnation of the Son of God, just because it is true, cannot be in itself complete. It erects a bridge, so to speak, rather than a home. And yet the bridge must afford the vision of the home, or it is no true bridge.

OLIVER C. QUICK

1638 The fount of Mary's joy
    Revealed now lies,
For, lo, has not the Boy
    His Father's eyes?

CHARLES L. O'DONNELL

JESUS

1639 Jesus was the seed rather than the founder of Christianity.

H.G. WELLS

1640 Jesus was not a Christian; he was a Jew. He did not preach a new faith, but taught men to do the will of God; and in his opinion, as also that of the Jews, the will of God was to be found in the Law of Moses and in the other books of Scripture.

JULIUS WELLHAUSEN

1641 Tell me the picture of Jesus you have reached and I will tell you some important traits about your nature.

OSCAR PFISTER

1642 "Gentle Jesus, meek and mild" is a sniveling modern invention, with no warrant in the Gospels.

GEORGE BERNARD SHAW

1643 If Jesus had been indicted in a modern court, he would have been examined by two doctors; found to be obsessed by a delusion; declared to be incapable of pleading; and sent to an asylum. . . .
GEORGE BERNARD SHAW

1644 No man dared to take liberties with him.
WILLIAM RALPH INGE

1645 That a few simple men should in one generation have invented so powerful and appealing a personality, so lofty an ethic and so inspiring a vision of human brotherhood, would be a miracle far more incredible than any recorded in the Gospel.
WILL DURANT

1646 A radical revolution, embracing even nature itself, was the fundamental idea of Jesus.
ERNEST RENAN

1647 In his life Christ is an example, showing us how to live; in his death he is a sacrifice, satisfying for our sins; in his resurrection, a conqueror; in his ascension, a king; in his intercession, a high priest.
MARTIN LUTHER

1648 Jesus Christ came into my prison cell last night, and every stone flashed like a ruby.
SAMUEL RUTHERFORD

1649 If Jesus Christ were to come today people would not even crucify him. They would ask him to dinner, and hear what he has to say, and make fun of it.
THOMAS CARLYLE

1650 Something fiery and star-like gleamed from his eyes and the majesty of Godhead shone from his countenance.
ST. JEROME

1651 Had the doctrines of Jesus been preached always as pure as they came from his lips, the whole civilized world would now have been Christian.
THOMAS JEFFERSON

1652 Power is the reward of sadness. It was after the Christ had wept over Jerusalem that he uttered some of his most august words; it was when his soul had been sorrowful even unto death that his enemies fell prostrate before his voice. Who suffers, conquers. The bruised is the breaker.
FRANCIS THOMPSON

1653 A God on the cross! That is all my theology.
JEAN LACORDAIRE

1654 "There is only one person I can think of after this," continued H——, but without mentioning a name that once put on a semblance of mortality. "If Shakespeare was to come into the room, we should all rise up to meet him; but if that person was to come into it, we should all fall down and try to kiss the hem of his garment." As a lady present seemed now to get uneasy at the turn the conversation had taken, we rose up to go.
WILLIAM HAZLITT

1655 Jesus alone is able to offer himself as the sufficient illustration of his own doctrine.
HENSLEY HENSON

1656 If Jesus Christ is not true God, how could he *help* us? If he is not true man, how could he help *us?*

DIETRICH BONHOEFFER

1657 For the Christian, the norm is made flesh in the person of Christ. Normality is not what the average sensual man ordinarily possesses; it is what he ought to try to possess.

RUSSELL KIRK

1658 And Christ himself, who preached the life of love, was yet as lonely as any man who ever lived.

THOMAS WOLFE

1659 No revolution that has ever taken place in society can be compared to that which has been produced by the words of Jesus Christ.

MARK HOPKINS

1660 "Heaven and earth shall pass away, but my words shall not pass away." If anyone believes that to be true, then he believes at the same time it is God who said it. Those who know anything about words know how ridiculous it is for a *man* to appeal to the everlastingness of his words.

THEODOR HAECKER

1661 The meaning of history is not Caesar but Jesus. History tends not toward Caesar but toward Jesus.

THOMAS MASARYK

1662 We conceive that Jesus of Nazareth lived and died, not to *persuade* the Father, not to *appease* the Father, not to make a sanguinary *purchase* from the Father, but simply to "*show* us the Father"; to leave upon the human heart a new, deep, vivid impression of what God is in himself, and of what he designs for his creature, man; to become, in short, the accepted interpreter of heaven and life. And this he achieved, in the only way of which we can conceive as practicable, by a new disclosure in his own person of all that is holy and godlike in character—startling the human soul with the sudden apparition of a being diviner far than it had yet beheld, and lifting its faith at once into quite another and purer region. . . . And so Christ, standing in solitary greatness, opens at once the eye of conscience to perceive and know the pure and holy God the Father who dwelt in him and made him so full of truth and grace. . . . Of anything *more perfect* than the meek but majestic Jesus, no heart can ever dream.

JAMES MARTINEAU

1663 Many teachers of the world have tried to explain everything—they have changed little or nothing. Jesus explained little and changed everything.

E. STANLEY JONES

1664 In proportion as we have the Spirit of Jesus we have the true knowledge of Jesus.

ALBERT SCHWEITZER

1665 If the life and death of Socrates were those of a man, the life and death of Jesus were those of a God.

JEAN JACQUES ROUSSEAU

1666 Alexander, Caesar, Charlemagne and I founded empires; but upon what did we rest the creations of our genius? Upon force. Jesus Christ alone founded his empire upon love; and at this hour millions of men would die for him.

NAPOLEON BUONAPARTE

1667 He was the first gentleman of recorded history and the greatest gentleman who ever lived.

IRVIN S. COBB

1668 He that cried in the manger, that
sucked the paps of a woman, that
hath exposed himself to poverty,
and a world of inconveniences, is
the Son of the living God, of the
same substance with his Father, begotten before all ages, before the
morning-stars: he is God eternal.

JEREMY TAYLOR

KINGDOM OF GOD

1669 See, this kingdom of God is now
found within us. The grace of the
Holy Spirit shines forth and warms
us, and, overflowing with many and
varied scents into the air around us,
regales our senses with heavenly
delight, as it fills our hearts with joy
inexpressible.

SERAPHIM OF SAROV

1670 Though we achieve social justice,
liberty, peace itself, though we give
our bodies to be burned for these
admirable causes, if we lack this—
the transformation of the natural
order by the Eternal Charity—we
are nothing. For the Kingdom is the
Holy not the moral; the Beautiful
not the correct; the Perfect not the
adequate; Charity not law.

EVELYN UNDERHILL

1671 In the Gospel Jesus is *autobasileia,*
the kingdom himself.

ORIGEN OF ALEXANDRIA

1672 When in the darkest depths the
miner striving,

Feels in his arms the vigor of the
Lord,
Strikes for a Kingdom and his
King's arriving,
Holding his pick more splendid than
the sword.

G.A. STUDDERT-KENNEDY

1673 If you want to work for the kingdom
of God, and to bring it, and to enter
into it, there is just one condition to
be first accepted. You must enter it
as children, or not at all.

JOHN RUSKIN

1674 The kingdom of God is a kingdom
of love; and love is never a stagnant
pool.

HENRY W. DU BOSE

1675 The kingdom of God is not meat
and drink; but righteousness, and
peace, and joy in the Holy Ghost.

Romans 14:17

1676 Is the Kingdom of God a big family? Yes, in a sense it is. But in
another sense it is a prodigious
biological operation—that of the
Redeeming Incarnation.

PIERRE TEILHARD DE CHARDIN

1677 There is no escape from the para-
doxical relation of history to the
kingdom of God. History moves
toward the realization of the kingdom but yet the judgment of God is
upon every new realization.

REINHOLD NIEBUHR

1678 The kingdom of heaven is like unto
leaven, which a woman took, and
hid in three measures of meal, till
the whole was leavened.

Matthew 13:33

1679 To want all that God wants, always

to want it, for all occasions and without reservations, this is the kingdom of God which is all within.

FRANÇOIS FÉNELON

1680 Wherever Christ's will is done, God's will is done, and the kingdom appears then and there. Such appearances of the kingdom in this present world actually occur, but they are only sporadic. They are the exception, not the rule. St. Paul's way of putting it, "He must reign till he hath put all enemies under his feet," exactly describes things as they now are in Christ's kingdom on earth. A soldier lays down his life that his countrymen might live: there is the kingdom. A woman slanders her neighbor at a bridge party: there the kingdom is defied and set at naught. A churchman foregoes luxuries for a month so that he will have more money to give for famine relief: there is the kingdom. An auto mechanic charges a customer for work he did not do: there the kingdom is defied and rejected. All human works and ways, thoughts, words, and deeds, are either manifestations—acceptances—of the kingdom and rule of Christ, or denials and defiances of it; and Christ must reign till he has put *all* enemies—rebel wills—under his feet.

CARROLL E. SIMCOX

LORD'S PRAYER

1681 Its very first words are *Our Father*. Do you see what these words mean? They mean quite frankly that you are putting yourself in the place of a son of God. To put it bluntly, you are *dressing up as Christ*.

C.S. LEWIS

1682 Lead us not into temptation! What can this prayer mean, since God certainly cannot tempt any creature to evil? And yet a request simply cannot be so utterly unintelligible to us as to have virtually no meaning at all. We may and must try to give it some meaning. Personally, I interpret it in the following sense: that God should not conceal himself entirely, or for too long, in the ordering of things public and private, in order that the believer may perceive the outward covering of the thread, that is hidden to the "world." If God were to withdraw himself entirely, who could keep the faith? According to his promise, he will not do so; but in order to avert this temptation, into which, unlike all others, God himself can lead us, it is taken up into the great world of prayer: "Lead us not into temptation!" Show thyself! That thy mills do *not* grind *too* slowly! Show us thy love *and* thy justice. Let no one doubt that thou art *the Lord,* let no one despair!

THEODOR HAECKER

1683 "Our kingdom go" is the necessary and unavoidable corollary of "Thy kingdom come." For the more there is of self, the less there is of God. The divine eternal fulness of life can be gained only by those who have deliberately lost the partial, separative life of craving and self-interest, of egocentric thinking, feeling, wishing and acting.

ALDOUS HUXLEY

1684 The liturgical prayer often becomes

mechanical or incomprehensible or both. The history of the church has shown that this was the fate even of the Lord's Prayer. Paul certainly knew the "Our Father" when he wrote that we do not know how to pray.

PAUL TILLICH

1685 The Lord's Prayer may be committed to memory quickly, but it is slowly learnt by heart.

FREDERICK DENISON MAURICE

1686 While the Spanish civil war was raging, the chaplain of one of Franco's troops arranged a requiem mass for those fallen in battle. He was announcing the intention of the mass as "for our fallen" when one of the men interrupted him: "Just a moment, Father. We want it 'for our fallen and for their fallen.' " Here was a man who had learned the meaning of the "our" in "Our Father." He was *sane*.

CARROLL E. SIMCOX

MARTYRDOM

1687 It is not the pain but the purpose that makes the martyr.

AUGUSTINE OF HIPPO

1688 Martyrdom is a readiness of mind rather to suffer any evil than to do any.

JEREMY TAYLOR

1689 Some that will hold a creed unto martyrdom will not hold the truth against a sneering laugh.

AUSTIN O'MALLEY

The only method by which religious 1690 truth can be established is by martyrdom.

SAMUEL JOHNSON

The way of the world is to praise 1691 dead saints and persecute living ones.

NATHANIEL HOWE

It is more difficult, and it calls for 1692 higher energies of soul, to live a martyr than to die one.

HORACE MANN

Love makes all the difference be- 1693 tween an execution and a martyrdom.

EVELYN UNDERHILL

The prophet and the martyr do not 1694 see the hooting throng. Their eyes are fixed on the eternities.

BENJAMIN N. CARDOZO

Martyrdom has always been a proof 1695 of the intensity, never of the correctness of a belief.

ARTHUR SCHNITZLER

The blood of the martyrs is the seed 1696 of the church.

TERTULLIAN

MARY

How well her name an ARMY doth 1697
    present
In whom the Lord of Hosts did
    pitch His tent.

GEORGE HERBERT

In order that the body of Christ 1698 might be shown to be a real body, he was born of a woman; but in order that his Godhead might be made clear he was born of a virgin.

THOMAS AQUINAS

1699 The feast we call *Annunciatio Mariae*, when the angel came to Mary and brought her the message from God, may be fitly called the Feast of Christ's Humanity; for then began our deliverance.

MARTIN LUTHER

1700 Born of the Father, Christ created his mother; formed as man in his mother, he glorified his Father. He, the son of Mary and the spouse of holy church, has made the church like to his mother, since he made it a mother for us and he kept it a virgin for himself. The church, like Mary, has inviolate integrity and incorrupt fecundity. What Mary merited physically the church has guarded spiritually, with the exception that Mary brought forth only one child while the church has many children destined to be gathered into one body.

AUGUSTINE OF HIPPO

1701 The real difficulty which prevents people from believing in the Virgin Birth is not want of evidence, but belief in a "closed universe" and in the impossibility of miracles. But who believes this cannot believe in the Incarnation, and therefore cannot be a Christian at all.

C.B. MOSS

1702 Our tainted nature's solitary boast.
WILLIAM WORDSWORTH *(of Mary)*

1703 We have sung *Magnificat* at every evensong, without noticing that rarely has the wildest Communist dared to utter words more contemptuous of our modern world and its standards than those of gentle Lady Mary.

BERNARD IDDINGS BELL

Every saint in God's household has 1704 his peculiar calling, and each is entitled to praise and thanks for what he has done for us. Mary gave us Christ our Savior. Has any human being ever given us more? St. Paul gave the Gospel to the whole world. St. Boniface gave the Gospel to the pagan Germans. St. Francis gave Europe a new face—fashioned upon the face of Christ. "St." Thomas Cranmer gave us the Book of Common Prayer. Our fathers and mothers gave us life. Mary gave us Christ. To each his due meed of praise. If we cherish Christ little we shall honor her little; if to us he is the Way, the Truth, and the Life, we shall give her all the honor a creature can bestow upon another creature.

CARROLL E. SIMCOX

The early church had the mother of 1705 Jesus in its midst. As apostolic times go on, the church speaks more and more about her. The latest gospels, Luke and John, speak of her at the most important places. At the Annunciation she symbolized the people of Israel. At Pentecost she appears as the symbol of the new people of God, the woman who after her birth-pangs thinks no more of her pain (Lk. 2:35; Jn. 19:25). The church of which Mary is thus the image consists of all of us. But the church is also a mother for each of us. And in this sense Mary is our mother, since she is the living personification of the church. We can address her with confidence, if this helps us to see Jesus with new eyes and reach him more easily. The life of the people of God in the East and in the West has, in fact, shown that this has been a way to the Lord. The believer hears Jesus saying to him, Son, behold your mother. But there are also the words, Mother, behold your son. Mary cherishes the children of the church. Our salvation is not only sublimer, but more human, than we think.

A New Catechism

1706   And Mary said, Behold the handmaid of the Lord; be it unto me according to thy word.

Luke 1:38

MINISTRY

1707   The three qualifications for the Ministry are the grace of God, knowledge of the Scriptures in the sacred tongues, and gumption.

Anonymous Scotsman

1708   One ought to think as follows about ministers. The office does not belong to Judas but to Christ alone. When Christ said to Judas, "Go, baptize," Christ himself was the baptizer and not Judas because the command comes from above even if it passes down through a stinking pipe. Nothing is taken from the office on account of the unworthiness of a minister.

MARTIN LUTHER

1709   It is the best part of the man, I sometimes think, that revolts most against his being a minister. His

good revolts from official goodness. The difficulty is that we do not make a world of our own, but fall into institutions already made, and have to accommodate ourselves to them to be useful at all, and this accommodation is, I say, a loss of so much integrity and, of course, of so much power. But how shall the droning world get on if all its *beaux esprits* recalcitrate upon its approved forms and accepted institutions, and quit them all in order to be single minded? The double refiners would produce at the other end the double damned.

RALPH WALDO EMERSON

"*We* bless the cup of blessing," "*we*   1710 break the bread," says St. Paul, speaking for the community: "*we* offer," "*we* present," is the language of the liturgies. But the ministry is the organ—the necessary organ—of these functions. It is the hand which offers and distributes; it is the voice which consecrates and pleads. And the whole body can no more dispense with its services than the natural body can grasp or speak without the instrumentality of hand and tongue. Thus the ministry is the instrument as well as the symbol of the church's unity, and no man can share her fellowship except in acceptance of its offices.

CHARLES GORE

The office of a minister of Christ is   1711 weighty; and they, who go forth as watchmen, have need to be steadily on their guard against the snares of prosperity and an outside friendship.

JOHN WOOLMAN

We are stewards of the mysteries of   1712

God. The faithful steward will say with Paul, "Behold, I show you a mystery," and not denature it into platitudes for retarded or tired minds. If anyone says to you that you are preaching over his head, there is a good answer in three words. It is, "Raise your head."

HALFORD E. LUCCOCK

1713 There is not in the universe a more ridiculous, nor a more contemptible animal, than a proud clergyman.

HENRY FIELDING

1714 St. Paul's injunction to us to put off the Old Man does not mean to put on the Old Woman.

BISHOP HENSLEY HENSON,
to his ordinands

1715 Popular religion may be summed up as respect for ecclesiastics.

BARUCH SPINOZA

1716 Anyone who takes his calling seriously seldom escapes the marks of it, and, within due limits, there is no reason why he should. But there is a great difference in the kind of professional parson he is taken to be, whether one who, as Seeley described him, regards God as the head of the clerical profession, or one who in all his ways plainly shows that he regards God as the Father of all men.

JOHN OMAN

1717 I never saw, heard, nor read, that the clergy were beloved in any nation where Christianity was the religion of the country. Nothing can render them popular but some degree of persecution.

JONATHAN SWIFT

The parish priest   1718
Of Austerity,
Climbed up in a high church steeple
To be nearer God,
So that he might hand
His word down to His people.

When the sun was high,
When the sun was low,
The good man sat unheeding
Sublunary things,
From transcendency
Was he forever reading.

And now and again
When he heard the creak
Of the weather vane a-turning,
He closed his eyes
And said, "Of a truth
From God I now am learning."

And in sermon script
He daily wrote
What he thought was sent from heaven,
And he dropped this down
On his people's head
Two times one day in seven.

In his age God said,
"Come down and die!"
And he cried out from the steeple,
"Where art thou, Lord?"
And the Lord replied,
"Down here among my people."

BREWER MATTOCKS

I have always considered a clergy- 1719
man as the father of a larger family
than he is able to maintain.

SAMUEL JOHNSON

The Christian ministry is the worst 1720
of all trades, but the best of all
professions.

JOSEPH FORT NEWTON

'Twas August, and the fierce sun 1721
overhead

Smote on the squalid streets of
Bethnal Green,

And the pale weaver, through his
windows seen

In Spitalfields, look'd thrice dispir-
ited.

I met a preacher there I knew, and
said:

'Ill and o'erworked, how fare you in
this scene?'—

'Bravely!' said he; 'for I of late have
been

Much cheer'd with thoughts of
Christ, *the living bread.*'

O human soul! as long as thou canst
so

Set up a mark of everlasting light,

Above the howling senses' ebb and
flow,

To cheer thee, and to right thee if
thou roam—

Not with lost toil thou laborest
through the night!

Thou mak'st the heaven thou hop'st
indeed thy home.

MATTHEW ARNOLD

1722 The servant of the Lord must not
strive; but be gentle unto all men,
apt to teach, patient, in meekness
instructing those that oppose themselves.

II Timothy 2:24–25

1723 We are ambassadors for Christ.
II Corinthians 5:20a

1724 Follow me, and I will make you
fishers of men.

Matthew 4:19

1725 O Lord Jesus Christ, who at thy first
coming didst send thy messenger to
prepare thy way before thee; grant
that the ministers and stewards of
thy mysteries may likewise so prepare and make ready thy way, by
turning the hearts of the disobeient
to the wisdom of the just, that at thy
second coming to judge the world
we may be found an acceptable
people in thy sight, who livest and
reignest with the Father and the
Holy Spirit ever, one God, world
without end.

Book of Common Prayer

MISSION

The church exists by mission, as fire
exists by burning.

EMIL BRUNNER

1726

Missions is the church in love with
the whole world.

CHARLES L. SLATTERY

1727

If people ask, "Why did he not
appear by means of other parts of
creation, and use some nobler instrument, as the sun or moon or
stars or fire or air, instead of man
merely?" let them know that the
Lord came not to make a display,
but to teach and heal those who
were suffering.

ATHANASIUS OF ALEXANDRIA

1728

God had an only Son, and he was a
missionary and a physician.

DAVID LIVINGSTONE

1729

Those who deblaterate against missions have only one thing to do: to
come and see them on the spot.

ROBERT LOUIS STEVENSON

1730

And a vision appeared to Paul in the
night; There stood a man of Macedonia, and prayed him, saying,
Come over into Macedonia, and
help us.

Acts 16:9

1731

1732 Our advancing troops always know when they are nearing one of these mission stations, because the natives are friendly and trustful. There, some selfless man, serene in the face of death, has pursued his task of spreading education, loyalty, cleanliness, and Christian principles among flocks once turbulent and discontented. They are forerunners of the many who must soon take up the work of rehabilitation of the submerged populations who have lived through the storm sweeping Asia. They have cut a pathway of grace through the wilderness. Their weary hands need sustaining now more than ever.

The New York Times,
editorial, Oct. 13, 1944

1733 The church is not a company on a summer hotel porch; it is a lifesaving crew.

HALFORD E. LUCCOCK

1734 Then said Jesus to them again, Peace be unto you: as my Father hath sent me, even so send I you.

John 20:21

conclusions, and their failures are due to individual perversity. The fact remains that the knowledge which is to be obtained through the study of theology makes mightily for righteousness.

FRANCIS J. HALL

It is as difficult to be quite orthodox **1737** as to be quite healthy. Yet the need for orthodoxy, like the need for health, is imperative.

CHARLES WILLIAMS

Orthodoxy is my doxy; heterodoxy **1738** is another man's doxy.

WILLIAM WARBURTON

All advanced thinkers, sceptical or **1739** otherwise, are apt to be intolerant, in the past and also now. On the whole, tolerance is more often found in connection with a genial orthodoxy.

ALFRED NORTH WHITEHEAD

Tradition by itself is not enough; it **1740** must be perpetually criticized and brought up to date under the supervision of what I call orthodoxy.

T.S. ELIOT

ORTHODOXY

(See *Belief, Faith, Theology*)

1735 You may be as orthodox as the devil, and as wicked.

JOHN WESLEY

1736 Orthodoxy and righteousness are not the same, and they may be divorced from each other in individual lives. But unworthy theologians are apt to be unsound in their

PREACHING

A sermon is a proclamation of the **1741** generous love of God in Christ, or it is not a Christian sermon.

NORMAN PITTENGER

Preaching is truth through personality.   **1742**

PHILLIPS BROOKS

Actors speak of things imaginary as **1743**

if they were real, while preachers too often speak of things real as if they were imaginary.

THOMAS BETTERTON
(actor, ob. 1710)

1744 I preached as never sure to preach again,
And as a dying man to dying men.
RICHARD BAXTER

1745 Unless those who are in the office of preacher find joy in him who sent them, they will have much trouble. Our Lord God had to ask Moses as much as six times. He also led me into the office the same way.
MARTIN LUTHER

1746 The half-baked sermon causes spiritual indigestion.
AUSTIN O'MALLEY

1747 The free pulpit is not a nagging pulpit. Like a skilful dentist the preacher does a good deal of his work away from the regions of the sensitive nerves.
LYNN HAROLD HOUGH

1748 We are forever hearing sermons about what ought to be done from people who do not stop to consider whether what they preach can be done. As a result, the exhortations, which are tautological reiterations of the rule which everyone knows already, prove terribly boring. They express nothing that we are not already familiar with, and sermons consisting of such exhortations are very empty, unless the preacher has an eye to practical wisdom at the same time.
IMMANUEL KANT

1749 When you preach the Gospel, be-

ware of preaching it as the religion which explains everything.
ALBERT SCHWEITZER

1750 Our business is to present that which is timeless (the same yesterday, today, and tomorrow) in the particular language of our own age. The bad preacher does exactly the opposite: he takes the ideas of our own age and tricks them out in the traditional language of Christianity.
C.S. LEWIS

1751 I am convinced if I asked any one of you suddenly to recall five sermons you have listened to, you would be hard put to answer. But if I should ask you to name five persons through whom God has put his hand on your life, you would not hesitate a moment.
HALFORD E. LUCCOCK

1752 The aim of preaching is not the elucidation of a subject, but the transformation of a person.
HALFORD E. LUCCOCK

1753 To love to preach is one thing—to love those to whom we preach, quite another.
RICHARD CECIL

1754 Preaching is not the art of making a sermon and delivering it. Preaching is the art of making a preacher and delivering that.
WILLIAM A. QUAYLE

1755 Preaching is thirty minutes in which to raise the dead.
JOHN RUSKIN

1756 I won't take my religion from any man who never works except with his mouth and never cherishes any memory except the face of the woman on the American silver dollar.

CARL SANDBURG

1757 Only the sinner has a right to preach.

CHRISTOPHER MORLEY

1758 The world is dying for want, not of good preaching, but of good hearing.

GEORGE DANA BOARDMAN

1759 One of the proofs of the divinity of our gospel is the preaching it has survived.

WOODROW WILSON

1760 The test of a preacher is that his congregation goes away saying, not "What a lovely sermon!" but, "I will do something!"

FRANCIS DE SALES

RECONCILIATION

1761 The emptiness and futility of life, the resentment and fear that keep us from inward serenity in the face of life's ills, the lovelessness that fills the earth with conflict, all find their cure in our reconciliation with God. Nothing less will bridge those seas of misunderstanding across which we "shout to one another." The antagonisms that divide the world are due to our own inner conflicts. Peace is one of the by-products that come from seeking God's rule and his righteousness. God has now entrusted to us this ministry of reconciliation.

JAMES REID

1762 It takes two sides to make a lasting peace, but it only takes one to make the first step.

EDWARD M. KENNEDY

1763 Reconciliation sounds a large theological term, but it simply means coming to ourselves and arising and going to our Father.

JOHN OMAN

1764 If thou bring thy gift to the altar, and there rememberest that thy brother hath ought against thee; leave there thy gift before the altar, and go thy way; first be reconciled to thy brother, and then come and offer thy gift.

Matthew 5:23–24

1765 Word over all, beautiful as the sky!
Beautiful that war, and all its deeds
     of carnage,
must in time be utterly lost;
That the hands of the sisters Death
     and Night, incessantly softly wash again, and ever
     again, this soil'd world:
. . . For my enemy is dead—a man
     divine as myself is dead;
I look where he lies, white-faced and
     still, in the coffin—
I draw near;
I bend down, and touch lightly with
     my lips the white face
in the coffin.

WALT WHITMAN

1766 Be ye reconciled to God.
II Corinthians 5:20b

RESURRECTION

1767 Why should it be thought a thing

incredible with you, that God should raise the dead?

Acts 26:8

1768 Taking all the evidence together, it is not too much to say that there is no single historic incident better or more variously supported than the resurrection of Christ.

B.F. WESTCOTT

1769 The Gospels do not explain the resurrection; the resurrection explains the Gospels. Belief in the resurrection is not an appendage to the Christian faith; it *is* the Christian faith.

J.S. WHALE

1770 Christ has conquered death, not only by suppressing its evil effects, but by reversing its sting. By virtue of the Resurrection, nothing any longer kills inevitably but everything is capable of becoming the blessed touch of the divine hands, the blessed influence of the will of God upon our lives. However compromised by our faults, or however cast down by circumstances, our position may be, we can at any moment, by a total redressment, wholly readjust the world around us and take up our lives again in a favorable sense. To those who love God all things are turned to good.

PIERRE TEILHARD DE CHARDIN

1771 How shall the dead arise, is no question of my faith; to believe only possibilities, is not faith, but mere philosophy.

THOMAS BROWNE

1772 Naturally we cannot say much about the spiritual body, because we cannot imagine what it would be like to have a body different from that which we now inhabit, but it seems to me reasonable to believe that we are weaving our spiritual bodies as we go along. They are being formed by our thoughts and acts of will and imaginations during this life.

W.R. MATTHEWS

1773 Fellowship with Christ is participation in the divine life which finds its fullest expression in triumph over death. Life is a larger word than Resurrection; but Resurrection is, so to speak, the crucial quality of life.

WILLIAM TEMPLE

1774 The basic meaning of the Resurrection is the liberation of Jesus Christ. John Masefield in his play tells in imagination how Procla, the wife of Pilate, sent for Longinus, the centurion in charge of the crucifixion, and asked him what had happened. "He was a fine young man," said Longinus, "but when we were finished with him he was a poor broken thing on a cross." "So you think," said Procla, "that he is finished and ended?" "No, madam, I do not," said Longinus. "He is set free throughout the world where neither Jew nor Greek can stop his truth."

WILLIAM BARCLAY

1775 The resurrection did not result in a committee with a chairman, but in a fellowship with an experience.

Anonymous

1776 Easter, like all deep things, begins in mystery and it ends, like all high things, in a great courage.

BLISS PERRY

1777 The Easter message is a word about God, a grand *Te Deum* that joyfully declares God is still master in his own household.

ERNEST W. SAUNDERS

SACRAMENTS

1778 *Question.* What meanest thou by this word *Sacrament?*
Answer. I mean an outward and visible sign of an inward and spiritual grace given unto us; ordained by Christ himself, as a means whereby we receive the same, and a pledge to assure us thereof.

Book of Common Prayer

1779 The use of sacraments is but only in this life, yet so that here they concern a far better life than this, and are for that cause accompanied with "grace which worketh salvation." Sacraments are the powerful instruments of God to eternal life. For as our natural body consisteth in the union of the body with the soul, so our life supernatural is in the union of the soul with God.

RICHARD HOOKER

1780 In all sacramental doctrine and practice the original and ultimate authority is Christ himself.

Edinburgh Conference

1781 Let me ask you a question: are we still able to understand what a sacrament means? The more we are estranged from nature, the less we can answer affirmatively. That is why, in our time, the sacraments have lost so much of their significance for individuals and churches. For in the sacraments nature participates in the process of salvation. Bread and wine, water and light, and all the great elements of nature become the bearers of spiritual meaning and saving power. Natural and spiritual powers are united—re-united—in the sacrament. The word appeals to our intellect and may move our will. The sacrament, if its meaning is alive, grasps our unconscious as well as our conscious being. It grasps the creative ground of our being. It is the symbol of nature and spirit, united in salvation.

PAUL TILLICH

SALVATION

1782 We must never separate what God does for us from what God does in us.

CHARLES GORE

1783 To follow the Saviour is to participate in salvation, to follow the light is to perceive the light.

IRENAEUS

1784 No one who is convinced of his own salvation is as yet even safe, let alone "saved." Salvation is the state of him who has ceased to be interested in whether he is saved or not, provided that what takes the place of that supreme self-interest is not a lower form of self-interest but the glory of God.

WILLIAM TEMPLE

1785 The terms for "salvation" in many languages are derived from roots like *salvus, saos,* whole, *heil,* which all designate health, the opposite of disintegration and disruption. Salvation is healing in the ultimate sense; it is final cosmic and individual healing.

PAUL TILLICH

1786 Consider yourself a refractory pupil for whom you are responsible as mentor and tutor. To sanctify sinful nature, by bringing it gradually under control of the angel within us, by the help of a holy God, is really the whole of Christian pedagogy and of religious morals. Our work— my work—consists in taming, subduing, evangelizing, and *angelizing* the evil self; and in restoring harmony with the good self. Salvation lies in abandoning the evil self in principle, and in taking refuge with the other, the divine self—in accepting with courage and prayer the task of living with one's own demon, and making it into a less and less rebellious instrument of good. The Abel in us must labor for the salvation of the Cain. To undertake it is to be converted, and this conversion must be repeated day by day. Abel only redeems and touches Cain by exercising him constantly in good works. To do right is in one sense an act of violence: it is suffering, expiation, a cross, for it means the conquest and enslavement of self. In another sense it is the apprenticeship to heavenly things, sweet and secret joy, contentment and peace.

HENRI FRÉDÉRIC AMIEL

1787 Everything was so dark in my life and God illuminated it. Do not forget it, O my heart! Do not forget it!

THEODOR HAECKER

In the certainty that he is enlisted   *1788* with God, man finds not only comfort in defeat, not only an ideal of holiness which persuades him to renounce his immediate desires, but an ecstatic mobilizing of all his scattered energies in one triumphant sense of his own infinite importance.

WALTER LIPPMANN

Salvation is seeing that the universe   *1789* is good, and becoming a part of that goodness.

CLUTTON BROCK

Nothing worth doing is completed   *1790* in our lifetime; therefore, we must be saved by hope. Nothing true or beautiful or good makes complete sense in any context of history; therefore, we must be saved by faith. Nothing we do, however virtuous, can be accomplished alone; therefore, we are saved by love. No virtuous act is quite as virtuous from the standpoint of our friend or foe as from our standpoint. Therefore, we must be saved by the final form of love which is forgiveness.

REINHOLD NIEBUHR

Salvation is nothing if it does not   *1791* deliver us from death.

GABRIEL MARCEL

God did not save you to be a   *1792* sensation. He saved you to be a servant.

JOHN E. HUNTER

To know Christ is not to speculate   *1793* about the mode of his incarnation, but to know his saving benefits.

PHILIP MELANCHTHON

TRADITION

1794   Continuity with the past is a necessity, not a duty.

OLIVER WENDELL HOLMES, JR.

1795   If I have seen further [than you and Descartes] it is by standing on the shoulders of giants.

ISAAC NEWTON, *to Robert Hooke*

1796   Do not seek to follow in the footsteps of the men of old; seek what they sought.

MATSUO BASHO

1797   Tradition may be defined as an extension of the franchise. Tradition means giving votes to the most obscure of all classes, our ancestors. It is the democracy of the dead.

GILBERT KEITH CHESTERTON

1798   Tradition is the living faith of the dead; traditionalism is the dead faith of the living.

JAROSLAV PELIKAN

1799   Tradition is an important help to history, but its statements should be carefully scrutinized before we rely on them.

JOSEPH ADDISON

1800   There is no greater disloyalty to the great pioneers of human progress than to refuse to budge an inch from where they stood.

WILLIAM RALPH INGE

1801   Every man of us has all the centuries in him.

JOHN, VISCOUNT MORLEY

1802   The general and perpetual voice of men is as the sentence of God himself. For that which all men have at all times learned, Nature herself must needs have taught; and God being the author of Nature, her voice is but his instrument.

RICHARD HOOKER

1803   Tradition and conscience are the two wings given to the human soul to reach the truth.

GIUSEPPE MAZZINI

1804   Piety to the past is not for its own sake nor for the sake of the past, but for the sake of a present so secure and enriched that it will create a yet better future.

JOHN DEWEY

1805   Hearken to me, ye that follow after righteousness, ye that seek the Lord: look unto the rock whence ye are hewn, and to the hole of the pit whence ye are digged.

Isaiah 51:1

V

Life in the Spirit

He which hath begun a good work in you will perform it until the day of Jesus Christ.

Philippians 1:6

The renewal of creation has been wrought by the self-same Word who made it from the beginning.

Athanasius of Alexandria

Creation's Lord, we give thee thanks
That this thy world is incomplete;
That battle calls our marshaled ranks;
That work awaits our hands and feet;

That thou hast not yet finished man;
That we are in the making still,
As friends who share the Maker's plan,
As sons who know the Father's will.

William De Witt Hyde

ACCEPTANCE

1806   Naked came I out of my mother's womb, and naked shall I return thither: the Lord gave, and the Lord hath taken away; blessed be the name of the Lord. In all this Job sinned not, nor charged God foolishly.

Job 1:21–22

1807   God is the master of the scenes; we must not choose what part we shall act; it concerns us only to be careful that we do it well, always saying, "If this please God, let it be as it is."

JEREMY TAYLOR

1808   He who is in a state of rebellion cannot receive grace, to use the phrase of which the Church is so fond—so rightly fond, I dare say—for in life as in art the mood of rebellion closes up the channels of the soul, and shuts out the airs of heaven.

OSCAR WILDE

1809   God grant me the serenity to accept the things I cannot change, the courage to change the things I can, and the wisdom to distinguish the one from the other.

Prayer of Alcoholics Anonymous

1810   As in a game of cards, so in the game of life we must play with what is dealt out to us; and the glory consists not so much in winning as in playing a poor hand well.

JOSH BILLINGS

1811   I sighed because the day was dark—
       and then I met a child who had
          no eyes.
       I complained because the walk was

long—until I met a man who had
   no legs.
I prayed for wealth beyond my
   need—and then I met a poor soul
   with no bread at all.
O God, forgive me—for the world is
   mine.

Anonymous

When his life's work was threatened, 1812
St. Ignatius Loyola was asked what he would do if Pope Paul IV dissolved or otherwise acted against the Society of Jesus, to which he had devoted his energy and gifts; and he replied: "I would pray for fifteen minutes, then I would not think of it again."

ALAN PATON

I have learned, in whatsoever state I 1813
am, therewith to be content. I know both how to be abased, and I know how to abound: every where and in all things I am instructed both to be full and to be hungry, both to abound and to suffer need. I can do all things through Christ which strengtheneth me.

Philippians 4:11–13

ACTION

Inasmuch as ye have done it unto 1814
one of the least of these my brethren, ye have done it unto me.

Matthew 25:40

Every man feels instinctively that all 1815
the beautiful sentiments in the world weigh less than a single lovely action.

JAMES RUSSELL LOWELL

1816 Wisdom is knowing what to do next, skill is knowing how to do it, and virtue is doing it.

DAVID STARR JORDAN

1817 Do little things as if they were great, because of the majesty of the Lord Jesus Christ who dwells in thee; and do great things as if they were little and easy, because of his omnipotence.

BLAISE PASCAL

1818 Have thy tools ready; God will find thee work.

CHARLES KINGSLEY

1819 It is better to wear out than to rust out.

BISHOP RICHARD CUMBERLAND

1820 I think that, as life is action and passion, it is required of a man that he should share the passion and action of his time at peril of being judged not to have lived.

OLIVER WENDELL HOLMES, JR.

1821 I have always loved to think of devoted suffering as the highest, purest, perhaps the only quite pure form of action.

FRIEDRICH VON HÜGEL

1822 Love's secret is always to be doing things for God, and not to mind because they are such very little ones.

FREDERICK W. FABER

1823 A Christian should always remember that the value of his good works is not based on their number and excellence, but on the love of God which prompts him to do these things.

JOHN OF THE CROSS

1824 I have never heard anything about the resolutions of the Apostles, but a great deal about their Acts.

HORACE MANN

1825 No man has a right to lead such a life of contemplation as to forget in his own ease the service due to his neighbor; nor has any man a right to be so immersed in active life as to neglect the contemplation of God.

AUGUSTINE OF HIPPO

1826 To give our Lord a perfect hospitality, Mary and Martha must combine.

TERESA OF AVILA

ADVERSITY

1827 We glory in tribulations also: knowing that tribulation worketh patience; and patience, experience; and experience, hope.

Romans 5:3–4

1828 God says to man: "With thy very wounds I will heal thee."

The Talmud

1829 It has done me good to be somewhat parched by the heat and drenched by the rain of life.

HENRY WADSWORTH LONGFELLOW

1830 It is not miserable to be blind; it is miserable to be incapable of enduring blindness.

JOHN MILTON

1831 It is good for us that we sometimes have sorrows and adversities, for they often make a man lay to heart that he is only a stranger and sojourner, and may not put his trust in any worldly thing. It is good that we sometimes endure contradictions, and are hardly and unfairly judged, when we do and mean what is good. For these things help us to be humble and shield us from vainglory. For then we seek more earnestly the witness of God, when men speak evil of us falsely, and give us no credit for good.

THOMAS À KEMPIS

1832 Relating a clubfoot to God may be the ruin of a man's religion. Relating God to a clubfoot may be the making of a man's life.

PAUL SCHERER

1833 Many can bear adversity, but few contempt.

English proverb

1834 He that pricketh the eye will make tears to fall; and he that pricketh the heart maketh it to show her knowledge.

Ecclesiasticus 22:19

1835 Prosperity is not without many fears and distastes; and adversity is not without comforts and hopes. The virtue of prosperity is temperance, but the virtue of adversity is fortitude, which in morals is the more heroical virtue. Prosperity is the blessing of the Old Testament, adversity is the blessing of the New, which carrieth the greater benediction, and the clearer revelation of God's favor.

FRANCIS BACON

1836 Grace grows best in the winter.

SAMUEL RUTHERFORD

1837 As sure as ever God puts his chil-

dren in the furnace he will be in the furnace with them.

CHARLES H. SPURGEON

1838 A wise man struggling with adversity is said by some heathen writer to be a spectacle on which the gods might look down with pleasure.

SYDNEY SMITH

1839 I'll say this for adversity: people seem to be able to stand it, and that's more than I can say for prosperity.

FRANK MC KINNEY HUBBARD

1840 Afflictions are but the shadow of God's wings.

GEORGE MAC DONALD

1841 You may not realize it when it happens, but a kick in the teeth may be the best thing in the world for you.

WALT DISNEY

1842 They took away what should have
   been my eyes,
(But I remembered Milton's Paradise).
They took away what should have
   been my ears,
(Beethoven came and wiped away
   my tears).
They took away what should have
   been my tongue,
(But I had talked with God when I
   was young).
He would not let them take away
   my soul—
Possessing that, I still possess the
   whole.

HELEN KELLER

BROKENNESS

(See *Adversity, Cross, Suffering*)

1843 We must be broken into life.
CHARLES E. RAVEN

1844 It is the crushed grape that yields the wine.
Anonymous

1845 Every story of conversion is the story of a blessed defeat.
C.S. LEWIS

1846 God creates out of nothing. Therefore until a man is nothing, God can make nothing out of him.
MARTIN LUTHER

1847 How else but through a broken heart may Lord Christ enter in?
OSCAR WILDE

1848 The sacrifice of God is a troubled spirit: a broken and contrite heart, O God, shalt thou not despise.
Psalm 51:17

CHARITY

1849 Charity is the great channel through which God passes all his mercy upon mankind. For we receive absolution of our sins in proportion to our forgiving our brother. This is the rule of our hopes, and the measure of our desire in this world; and in the day of death and judgment the great sentence upon mankind shall be transacted according to our alms, which is the other part of charity. Certain it is, that God cannot, will not, never did, reject a charitable man in his greatest needs and in his most passionate prayers; for God himself is love, and every degree of charity that dwells in us is the participation of the Divine Nature.
JEREMY TAYLOR

1850 This is charity, to do all, all that we can.
JOHN DONNE

1851 Although I am far from thee, may no one else be far from thee.
HAFIZ

1852 I rather think there is an immense shortage of Christian charity among so-called Christians.
HARRY S. TRUMAN

1853 Feel for others—in your pocket.
CHARLES H. SPURGEON

1854 You can give without loving, but you cannot love without giving.
AMY CARMICHAIEL

1855 I feel that God would sooner we did wrong in loving than never love for fear we should do wrong.
FATHER ANDREW

1856 Charity begins at home, and justice begins next door.
CHARLES DICKENS

1857 Our Lord does not care so much for the importance of our works as for the love with which they are done.
TERESA OF AVILA

1858 Almighty God, have mercy on N and N and on all that bear me evil will, and would do me harm, and their faults and mine together, by such easy, tender, merciful means as thine infinite wisdom best can divine, vouchsafe to attend and redress, and make us saved souls in heaven together where we may ever live and love together with thee and thy blessed saints, O glorious Trinity, for the bitter passion of our sweet Saviour Christ. Amen.

Ascribed to THOMAS MORE

1859 The Christians know one another by secret marks and signs, and they love one another almost before they know one another.

STATIUS CAECILIUS

1860 No sound ought to be heard in the church but the healing voice of Christian charity.

EDMUND BURKE

1861 If charity were less important, the deviations from charity would not only be less serious but would also be less liable to call themselves by any name except the honest one of sin. All virtue is loving right, all sin is loving wrong.

HUBERT VAN ZELLER

1862 The best thing to give to your enemy is forgiveness; to an opponent, tolerance; to a friend, your heart; to your child, a good example; to a father, deference; to your mother, conduct that will make her proud of you; to yourself, respect; to all men, charity.

JOHN BALFOUR

1863 Lord of the world, I beg you to redeem Israel. And if you do not want to do that, then redeem the Gentiles.

RABBI ISRAEL OF KOZNITZ.

1864 Above all things have fervent charity among yourselves: for charity shall cover the multitude of sins.

I Peter 4:8.

O Lord, who hast taught us that all   1865
our doings without charity are nothing worth; send thy Holy Ghost, and pour into our hearts that most excellent gift of charity, the very bond of peace and of all virtues, without which whosoever liveth is counted dead before thee. Grant this for thine only Son Jesus Christ's sake.

Book of Common Prayer

CHASTITY

The essence of chastity is not the   1866
suppression of lust, but the total orientation of one's life towards a goal. Without such a goal, chastity is bound to become ridiculous. Chastity is the *sine qua non* of lucidity and concentration.

DIETRICH BONHOEFFER

Not in flight from (by suppressing   1867
them) but in mastery of (by sublimating them) the unfathomable spiritual forces that still lie dormant beneath the mutual attraction of the sexes—there lie the hidden essence of chastity and the grand task it will have to face.

PIERRE TEILHARD DE CHARDIN

Chastity is that duty which was   1868
mystically intended by God in the law of circumcision. It is the circumcision of the heart, the cutting off all superfluity of naughtiness, and a suppression of all irregular desires in the matters of sensual or carnal

pleasure. I call all desires irregular and sinful that are not sanctified: (1) by the holy institution or by being within the protection of marriage; (2) by being within the order of nature; (3) by being within the moderation of Christian modesty.

JEREMY TAYLOR

1869 Chastity is the most unpopular of the Christian virtues. There is no getting away from it: the Christian rule is, "Either marriage, with complete faithfulness to your partner, or else total abstinence." Now this is so difficult and so contrary to our instincts, that obviously either Christianity is wrong or our sexual instinct, as it now is, has gone wrong. One or the other. Of course, being a Christian, I think it is the instinct which has gone wrong.

C.S. LEWIS

1870 To be chaste is to have the body in the keeping of the heart. Their divorce is the one thing which in the end makes unchastity.

F.H. BRADLEY

1871 Even from the body's purity, the mind
Receives a secret sympathetic aid.

JAMES THOMSON

CHEERFULNESS

(See *Happiness, Honor, Joy, Laughter*)

1872 Cheerfulness and content are great beautifiers, and are famous preservers of good looks.

CHARLES DICKENS

A cheerful look makes a dish a feast.   1873

GEORGE HERBERT

One of the most effectual ways of   1874 pleasing and of making one's self loved is to be cheerful: joy softens more hearts than tears.

MME. DE SARTORY

A good laugh is sunshine in a house.   1875

WILLIAM MAKEPEACE THACKERAY

Cheerfulness in most cheerful peo-   1876 ple is the rich and satisfying result of strenuous discipline.

EDWIN PERCY WHIPPLE

A merry heart doeth good like a   1877 medicine.

Proverbs 17:22

Be of good cheer: I have overcome   1878 the world.

John 16:33

COMPASSION

(See *Charity, Kindness*)

A righteous man regardeth the life   1879 of his beast: but the tender mercies of the wicked are cruel.

Proverbs 12:10

We must learn to regard people less   1880 in the light of what they do or omit to do, and more in the light of what they suffer.

DIETRICH BONHOEFFER

He that hath pity upon the poor   1881 lendeth unto the Lord.

Proverbs 19:17

1882 A dog starv'd at his master's gate
Predicts the ruin of the State,
A horse misus'd upon the road
Calls to Heaven for human blood.
Each outcry of the hunted hare
A fibre from the brain does tear,
A skylark wounded on the wing,
A cherubim does cease to sing.
WILLIAM BLAKE

1883 The root of the matter, if we want a stable world, is a very simple and old-fashioned thing, a thing so simple that I am almost ashamed to mention it for fear of the derisive smile with which wise cynics will greet my words. The thing I mean is love, Christian love, or compassion. If you feel this, you have a motive for existence, a reason for courage, an imperative necessity for intellectual honesty.
BERTRAND RUSSELL

1884 Of what avail is an open eye, if the heart is blind?
SOLOMON IBN GABIROL

1885 That person is cultured who is able to put himself in the place of the greatest number of other persons.
JANE ADDAMS

1886 Man is never nearer the Divine than in his compassionate moments.
JOSEPH H. HERTZ

1887 Compassion is the basis of all morality.
ARTHUR SCHOPENHAUER

1888 It is not written, blessed is he that *feedeth* the poor, but he that *considereth* the poor. A little thought and a little kindness are often worth more than a great deal of money.
JOHN RUSKIN

What is a charitable heart? It is the 1889
heart of him who burns with pity for all creation—for every human being, every bird, every animal, every demon. He looks at the creatures, or remembers them, and his eyes are filled with tears. His heart is also filled with deep compassion and limitless patience; it overflows with tenderness, and cannot bear to see or hear any evil or the least grief endured by the creature.
Therefore he offers his prayers constantly for the dumb creatures and for the enemies of truth and for those who do him harm, that they may be preserved and pardoned. And for the reptiles also he prays with great compassion, which rises without measure from the depths of his heart till he shines again and is glorious like God.
ISAAK OF SYRIA

CONCERN

Christianity taught us to care. Caring is the greatest thing, caring matters most. 1890
FRIEDRICH VON HÜGEL,
his last words

The thing that drove Dickens forward . . . was simply the fact that he was a moralist, the consciousness of his "having something to say." He is always preaching a sermon, and that is the final secret of his inventiveness. For you can create only if you can *care*. 1891
GEORGE ORWELL

Wherever there is lost the consciousness that every man is an object of 1892 concern for us just because he is a man, civilization and morals are shaken, and the advance to fully developed inhumanity is only a question of time.

ALBERT SCHWEITZER

1893 He [John Brown] did not go to the college called Harvard; good old Alma Mater as she is. . . . He would have left a Greek accent slanting the wrong way, and righted up a falling man.

HENRY DAVID THOREAU

1894 Before any cosmic act of reform we must have a cosmic oath of allegiance. A man must be interested in life, then he could be disinterested in his views of it. "My son, give me thy heart"; the heart must be fixed on the right thing: the moment we have a fixed heart we have a free hand.

GILBERT KEITH CHESTERTON

CONTENTMENT

1895 No form of society can be reasonably stable in which the majority of the people are not fairly content. People cannot be content if they feel that the foundations of their lives are wholly unstable.

JAMES TRUSLOW ADAMS

1896 True contentment is a real, even an active, virtue—not only affirmative but creative. It is the power of getting out of any situation all there is in it.

GILBERT KEITH CHESTERTON

Better is a dry morsel, and quietness   1897
therewith, than an house full of sacrifices with strife.

Proverbs 17:1

When we cannot find contentment   1898
in ourselves it is useless to seek it elsewhere.

FRANÇOIS DE LA ROCHEFOUCAULD

True contentment depends not on   1899
what we have; a tub was large enough for Diogenes, but a world was too little for Alexander.

CHARLES CALEB COLTON

COURAGE

Courage is what it takes to stand up   1900
and speak; courage is also what it takes to sit down and listen.

Anonymous

Courage without discipline is nearer   1901
beastliness than manhood.

PHILIP SIDNEY

A very popular error—having the   1902
courage of one's convictions: rather it is a matter of having the courage for an attack upon one's convictions.

FRIEDRICH WILHELM NIETZSCHE

Whistling to keep up courage is   1903
good practice for whistling.

HENRY S. HASKINS

By faith he forsook Egypt, not fear-   1904
ing the wrath of the king: for he endured, as seeing him who is invisible.

Hebrews 11:27

1905 Courage is a virtue only insofar as it is directed by prudence.

FRANÇOIS FÉNELON

1906 Courage is doing what you're afraid to do. There can be no courage unless you're scared.

EDDIE RICKENBACKER

1907 A close friend of mine was the chief of the London police force. Once a crowd in Trafalgar Square began to get out of hand. He walked slowly toward it, wearing his old fatigue jacket with its three bars of decorations. On reaching the crowd, and in the sight of all, he laid his jacket on the pavement. Then he turned, faced the crowd, and walked slowly towards and into it. By the time he had reached the other side, the crowd had begun to fritter away at the edges and disperse. This walking slowly through a crowd is common police training, I am told. I asked him, "Weren't you afraid?" "No," he answered, "I represent the King, and they knew it!"

RICHARDSON WRIGHT

1908 Workman of God! oh, lose not heart,
    But learn what God is like,
And in the darkest battle-field,
    Thou shalt know where to strike.

Thrice blest is he to whom is given
    The instinct that can tell
That God is on the field when He
    Is most invisible.

FREDERICK W. FABER

1909 In God I have put my trust; I will not fear what flesh can do unto me.
Psalm 56:4 (AV)

1910 Where I could not be honest I never yet was valiant.

WILLIAM SHAKESPEARE

1911 Not to mention his [John Brown's] other successes, was it a failure, or did it show a want of good management, to deliver from bondage a dozen human beings, and walk off with them by broad daylight, for weeks if not months, at a leisurely pace, through one state after another, for half the length of the North, conspicuous to all parties, with a price set upon his head, going into a court-room on his way and telling what he had done, thus convincing Missouri that it would not be profitable to try to hold slaves in his neighborhood?—and this, not because the government menials were lenient, but because they were afraid of him.

Yet he did not attribute his success, foolishly, to "his star," or to any magic. He said, truly, that the reason why such greatly superior numbers quailed before him was, as one of his prisoners confessed, because they *lacked a cause,*—a kind of armor which he and his party never lacked. When the time came, few men were found willing to lay down their lives in defense of what they knew to be wrong; they did not like that this should be their last act in this world.

HENRY DAVID THOREAU

1912 Fear ye not, stand still, and see the salvation of the Lord.
Exodus 14:13

1913 The Lord is my light and my salvation; whom shall I fear? the Lord is the strength of my life; of whom shall I be afraid?
Psalm 27:1

1914 If God be for us, who can be against us?

Romans 8:31

1915 Perfect love casteth out fear.

I John 4:18

COURTESY

(See *Manners*)

1916 There is a politeness of the heart, and it is allied to love. It produces the most agreeable politeness of outward behavior.

JOHANN WOLFGANG VON GOETHE

1917 Good manners is the art of making those people easy with whom we converse. Whoever makes the fewest people uneasy is the best bred in the company.

JONATHAN SWIFT

1918 Politeness is to human nature what warmth is to wax.

ARTHUR SCHOPENHAUER

1919 To dispense with ceremony is the most delicate mode of conferring a compliment.

EDWARD BULWER-LYTTON

1920 We must be courteous to a man as we are to a picture, which we are willing to give the advantage of a good light.

RALPH WALDO EMERSON

1921 A soft answer turneth away wrath.

Proverbs 15:1

1922 Of courtesy, it is much less
Than courage of heart or holiness.

Yet in my walks it seems to me
That the grace of God is in courtesy.

HILAIRE BELLOC

DAILY LIVING

Our task as moral beings is to lead a "dying life"; to rest on our oars would mean a "living death," a very different thing. 1923

A.E. TAYLOR

We die daily. Happy those who daily come to life as well. 1924

GEORGE MAC DONALD

If a man cannot be a Christian where he is, he cannot be a Christian anywhere. 1925

HENRY WARD BEECHER

Every day is a messenger of God. 1926
Russian proverb

We do not live in order to eat; we eat in order to live. 1927

Greek proverb

Life is like playing a violin solo in public and learning the instrument as one goes on. 1928

EDWARD BULWER-LYTTON

Life is the art of drawing sufficient conclusions from insufficient premises. 1929

SAMUEL BUTLER

The problem of life is not to make life easier, but to make men stronger. 1930

DAVID STARR JORDAN

"Give us our daily bread" (not an 1931

annuity for life) applies to spiritual gifts too; the little *daily* support for the *daily* trial. Life has to be taken day by day and hour by hour.

C.S. LEWIS

1932 Relying on God has to begin all over again every day as if nothing had yet been done.

C.S. LEWIS

1933 This is the day which the Lord hath made; we will rejoice and be glad in it.

Psalm 118:24

1934 Almighty God, our heavenly Father, who declarest thy glory and showest forth thy handiwork in the heavens and in the earth; deliver us, we beseech thee, in our several callings, from the service of mammon, that we may do the work which thou givest us to do, in truth, in beauty, and in righteousness, with singleness of heart as thy servants, and to the benefit of our fellow men; for the sake of him who came among us as one that serveth, thy Son Jesus Christ our Lord.

Book of Common Prayer

DISSATISFACTION

1935 It is better to be Socrates dissatisfied than a pig satisfied.

JOHN STUART MILL

1936 To be discontented with the divine discontent, and to be ashamed with the noble shame, is the very germ and first upgrowth of all virtue.

CHARLES KINGSLEY

The voice of protest, of warning, of 1937 appeal is never more needed than when the clamor of fife and drum, echoed by the press and too often by the pulpit, is bidding all men fall in and keep step and obey in silence the tyrannous word of command. Then, more than ever, it is the duty of the good citizen not to be silent.

CHARLES ELIOT NORTON

The world owes all its onward im- 1938 pulses to men ill at ease. The happy man inevitably confines himself within ancient limits.

NATHANIEL HAWTHORNE

DUTY

Duty is the sublimest word in our 1939 language. Do your duty in all things. You cannot do more. You should never wish to do less.

ROBERT E. LEE

Let us have faith that right makes 1940 might, and in that faith let us to the end dare to do our duty as we understand it.

ABRAHAM LINCOLN

The destiny of mankind is not de- 1941 cided by material computation. When great causes are on the move in the world . . . we learn that we are spirits, not animals, and that something is going on in space and time, and beyond space and time, which, whether we like it or not, spells duty.

WINSTON CHURCHILL

Duty: where a man loves what he 1942 commands himself to do.

JOHANN WOLFGANG VON GOETHE

1943 The right, practical divinity is this: Believe in Christ, and do your duty in that state of life to which God has called you.

MARTIN LUTHER

1944 When praying, do not give God instructions—report for duty!

Anonymous

1945 The reward of one duty done is the power to fulfill another.

GEORGE ELIOT

1946 I fancy that it is just as hard to do your duty when men are sneering at you as when they are shooting at you.

WOODROW WILSON

1947 A scholar profanes the Name of God if he does not pay the butcher at once.

The Talmud

1948 One has two duties—to be worried and not to be worried.

E.M. FORSTER

1949 Exactness in little duties is a wonderful source of cheerfulness.

FREDERICK WILLIAM FABER

1952 I have never seen a man who could do real work except under the stimulus of encouragement and enthusiasm and the approval of the people for whom he is working.

CHARLES M. SCHWAB

1953 One of the highest of human duties is the duty of encouragement. There is a regulation of the Royal Navy which says: "No officer shall speak discouragingly to another officer in the discharge of his duties." Eliphaz unwillingly paid Job a great tribute. As Moffatt translates it: "Your words have kept men on their feet" (Job 4:4). Barrie somewhere wrote to Cynthia Asquith: "Your first instinct is always to telegraph to Jones the nice thing Brown said about him to Robinson. You have sown a lot of happiness that way." It is easy to laugh at men's ideals; it is easy to pour cold water on their enthusiasm; it is easy to discourage others. The world is full of discouragers. We have a Christian duty to encourage one another. Many a time a word of praise or thanks or appreciation or cheer has kept a man on his feet. Blessed is the man who speaks such a word.

WILLIAM BARCLAY

ENCOURAGEMENT

1950 Correction does much, but encouragement does more. Encouragement after censure is as the sun after a shower.

JOHANN WOLFGANG VON GOETHE

1951 David encouraged himself in the Lord his God.

I Samuel 30:6

EXPERIENCE

1954 Experience is not what happens to a man. It is what a man does with what happens to him.

ALDOUS HUXLEY

1955 To most men, experience is like the stern lights of a ship, which illumine only the track it has passed.

SAMUEL TAYLOR COLERIDGE

1956 All experience is an arch, to build upon.

HENRY ADAMS

1957 A new broom sweeps clean, but the old brush knows the corners.

Irish proverb

1958 To a great experience one thing is essential—an experiencing nature.

WALTER BAGEHOT

1959 The life of the law has not been logic: it has been experience.

OLIVER WENDELL HOLMES, JR.

1960 Experience is the name everyone gives to his mistakes.

OSCAR WILDE

1961 I have but one lamp by which my feet are guided, and that is the lamp of experience. I know of no way of judging the future but by the past.

PATRICK HENRY

1962 Experience is the best of schoolmasters, only the school fees are heavy.

THOMAS CARLYLE

1963 The long experience of the church is more likely to lead to correct answers than the experience of the lone individual.

ELTON TRUEBLOOD

FAITH

1964 Faith is awe in the presence of the divine incognito.

KARL BARTH

1965 Faith, like a jackal, feeds among the tombs, and even from these dead doubts she gathers her most vital hope.

HERMAN MELVILLE

Religions die when they are proved *1966* to be true.

OSCAR WILDE

I believe in an ultimate decency of *1967* things; ay, if I woke in hell, I should still believe it.

ROBERT LOUIS STEVENSON

For the most part the knowledge of *1968* things divine escapes us because of our unbelief.

HERACLITUS OF EPHESUS

Faith is one of the feelings which a *1969* too civilized society can least forgive: for it has lost it and hates others to possess it.

ROMAIN ROLLAND

Faith which does not doubt is dead *1970* faith.

MIGUEL DE UNAMUNO

If we believe, everything can be *1971* transformed into our Lord.

PIERRE TEILHARD DE CHARDIN

Faith is the substance of things *1972* hoped for, the evidence of things not seen.

Hebrews 11:1

Trust in the Lord with all thine *1973* heart; and lean not unto thine own understanding.

Proverbs 3:5

Do not preach the duty of love, but *1974* the duty of faith. Do not begin by telling men in God's name that they should love one another. That is no more than an amiable gospel. And it is an impossible gospel till faith gives the power to love. They cannot do it. Tell them God has loved them. . . . Preach faith and the love will grow out of it itself.

P.T. FORSYTH

1975 Columbus found a world and had no chart,
Save one that faith deciphered in the skies;
To trust the soul's invincible surmise
Was all his science and his only art.

GEORGE SANTAYANA

1976 Faith is a living, daring confidence in God's grace. It is so sure and certain that a man could stake his life on it a thousand times.

MARTIN LUTHER

1977 Faith is the resolution to stand or fall by the noblest hypothesis.

F.W.H. MYERS

1978 Faith is a power, pre-eminently, of *holding fast to an unseen power of goodness.*

MATTHEW ARNOLD

1979 Faith is not belief in spite of evidence, but life in scorn of consequences.

KIRSOPP LAKE

1980 Faith does not consist in the belief that we are saved; it consists in the belief that we are loved.

ALEXANDRE VINET

1981 Think not the faith by which the just shall live
Is a dead creed, a map correct of heaven,
Far less a feeling fond and fugitive,

A thoughtless gift, withdrawn as soon as given:
It is an affirmation and an act
That bids eternal truth be present fact.

HARTLEY COLERIDGE

If a man have a strong faith he can 1982 indulge in the luxury of scepticism.

FRIEDRICH WILHELM NIETZSCHE

You can do very little with faith, but 1983 you can do nothing without it.

NICHOLAS MURRAY BUTLER

The great act of faith is when a man 1984 decides that he is not God.

OLIVER WENDELL HOLMES, JR.

O taste and see that the Lord is 1985 good: blessed is the man that trusteth in him.

Psalm 34:8 (AV)

The just shall live by faith. 1986
Romans 1:17

Your faith should not stand in the 1987 wisdom of men, but in the power of God.

I Corinthians 2:5

We walk by faith, not by sight. 1988
II Corinthians 5:7

He that cometh to God must believe 1989 that he is, and that he is a rewarder of them that diligently seek him.

Hebrews 11:6

FASTING

Fasting is the attitude of, "Lord, 1990 empty me of self." Prayer is the insistent cry of one's soul, "Lord, fill me with thyself."

H.H. LEAVITT

1991 As to the repugnance felt by our (modern) Catholics for fasting, it is not without some interest to note that it is occurring in the very time when the disciples of Gandhi have demonstrated the virtues of fasting on the level of natural mystique and non-violent resistance.

JACQUES MARITAIN

1992 Is this a Fast, to keep
    The larder lean?
      And clean
From fat of veals or sheep?

Is it to quit the dish
    Of flesh, and still
      To fill
The platter high with fish?

Is it to fast an hour,
    Or ragg'd to go,
      Or show
A down-cast look and sour?

No: 'tis a Fast to dole
    Thy sheaf of wheat
      And meat
Unto the hungry soul.

It is to fast from strife
    And old debate
      And hate;
To circumcise thy life.

To show a heart grief-rent;
    To starve thy sin,
      Not bin;
And that's to keep thy Lent.

ROBERT HERRICK

1993 Is not this the fast that I have chosen? to loose the bands of wickedness, to undo the heavy burdens, and to let the oppressed go free, and that ye break every yoke? Is it not to deal thy bread to the hungry, and that thou bring the poor that are cast out to thy house? when thou seest the naked, that thou cover him; and that thou hide not thyself from thine own flesh?

Isaiah 58:6–7

FREEDOM

Men are free when they are in a living homeland, not when they are straying and breaking away. Men are free when they belong to a living, organic, believing community, active in fulfilling some unfulfilled, perhaps some unrealized purpose.   *1994*

D.H. LAWRENCE

There are two freedoms—the false, where a man is free to do what he likes; the true, where a man is free to do what he ought.   *1995*

CHARLES KINGSLEY

No man in this world attains to freedom from any slavery except by entrance into some higher servitude. There is no such thing as an entirely free man conceivable.   *1996*

PHILLIPS BROOKS

It is better for a man to go wrong in freedom than to go right in chains.   *1997*

THOMAS HENRY HUXLEY

A Christian man is the most free lord of all, and subject to none; a Christian man is the most dutiful   *1998* servant of all, and subject to every-one.

MARTIN LUTHER

1999 The Constitution gives us the right to do our own thinking. It's up to us to acquire the ability.

B.H. MC CORMICK

2000 Christianity promises to make men free; it never promises to make them independent.

WILLIAM RALPH INGE

2001 Freedom is participation in power.

MARCUS TULLIUS CICERO

2002 Freedom is not worth having if it does not connote freedom to err.

MOHANDAS GANDHI

2003 Freedom is that faculty which enlarges the usefulness of all other faculties.

IMMANUEL KANT

2004 Private property was the original source of freedom. It still is its main bulwark.

WALTER LIPPMANN

2005 There is no freedom for the weak.

GEORGE MEREDITH

2006 The secret of happiness is freedom, and the secret of freedom, courage.

THUCYDIDES

2007 We are subject to the men who rule over us, but subject only in the Lord. If they command anything against him, let us not pay the least regard to it.

JOHN CALVIN

GENTILITY

(See *Courtesy, Manners*)

This is the final test of a gentleman: 2008 his respect for those who can be of no possible use to him.

WILLIAM LYON PHELPS

Well-bred thinking means kindly 2009 and sensitive thoughts.

FRANÇOIS DE LA ROCHEFOUCAULD

Nothing is so strong as gentleness, 2010 nothing so gentle as real strength.

FRANCIS DE SALES

A true man of honor feels humbled 2011 himself when he cannot help humbling others.

ROBERT E. LEE

A gentleman is a man who can 2012 disagree without being disagreeable.

Anonymous

A gentleman makes no noise; a lady 2013 is serene.

RALPH WALDO EMERSON

GETTING AND GIVING

Drink waters out of thine own cis- 2014 tern, and running waters out of thine own well. Let thy fountains be dispersed abroad, and rivers of waters in the streets.

Proverbs 5:15–16

Unto whomsoever much is given, of 2015 him shall be much required: and to whom men have committed much, of him they will ask the more.

Luke 12:48

2016 What I gave, I have; what I spent, I had; what I kept, I lost.

Old epitaph

2017 The more he cast away the more he had.

JOHN BUNYAN

2018 We make a living by what we get, but we make a life by what we give.

WINSTON CHURCHILL

2019 God has given us two hands—one for receiving and the other for giving.

BILLY GRAHAM

2020 One can know nothing of giving aught that is worthy to give unless one knows also how to take.

HAVELOCK ELLIS

2021 The only gift is a portion of thyself.

RALPH WALDO EMERSON

2022 Blessed is he that considereth the poor: the Lord will deliver him in time of trouble.

Psalm 41:1

2023 Cast thy bread upon the waters: for thou shalt find it after many days.

Ecclesiastes 11:1

2024 Freely ye have received; freely give.

Matthew 10:8

2025 He that giveth, let him do it with simplicity.

Romans 12:8

2026 God loveth a cheerful giver.

II Corinthians 9:7

GODLINESS

(See *Communion with God*)

I am my Father's child, not his counselor. 2027

GERHARD TERSTEEGEN

I would fain be to the Eternal Goodness what a man's hand is to a man. 2028

Theologia Germania

My son, forget not my law; but let thine heart keep my commandments: for length of days, and long life, and peace, shall they add to thee. Let not mercy and truth forsake thee: bind them about thy neck; write them upon the table of thine heart: so shalt thou find favor and good understanding in the sight of God and man. 2029

Proverbs 3:1–4

It never frightened a Puritan when you bade him stand still and listen to the speech of God. His closet and his church were full of the reverberations of the awful, gracious, beautiful voice for which he listened. 2030

PHILLIPS BROOKS

GOODNESS

Certainly it is heaven upon earth to have a man's mind move in charity, rest in Providence, and turn upon the poles of truth. 2031

FRANCIS BACON

He who is too much afraid of being 2032

duped has lost the power of being magnanimous.

HENRI FRÉDÉRIC AMIEL

2033 He hath showed thee, O man, what is good; and what doth the Lord require of thee, but to do justly, and to love mercy, and to walk humbly with thy God?

Micah 6:8

2034 To be honest, to be kind—to earn a little and to spend a little less, to make upon the whole a family happier for his presence, to renounce when that shall be necessary and not to be embittered, to keep a few friends, but these without capitulation—above all, on the same grim condition, to keep friends with himself—here is a task for all that a man has of fortitude and delicacy.

ROBERT LOUIS STEVENSON

2035 It is easier to make certain things legal than to make them legitimate.

NICOLAS DE CHAMFORT

2036 If some great Power would agree to make me always think what is true and do what is right, on condition of being turned into a sort of clock and wound up every morning before I went to bed, I should instantly close with the offer.

THOMAS HENRY HUXLEY

2037 Goodness in actions is like unto straightness; wherefore that which is done well we term *right*. For as the straight way is most acceptable to him that travelleth, because by it he cometh soonest to his journey's end; so in action, that which doth lie the evenest between us and the end we desire must needs be fittest for our use. Besides which fitness for use, there is also in rectitude, beauty; as contrariwise in obliquity, deformity. And that which is good in the actions of men, doth not only delight as profitable, but as amiable also. In which consideration the Grecians most divinely have given to the active perfection of men a name expressing both beauty and goodness, because goodness in ordinary speech is for the most part applied only to that which is beneficial. But we in the name of goodness do here imply both.

RICHARD HOOKER

Nothing in the world—indeed, 2038 nothing even beyond the world— can possibly be conceived which could be called good without qualification except a *good will.*

IMMANUEL KANT

When God crowns our merits, it is 2039 nothing other than his own gifts that he crowns.

AUGUSTINE OF HIPPO

I cannot praise a fugitive and clois- 2040 tered virtue, unexercised and unbreathed, that never sallies out and sees her adversary, but slinks out of the race where that immortal garland is to be run for, not without dust and heat.

JOHN MILTON

The good is what preserves and 2041 enhances life; evil is what hinders or destroys it. We are ethical if we abandon our stubbornness, if we surrender our strangeness toward other creatures and share in the life and the suffering that surround us. Only this quality makes us truly men. Only then do we possess an inalienable, continuously developing, and self-orienting ethic of our own.

ALBERT SCHWEITZER

2042 It is very hard to be simple enough to be good.

RALPH WALDO EMERSON

2043 I believe in getting into hot water. I think it keeps you clean.

GILBERT KEITH CHESTERTON

2044 Your goody-goody people are the thieves of virtue.

CONFUCIUS

2045 Dear God, make all bad people good, and all good people nice.

A little girl's prayer

2046 What is beautiful is good, and who is good will soon also be beautiful.

SAPPHO

2047 It takes courage for a man to listen to his own goodness and act upon it.

PABLO CASALS

2048 He who would do good to another must do it in minute particulars.

WILLIAM BLAKE

2049 And when we come to think of it, goodness *is* uneventful. It does not flash, it glows. It is deep, quiet, and very simple. It passes not with oratory, it is commonly foreign to riches, nor does it often sit in the places of the mighty: but may be felt in the touch of a friendly hand or the look of a kindly eye.

DAVID GRAYSON

2050 The first condition of human goodness is something to love; the second, something to reverence.

GEORGE ELIOT

2051 Real goodness does not attach itself merely to this life—it points to another world.

DANIEL WEBSTER

2052 The path of the just is as the shining light, that shineth more and more unto the perfect day.

Proverbs 4:18

GRATITUDE

(See *Thanksgiving*)

2053 It is the highest and holiest of the paradoxes that the man who really knows he cannot pay his debt will be forever paying it.

GILBERT KEITH CHESTERTON

2054 Gratitude is the heart's memory.

French proverb

2055 Thou that hast given so much to me,
Give one thing more—a grateful heart;
Not thankful when it pleaseth me,
As if thy blessings had spare days;
But such a heart, whose pulse may be
Thy praise.

GEORGE HERBERT

2056 Gratitude is not only the dominant note in Christian piety but equally the dominant motive of Christian action in the world. Such gratitude is for the grace that has been shown to us by God . . . A true Christian is a man who never for a moment forgets what God has done for him in Christ, and whose whole comportment and whole activity have their root in the sentiment of gratitude.

JOHN BAILLIE

2057 In the 1860s, Dr. Edson, rector of St. Anne's Church and best loved citizen of Lowell, Massachusetts, said to a friend, "Good morning, how are you today?" "I am very well, thank God," came the reply. "I am so glad to hear you thank God for it," said the old rector. "For twenty years everyone in Lowell has been thanking *me*. They always say, 'I am very well thank *you*, Dr. Edson.'"

Anonymous

2058 Gratitude is heaven itself.

WILLIAM BLAKE

2059 It is of grace not of ourselves that we lead civilized lives. There is sound sense in the old pagan notion that gratitude is the root of all virtue. Loyalty to whatever in the established environment makes a life of excellence possible is the beginning of all progress. The best we can accomplish for posterity is to transmit unimpaired and with some increment of meaning the environment that makes it possible to maintain the habits of decent and refined life. Our individual habits are links in forming the endless chain of humanity. Their significance depends upon the environment inherited from our forerunners, and it is enhanced as we foresee the fruits of our labors in the world in which our successors live.

JOHN DEWEY

2060 What hast thou that thou didst not receive?

I Corinthians 4:7

GREATNESS

2061 Great men are the true men, the men in whom nature has succeeded. They are not extraordinary—they are in the true order. It is the other species of men who are not what they ought to be.

HENRI FRÉDÉRIC AMIEL

2062 She never knew how to be famous.

ÈVE CURIE, *of her mother*

2063 A great man stands on God. A small man stands on a great man.

RALPH WALDO EMERSON

2064 We are very near to greatness; one step and we are safe; can we not take the leap?

RALPH WALDO EMERSON

2065 For us the great men are not those who solved the problems, but those who discovered them.

ALBERT SCHWEITZER

2066 Greatness after all, in spite of its name, appears to be not so much a certain size as a certain quality in human lives. It may be present in lives whose range is very small.

PHILLIPS BROOKS

2067 A great man represents a great ganglion in the nerves of society, or, to vary the figure, a strategic point in the campaign of history, and part of his greatness consists in his being *there*.

OLIVER WENDELL HOLMES, JR.

2068 He is invited to great things who receives small things greatly.

MAGNUS AURELIUS CASSIODORUS

2069 If a man seeks for greatness, let him forget greatness and ask for truth, and he will find both.

HORACE MANN

2070 The world is divided into people who do things and people who get the credit. Try, if you can, to belong to the first class. There's far less competition.

DWIGHT MORROW,
in a letter to his son

2071 Great men are nearly always the kindest; out of some instinctive knowledge they encourage the very people who do not elbow themselves ahead.

STEFAN ZWEIG

2072 Great hopes make great men.

THOMAS FULLER

2073 Cheap editions of great books may be delightful, but cheap editions of great men are absolutely detestable.

OSCAR WILDE

2074 If a great man says something that seems illogical, don't laugh; try to understand it.

The Talmud

2075 Should a great man be judged according to different principles from other men? People have often answered this question with Yes, but I think No. For a great man is great because he is a chosen instrument in the hand of God; but the moment he imagines that it is he himself who is acting, that he can look into the future and with that in mind let the end ennoble the means—then he is small. Rights and duties are valid for all and their transgression can no more be excused in the great than in politics, though people imagine that states are allowed to do wrong. Certainly wrongs such as these have often produced beneficial results, but for that we have to thank providence and not this man or that state.

SØREN KIERKEGAARD

The strong men keep coming on.   **2076**
They go down shot, hanged, sick, broken.
They live on fighting, singing, lucky as plungers.
The strong mothers pulling them on . . .
The strong mothers pulling them from a dark sea, a great prairie, a long mountain.
Call hallelujah, call amen, call deep thanks.
The strong men keep coming on.

CARL SANDBURG

GROWTH

Love slays what we have been that   **2077**
we may be what we were not.

AUGUSTINE OF HIPPO

The transition from the pleasure-   **2078**
principle to the reality-principle is one of the most important advances in the development of the ego.

SIGMUND FREUD

Do not entertain the notion that you   **2079**
ought to *advance* in prayer. If you do, you will only find that you have put on the brake instead of the accelerator. All real progress in spiritual things comes gently, imperceptibly, and is the work of God. Our crude efforts spoil it. Know yourself

for the childish, limited and dependent soul you are. Remember the only growth which matters happens without our knowledge and that trying to stretch ourselves is both dangerous and silly. Think of the Infinite Goodness, never of your own state. Realize that the very capacity to pray at all is the free gift of the Divine Love and be content with St. Francis de Sales' favorite prayer, in which all personal religion is summed up: "Yes, Father! Yes! and always Yes!"

EVELYN UNDERHILL

2080 As outward beauty disappears one must hope it goes in!

TENNESSEE WILLIAMS

2081 Childhood reveals tendencies. Youth develops personality. Maturity establishes character.

HUBERT VAN ZELLER

2082 The great majority of men are bundles of beginnings.

RALPH WALDO EMERSON

2083 There is nothing noble in being superior to some one else. The true nobility is in being superior to your previous self.

Hindu proverb

2084 Thank God every morning when you get up that you have something to do which must be done whether you like it or not. Being forced to work, and forced to do your best, will breed in you temperance, self-control, diligence, strength of will, content, and a hundred other virtues which the idle never know.

CHARLES KINGSLEY

2085 He is only advancing in life, whose heart is getting softer, his blood warmer, his brain quicker, and his spirit entering into living peace.

JOHN RUSKIN

HAPPINESS

(See *Humor, Joy, Laughter*)

Happiness is the practice of the virtues. 2086

CLEMENT OF ALEXANDRIA

Happiness in this world, when it comes, comes incidentally. Make it the object of pursuit, and it leads us on a wild-goose chase, and is never attained. 2087

NATHANIEL HAWTHORNE

Happiness never takes its own pulse. 2088

Anonymous

Happiness is neither virtue nor pleasure nor this thing nor that, but simply growth. We are happy when we are growing. 2089

J.B. YEATS

Those who wish to sing always find a song. 2090

Swedish proverb

Happiness consists in the attainment of our desires, and in our having only right desires. 2091

AUGUSTINE OF HIPPO

No person is either so happy or so unhappy as he imagines. 2092

FRANÇOIS DE LA ROCHEFOUCAULD

In vain do they talk of happiness who never subdued an impulse in obedience to a principle. He who 2093 never sacrified a present to a future good, or a personal to a general one, can speak of happiness only as the blind speak of colors.

HORACE MANN

2094 Happiness is the harvest of a quiet eye.

AUSTIN O'MALLEY

2095 The supreme happiness of life is the conviction of being loved for yourself, or, more correctly, of being loved in spite of yourself.

VICTOR HUGO

2096 What makes men happy is liking what they have to do. This is a principle on which society is not founded.

CLAUDE ADRIEN HELVÉTIUS

2097 Nobody can compel me to be happy in his own way. Paternalism is the greatest despotism.

IMMANUEL KANT

2098 Nothing is more hopeless than a scheme of merriment.

SAMUEL JOHNSON

2099 Happiness is no laughing matter.

RICHARD WHATELY,
onetime Archbishop of Dublin

2100 Happiness sneaks in through a door you didn't know you left open.

JOHN BARRYMORE

2101 That is happiness: to be dissolved into something complete and great.

WILLA CATHER

2102 I love such mirth as does not make friends ashamed to look upon one another next morning.

IZAAK WALTON

HEALING AND HEALTH

The voice of joy and health is in the dwellings of the righteous. 2103

Psalm 118:15

Health and cheerfulness mutually beget each other. 2104

JOSEPH ADDISON

I bandage, God heals. 2105

AMBROISE PARÉ

All disease of soul or body is a subtraction from human nature, a way of being sub-standard. There are no colds in Paradise. So, healing of any sort is a kind of creative or rather regenerating work, a direct expression and furtherance of God's will. It means bringing life back to what it ought to be, mending that which has broken down, healing our deep mental and spiritual wounds by the action of Christ's charity, giving new strength to the weak, new purity to the tainted. 2106

EVELYN UNDERHILL

The model doctor should be at once a genius, a saint, a man of God. 2107

HENRI FRÉDÉRIC AMIEL

Look to your health; and if you have it, praise God and value it next to a good conscience; for health is the second blessing that we mortals are capable of—a blessing that money cannot buy; therefore value it, and be thankful for it. 2108

IZAAK WALTON

Some people think that doctors and nurses can put scrambled eggs back into the shell. 2109

DOROTHY CANFIELD FISHER

2110 The temperature of the spiritual life of the church is the index of her power to heal.

EVELYN FROST

2111 Hear further, O man, of the work of resurrection going on in yourself, even though you were unaware of it. For perhaps you have sometimes fallen sick, and lost flesh, and strength, and beauty; but when you received again from God mercy and healing, you picked up again in flesh and appearance and recovered also your strength.

THEOPHILUS OF ANTIOCH

HEART

2112 Keep thy heart with all diligence; for out of it are the issues of life.

Proverbs 4:23

2113 A cheerful countenance is a token of a heart that is in prosperity.

Ecclesiasticus 13:26

2114 The heart is either a *grand seigneur* or a nobody.

MALCOLM DE CHAZAL

2115 Not all those who know their minds know their hearts as well.

FRANÇOIS DE LA ROCHEFOUCAULD

2116 Tact is the intelligence of the heart.

Anonymous

2117 To my God, a heart of flame; to my fellow men, a heart of love; to myself, a heart of steel.

AUGUSTINE OF HIPPO

2118 The heart has its reasons which reason does not know.

BLAISE PASCAL

2119 Hardening of the heart ages more people than hardening of the arteries.

Anonymous

2120 The capital of heaven is the heart in which Jesus Christ is enthroned as king.

SADHU SUNDAR SINGH

2121 A man's first care should be to avoid the reproaches of his own heart.

JOSEPH ADDISON

2122 The heart is a small thing, but desireth great matters. It is not sufficient for a kite's dinner, yet the whole world is not sufficient for it.

FRANCIS QUARLES

2123 Science is the power of man, and love his strength; man *becomes* man only by the intelligence, but he *is* man only by the heart. Knowledge, love, power—there is the complete life.

HENRI FRÉDÉRIC AMIEL

2124 Two things are bad for the heart— running up stairs and running down people.

BERNARD M. BARUCH

2125 The heart is forever making the head its fool.

FRANÇOIS DE LA ROCHEFOUCAULD

2126 A good heart is better than all the heads in the world.

EDWARD BULWER-LYTTON

2127 Plato located the soul of man in the head; Christ located it in the heart.

ST. JEROME

2128 As pride, vanity, hypocrisy, envy or malice don't take away from the mind its geometrical skill, so a man may be most mathematical in his demonstrations of the religion of reason when he has extinguished every good sentiment of his heart, and be the most zealous for its excellency and sufficiency when he has his passions in the most disordered state.

WILLIAM LAW

2129 The heart is the best logician.

WENDELL PHILLIPS

2130 "In my heart I have determined on it." And one is even inclined to point to one's breast as one says it. Psychologically this way of speaking should be taken seriously. Why should it be taken less seriously than the assertion that belief is a state of mind?

LUDWIG WITTGENSTEIN

2131 The head learns new things, but the heart forevermore practices old experiences.

HENRY WARD BEECHER

HONESTY

(See *Sincerity, Truth and Falsehood*)

2132 A false balance is abomination to the Lord: but a just weight is his delight.

Proverbs 11:1

Being entirely honest with oneself is 2133 a good exercise.

SIGMUND FREUD

How awful to reflect that what peo- 2134 ple say of us is true!

LOGAN PEARSALL SMITH

Honesty is the best policy; but he 2135 who is governed by that maxim is not an honest man.

RICHARD WHATELY,
onetime Archbishop of Dublin

He who says there is no such thing 2136 as an honest man, you may be sure is himself a knave.

GEORGE BERKELEY

An honest man's the noblest work 2137 of God.

ALEXANDER POPE

A small but honest mind is less 2138 wearisome in the end than a great but crooked one.

FRANÇOIS DE LA ROCHEFOUCAULD

Honesty is the first chapter of the 2139 book of wisdom.

THOMAS JEFFERSON

I hope I shall possess firmness and 2140 virtue enough to maintain what I consider the most enviable of all titles, the character of an honest man.

GEORGE WASHINGTON

Locks keep out only the honest. 2141
Jewish proverb

HOPE

If you do not hope, you will not find 2142 what is beyond your hopes.

CLEMENT OF ALEXANDRIA

2143 The virtue of hope is an orientation of the soul towards a transformation after which it will be wholly and exclusively love.

SIMONE WEIL

2144 Hope springs eternal in the human breast:
Man never is, but always to be blest.

ALEXANDER POPE

2145 Christian hope is the consecration of desire, and desire is the hardest thing of all to consecrate. When you positively hope for the Kingdom of God, then your desire becomes consecrated. That will only happen as you begin to think how lovely the life according to Christ is.

WILLIAM TEMPLE

2146 Every man contemplates an angel in his future self.

RALPH WALDO EMERSON

2147 Whatever enlarges hope will also exalt courage.

SAMUEL JOHNSON

2148 The setting of a great hope is like the setting of the sun.

HENRY WADSWORTH LONGFELLOW

2149 A religious hope does not only bear up the mind under her sufferings, but makes her rejoice in them.

JOSEPH ADDISON

2150 He who wants to enjoy the glory of the sunrise must live through the night.

Anonymous

2151 The *Encyclopaedia Britannica* devotes many columns to the topic of love, and many more to faith. But hope, poor little hope! She is not even listed!

KARL MENNINGER

2152 The future enters into us, in order to transform itself in us, long before it happens.

RAINER MARIA RILKE

2153 Hope is the struggle of the soul, breaking loose from what is perishable, and attesting her eternity.

HERMAN MELVILLE

2154 What oxygen is for the lungs, such is hope for the meaning of life.

EMIL BRUNNER

2155 The word *hope* I take for faith; and indeed hope is nothing else but the constancy of faith.

JOHN CALVIN

2156 The hope of the righteous shall be gladness.

Proverbs 10:28

2157 The righteous hath hope in his death.

Proverbs 14:32

2158 It is good that a man should both hope and quietly wait for the salvation of the Lord.

Lamentations 3:26

2159 The God of hope fill you with all joy and peace in believing, that ye may abound in hope.

Romans 15:13

HOSPITALITY

2160 Carried a new cloak to Johnny

Riordan. I found that the shanty was warmed by the simple social relations of the Irish. On Sunday they come from the town and stand in the doorway and so keep out the cold. One is not cold among his brothers and sisters. What if there is less fire on the hearth, if there is more in the heart!

HENRY DAVID THOREAU

2161 Hospitality is one form of worship.
Jewish proverb

2162 To welcome a fellow man is to welcome the *Shekhinah* [Divine Presence].
Jewish proverb

2163 The magnanimous know very well that they who give time, or money, or shelter, to the stranger,—so it be done for love and not for ostentation,—do, as it were, put God under obligation to them, so perfect are the compensations of the universe.
RALPH WALDO EMERSON

2164 The stranger that dwelleth with you shall be unto you as one born among you, and thou shalt love him as thyself.
Leviticus 19:34

2165 When thou makest a feast, call the poor, the maimed, the lame, the blind: and thou shalt be blessed.
Luke 14:13–14

2166 Receive ye one another, as Christ also received us to the glory of God.
Romans 15:7

HUMILITY

After all, man knows mighty little, 2167 and may some day learn enough of his own ignorance to fall down and pray.

HENRY ADAMS

If you find in the Holy Law or the 2168 Prophets or the Sages a hard saying which you cannot understand, stand fast in your faith and attribute the fault to your own want of intelligence. Place it in a corner of your heart for future consideration. Do not despise your religion because you are unable to understand one difficult matter.

MOSES MAIMONIDES

An able yet humble man is a jewel 2169 worth a kingdom.

WILLIAM PENN

Humbleness is always grace; always 2170 dignity.

JAMES RUSSELL LOWELL

I do not know what I may appear to 2171 the world; but to myself I seem to have been only a boy playing on the seashore, and diverting myself in now and then finding a smoother pebble or a prettier shell than ordinary whilst the great ocean of truth lay all undiscovered before me.

ISAAC NEWTON

Humility is the first of the virtues— 2172 for other people.

OLIVER WENDELL HOLMES

Humility is the garment of the 2173 Deity. The incarnate Word was clothed in it, and, through it, conversed with us in our bodies, covering the radiance of his greatness and his glory by this humility lest the creature be scorched by the sight of him. The creature could not have looked at him, had he not taken on some part of it and thus conversed with it. Therefore every man who clothes himself in garments of humility becomes clothed in Christ himself, since Christ desired to be clothed also in his inner man in that likeness in which he was seen by his creature and in which he lived with it.

ISAAK OF SYRIA

2174 Humility is pride in God.

AUSTIN O'MALLEY

2175 The sufficiency of my merit is to know that my merit is not sufficient.

AUGUSTINE OF HIPPO

2176 The humility of Christ is not the moderation of keeping one's exact place in the scale of being, but rather that of absolute dependence on God and absolute trust in him, with the consequent ability to move mountains. The secret of the meekness and the gentleness of Christ lies in his relation to God.

RICHARD NIEBUHR

2177 You will find angling to be like the virtue of humility, which has a calmness of spirit and a world of other blessings attending upon it.

IZAAK WALTON

2178 Most men descend to nameless graves. A few forget themselves into immortality.

WENDELL PHILLIPS

2179 Some American tourists one day visited the home of Beethoven. A young woman among them sat down at the great composer's piano and began to play his *Moonlight Sonata*. After she had finished she turned to the old caretaker and said: "I presume a great many musicians visit this place every year." "Yes," he replied. "Paderewski was here last year." "And did he play on Beethoven's piano?" "No, he said he wasn't worthy."

Anonymous

2180 Don't make yourself so big. You are not so small.

Jewish proverb

2181 We are all in the gutter, but some of us are looking at the stars.

OSCAR WILDE

2182 The true way to be humble is not to stoop until you are smaller than yourself, but to stand at your real height against some higher nature that will show you what the real smallness of your greatness is.

PHILLIPS BROOKS

2183 Humility must always be the portion of any man who receives acclaim earned in the blood of his followers and the sacrifices of his friends.

DWIGHT D. EISENHOWER

2184 Without humility there can be no humanity.

JOHN BUCHAN

2185 You grow up the day you have your first real laugh at yourself.

ETHEL BARRYMORE

2186 There is a story of a rabbi and a

cantor and a humble synagogue cleaner who were preparing for the Day of Atonement. The rabbi beat his breast, and said, "I am nothing, I am nothing." The cantor beat his breast, and said, "I am nothing, I am nothing." The cleaner beat his breast, and said, "I am nothing, I am nothing." And the rabbi said to the cantor, "Look who thinks he's nothing."

ALAN PATON

2187 Science seems to me to teach in the highest and strongest manner the great truth which is embodied in the Christian conception of entire surrender to the will of God. Sit down before facts as a little child, be prepared to give up every preconceived notion, follow humbly wherever and to whatever abysses nature leads you or you shall learn nothing. I have only begun to learn content and peace of mind since I have resolved at all risks to do this.

THOMAS HENRY HUXLEY, *in a letter to Charles Kingsley*

HUMOR

(See *Wit*)

2188 It is the test of a good religion whether you can make a joke of it.

GILBERT KEITH CHESTERTON

2189 There are people who think everything one does with a serious face is sensible.

GEORG CHRISTOPH LICHTENBERG

2190 The monkey wears an expression of seriousness that would do credit to any college student. But the monkey is serious because it itches.

ROBERT MAYNARD HUTCHINS

2191 Don't tell me of a man's being able to talk sense; everyone can talk sense. Can he talk nonsense?

WILLIAM PITT

2192 The humorist runs with the hare; the satirist hunts with the hounds.

RONALD KNOX

2193 A clown may be the first in the kingdom of heaven, if he has helped lessen the sadness of human life.

RABBI BAROKA

2194 You could read Kant by yourself, if you wanted to; but you must share a joke with someone else.

ROBERT LOUIS STEVENSON

2195 There ain't much fun in medicine, but there's a good deal of medicine in fun.

JOSH BILLINGS

2196 Good jests bite like lambs, not like dogs.

Anonymous

2197 The most valuable sense of humor is the kind that enables a person to see instantly what it isn't safe to laugh at.

Anonymous

2198 Humor is odd, grotesque, and wild,
Only by affectation spoil'd;
'Tis never by invention got,
Men have it when they know it not.

JONATHAN SWIFT

2199 True humor springs not more from the head than from the heart; it is not contempt, its essence is love.

THOMAS CARLYLE

2200 I have never understood why it should be considered derogatory to the Creator to suppose that he has a sense of humor.

WILLIAM RALPH INGE

which the wings of human nature have spread themselves have been flown for religious ideals.

WILLIAM JAMES

IDEALISM

2201 Ideals are like the stars—we never reach them, but like the mariners of the sea we chart our course by them.

CARL SCHURZ

2202 The true ideal is not opposed to the real but lies in it; and blessed are the eyes that find it.

JAMES RUSSELL LOWELL

2203 Some men can live up to their loftiest ideals without ever going higher than a basement.

THEODORE ROOSEVELT

2204 Some men see things as they are and say why. I dream things that never were and say, why not?

ROBERT F. KENNEDY

2205 If one advances confidently in the direction of his dreams, and endeavors to live the life which he imagined, he will meet with a success unexpected in common hours. In proportion as he simplifies his life, the laws of the universe will appear less complex, and solitude will not be solitude, nor poverty poverty, nor weakness weakness. If you have built castles in the air, your work need not be lost; that is where they should be. Now put foundations under them.

HENRY DAVID THOREAU

2206 The highest flights of charity, devotion, trust, patience, bravery, to

IMAGINATION

Must then a Christ perish in torment in every age to save those that have no imagination? 2207

GEORGE BERNARD SHAW

Imagination does not breed insanity. Exactly what does breed insanity is reason. Poets do not go mad; but chessplayers do. . . . Perhaps the strongest case of all is this: that only one great English poet went mad, Cowper. And he was definitely driven mad by logic, by the ugly and alien logic of predestination. Poetry was not the disease, but the medicine; poetry partly kept him in health. . . . He was damned by John Calvin; he was almost saved by John Gilpin. 2208

GILBERT KEITH CHESTERTON

The late Bishop Gore once defined Christian charity as "reading statistics with compassion." It might be equally well defined as "reading statistics with imagination." For we are not naturally so cold-hearted that if the imagination were granted to us, the compassion would not follow. 2209

JOHN BAILLIE

That minister of ministers,
    Imagination, gathers up
The undiscovered Universe,
    Like jewels in a jasper cup. 2210

JOHN DAVIDSON

2211 Imagination is not a talent of some men but is the health of every man.
RALPH WALDO EMERSON

2212 Science does not know its debt to imagination.
RALPH WALDO EMERSON

INFLUENCE

2213 The true teacher defends his pupils against his own personal influence.
BRONSON ALCOTT

2214 The death of a good man is like the putting out of a wax perfumed candle: he recompenses the loss of light with the sweet odor he leaves behind him.
OWEN FELLTHAM

2215 No man should think himself a zero, and think he can do nothing about the state of the world.
BERNARD M. BARUCH

2216 Blessed is the influence of one true, loving soul on another.
GEORGE ELIOT

2217 Professor Whitehead had a benign and beautiful presence, a voice and diction that made music of English speech, humor that lighted up dark places, humility that made the foolish wiser and evoked the wisdom of the taciturn.
FELIX FRANKFURTER

2218 They say in the traditions that Matthew the apostle constantly said, that "if the neighbor of an elect man sin, the elect man has sinned. For had he conducted himself as the Word prescribes, his neighbor also would have been filled with such reverence for the life he led as not to sin."
CLEMENT OF ALEXANDRIA

INTELLIGENCE

(See *Knowledge, Wisdom*)

Whoso shrinks from ideas ends by having nothing but sensations.   *2219*
JOHANN WOLFGANG VON GOETHE

In the study of ideas, it is necessary   *2220*
to remember that insistence on hardheaded clarity issues from sentimental feeling, as it were a mist, cloaking the perplexities of fact. Insistence on clarity at all costs is based on sheer superstition as to the mode in which the human intelligence functions.
ALFRED NORTH WHITEHEAD

Gird up the loins of your mind.   *2221*
I Peter 1:13

This intelligence-testing business re-   *2222*
minds me of the way they used to weigh hogs in Texas. They would get a long plank, put it over a crossbar, and somehow tie the hog on one end of the plank. They'd search all around till they found a stone that would balance the weight of the hog and they'd put that on the other end of the plank. Then they'd guess the weight of the stone.
JOHN DEWEY

Christianity has need of thought   *2223*
that it may come to the consciousness of its real self. For centuries it

treasured the great commandment of love and mercy as traditional truth without recognizing it as a reason for opposing slavery, witch-burning, torture, and all the other ancient and medieval forms of inhumanity.

ALBERT SCHWEITZER

2224 Behold, I send you forth as sheep among wolves: be ye therefore wise as serpents, and harmless as doves.
Matthew 10:16

2225 Goodness must be joined with knowledge. Mere goodness is not much use, as I have found in life. One must cultivate the fine discriminating quality which goes with spiritual courage and character.

MOHANDAS GANDHI

2226 The more intelligent a man is, the more originality he discovers in men. Ordinary people see no difference between men.

BLAISE PASCAL

2227 It is not the insurrections of ignorance that are dangerous, but the revolts of the intelligence.

JAMES RUSSELL LOWELL

2228 When you don't have an education, you've got to use your brains.
Anonymous

JOY

(See *Happiness*)

2229 Those who bring sunshine to the lives of others cannot keep it from themselves.

JAMES M. BARRIE

Joy is not in things, it is in us.   2230
RICHARD WAGNER

If there is joy in the world, surely   2231
the man of pure heart possesses it.
THOMAS À KEMPIS

It is good if man can bring about   2232
that God sings within him.
RABBI ELIMELECH OF LIZHENSK

The rule of joy and the law of duty   2233
seem to me all one.
OLIVER WENDELL HOLMES, JR.

"I have no name," said the infant   2234
Joy in Blake's poem. If her instinctive answer had been "My name is Miss Jemima Jones" we should have known what it was that struck the soul first. But Joy has no name. Its very being is lost in the great tide of selfless delight—creation's response to the infinite loving of God.
EVELYN UNDERHILL

Joy is the passage from a lesser to a   2235
greater perfection.
BARUCH SPINOZA

To enjoy, to create (which is to love)   2236
and to try to understand is all that at the moment I can see of duty.
JACQUETTA HAWKES

The only joy in the world is to   2237
begin.
CESARE PAVESE

The most profound joy has more of   2238
gravity than of gaiety in it.
MICHEL DE MONTAIGNE

Great joy, especially after a sudden   2239
change of circumstances, is apt to be silent, and dwells rather in the heart than on the tongue.
HENRY FIELDING

2240 Grief can take care of itself, but to get the full value of a joy you must have somebody to divide it with.
MARK TWAIN

2241 Joys impregnate, sorrows bring forth.
WILLIAM BLAKE

2242 The life without festival is a long road without an inn.
DEMOCRITUS OF ABDERA

2243 There's night and day, brother, both sweet things; sun, moon, and stars, brother, all sweet things; there's likewise a wind on the heath. Life is very sweet, brother, who would wish to die?
GEORGE BORROW

2244 How good is man's life, the mere living! how fit to employ
All the heart and the soul and the senses forever in joy!
ROBERT BROWNING

2245 There is no cure for birth and death save to enjoy the interval.
GEORGE SANTAYANA

2246 The joy of the Lord is your strength.
Nehemiah 8:10

2247 Weeping may endure for a night, but joy cometh in the morning.
Psalm 30:5 (AV)

2248 They that sow in tears shall reap in joy.
Psalm 126:6

2249 With joy shall ye draw water out of the wells of salvation.
Isaiah 12:3

2250 These things have I spoken unto you, that my joy might remain in you, and that your joy might be full.
John 15:11

JUSTICE

One law for the lion and ox is oppression.   2251
WILLIAM BLAKE

Justice is truth in action.   2252
BENJAMIN DISRAELI

Justice: to be ever ready to admit   2253
that another person is something quite different from what we read when he is there, or when we think about him. Or rather, to read in him that he is certainly something different, perhaps something completely different, from what we read in him. Every being cries out to be read differently.
SIMONE WEIL

Justice has nothing to do with expe-   2254
diency. It has nothing to do with any temporary standard whatever. It is rooted and grounded in the fundamental instincts of humanity.
WOODROW WILSON

Justice is the sum of all moral duty.   2255
WILLIAM GODWIN

All punishment is mischief. All pun-   2256
ishment in itself is evil. Upon the principle of utility, if it ought at all to be admitted, it ought only to be admitted in as far as it promises to exclude some greater evil.
JEREMY BENTHAM

All knowledge that is divorced from   2257

justice must be called cunning rather than wisdom.

PLATO

2258 Justice, I think, is the tolerable accommodation of the conflicting interests of society, and I don't believe there is any royal road to attain such accommodations concretely.

LEARNED HAND

2259 One hour of justice is worth a hundred of prayer.

Arab proverb

2260 Justice delayed is justice denied.

WILLIAM E. GLADSTONE

2261 It is just as well that justice is blind; she might not like some of the things done in her name if she could see them.

Anonymous

2262 When we demand justice, it is always justice on our behalf against other people. Nobody, I imagine, would ever ask for justice to be done *upon* him for every thing he ever did wrong. We do not want justice—we want revenge; and that is why, when justice is done upon us, we cry out that God is vindictive.

DOROTHY L. SAYERS

2263 Justice and power must be brought together, so that whatever is just may be powerful, and whatever is powerful may be just.

BLAISE PASCAL

2264 That which is unjust can really profit no one; that which is just can really harm no one.

HENRY GEORGE

Use every man after his desert, and 2265 who should 'scape whipping!

WILLIAM SHAKESPEARE

Justice, sir, is the great interest of 2266 man on earth.

DANIEL WEBSTER

Children are innocent and love justice, while most adults are wicked 2267 and prefer mercy.

GILBERT KEITH CHESTERTON

Injustice anywhere is a threat to 2268 justice everywhere.

MARTIN LUTHER KING, JR.

All things come to him who waits— 2269 even justice.

AUSTIN O'MALLEY

Justice being taken away, then what 2270 are kingdoms but great robberies? For what are robberies themselves, but little kingdoms?

AUGUSTINE OF HIPPO

There is no such thing as justice—in 2271 or out of court.

CLARENCE DARROW

The only justice is to follow the 2272 sincere intuition of the soul, angry or gentle. Anger is just, and pity is just, but judgment is never just.

D.H. LAWRENCE

To Sam "Golden Rule" Jones: 2273

What I know about your earthly career convinces me that you were not a politician of the "Honest John" sort but that you really earned your sobriquet. I know that once, while Mayor of Toledo, Ohio, you presided on the police court bench and heard the case of a man who had stolen food for his family.

You fined him $10 because he was guilty and you were not one of those sentimentalists who don't believe in the Majesty of the Law. Then you handed to the bailiff that big sombrero of yours and ordered him to pass it among the people in the courtroom, fining each of them 50 cents for living in a city where a man had to steal in order to feed his children. The hat came back very full; you gave its contents to the defendant and remitted his fine. That justice and mercy can coexist in one person, if he's big enough to contain them both, is a truth of which we can't be reminded too often, and the only effective reminders of it are people like you. Solomon said of all your blessed sort: "The path of the just is as the shining light, that shineth more and more unto the perfect day" (Prov. 4:18).

CARROLL E. SIMCOX

KINDNESS

(See *Charity, Love*)

2274 In this world, you must be a bit too kind in order to be kind enough.
PIERRE CARLET DE CHAMBLAIN DE MARIVAUX

2275 I expect to pass through this world but once. Any good thing, therefore, that I can do, or any kindness I can show a fellow being, let me do it now. Let me not defer or neglect it, for I shall not pass this way again.
STEPHEN GRELLET

2276 Where there is no truth there is no kindness.
NACHMAN OF BRATSLAV

The best portion of a good man's 2277
life,
His little, nameless, unremembered acts
Of kindness and of love.
WILLIAM WORDSWORTH

Kindness is in our power, but fond- 2278
ness is not.
SAMUEL JOHNSON

A man who lacks nobility cannot 2279
have kindliness, he can only have good nature.
NICOLAS DE CHAMFORT

The first thing a kindness deserves is 2280
acceptance, the second, transmission.
GEORGE MAC DONALD

To smile at a jest which plants a 2281
thorn in another's breast is to become a principal in the mischief.
WILLIAM B. SHERIDAN

A sufficient commentary on human 2282
nature is that a mob never rushes madly across town to do a needed kindness.
Anonymous

Kindness is the principle of tact, 2283
and respect for others the first condition of *savoir-vivre*.
HENRI FRÉDÉRIC AMIEL

You cannot do a kindness too soon, 2284
for you never know how soon it will be too late.
RALPH WALDO EMERSON

Kind words are the music of the 2285
world. They have a power which seems to be beyond natural causes, as though they were some angel's

song which had lost its way and come to earth.

FREDERICK W. FABER

2286 Kindness has converted more sinners than zeal, eloquence, or learning.

FREDERICK W. FABER

LIBERTY

(See *Freedom*)

2287 God grants liberty only to those who love it, and are always ready to guard and defend it.

DANIEL WEBSTER

2288 The natural progress of things is for liberty to yield and government to gain ground.

THOMAS JEFFERSON

2289 Liberty cannot be preserved without a general knowledge among the people.

JOHN ADAMS

2290 License they mean when they cry liberty,
For who loves that must first be wise and good.

JOHN MILTON

2291 If liberty is to be saved, it will not be by the doubters, the men of science, or the materialists; it will be by religious conviction, by the faith of individuals, who believe that God wills man to be free but also pure.

SAMUEL TAYLOR COLERIDGE

2292 Christianity is the companion of liberty in all its conflicts, the cradle of its infancy, and the divine source of its claims.

ALEXIS DE TOCQUEVILLE

Liberty is the power that we have over ourselves. 2293

HUGO GROTIUS

Liberty doesn't work as well in 2294 practice as it does in speeches.

WILL ROGERS

There should be more in American 2295 liberty than the privilege we enjoy of insulting the President with impunity.

AUSTIN O'MALLEY

Liberty, not communism, is the 2296 most contagious force in the world.

EARL WARREN

Liberty is the only thing you can't 2297 have unless you give it to others.

WILLIAM ALLEN WHITE

Liberty is always unfinished business. 2298

American Civil Liberties Union

Where the Spirit of the Lord is, 2299 there is liberty.

II Corinthians 3:17

LIKING AND LOVING

We like someone because. We love 2300 someone although.

HENRI DE MONTHERLANT

Dick Shepherd, the beloved, tempestuous, and eccentric vicar of St. Martin's-in-the-Fields, was asked by a friend how he could possibly love 2301 a certain person, to which Shepherd replied, "I do more than love him. I positively like him!"

ALAN PATON

2302   Since I dislike you,
    How can I then fulfil the law of
       love?
    Your speech, your ways, your very
       image in my eye,
    These all revolt me . . . (and it is
       little help
    That I am sure you care no whit the
       more for me!)

    Thus battle head and heart,
    The one reverberant with pique,
    The other incandescent in the light
       of love.
    But both, I think, must surely be of
       God,
    And so an acrid lesson says
    That head must love whom heart
       insists
    It cannot like.

    God help me try!

SAMUEL J. MILLER

2303   *To Will Rogers:*
    You were past 50 when you said that you had never met a man you didn't like. We know that you meant it, and we can only ponder your achievement (for that's what it was) with awe and envy. You had a peerless gift for friendship. What I'd like to know now is what you would say if you had met some of the world's nastiest people, and it occurs to me that, under the conditions of eternity, perhaps you have. My question: How do you like Adolf Hitler? Nabal the Carmelite (that fellow in *I Samuel 25*)? Or this one—the man who poisoned my dog, some 40 years ago? In my prayers I sometimes try to recall all who have ever hurt me and have now left this life. I ask for them God's pardon and peace. I include this man. It's the best I can do for him—to pray that he has changed. But if you have met him, and he has not changed, how do you like him? What is it to like somebody? Isn't it to be attracted to him, to enjoy his company, to give him brownie points, to approve of him? I find it incredible that you, of all people, would like an unrepentant dog poisoner. If ever I learn that you do, I shall be very disappointed in you. The man is entitled to our prayers, and our love; but surely not to our liking.

CARROLL E. SIMCOX

LOVE

(See *Charity, Kindness*)

Luf copuls gŏd & manne.   2304
RICHARD ROLLE OF HAMPOLE

Some day, after mastering the   2305
winds, the waves, the tides, and gravity, we shall harness for God the energies of love, and then, for the second time in the history of the world, man will have discovered fire.

PIERRE TEILHARD DE CHARDIN

Love consists in this, that two soli-   2306
tudes protect and touch and greet each other.

RAINER MARIA RILKE

Many waters cannot quench love,   2307
neither can the floods drown it.
Song of Solomon 8:7

2308 Let love be without dissimulation.
Romans 12:9

2309 He that loveth not knoweth not·
God; for God is love.
I John 4:8

2310 Love is infallible; it has no errors,
for all errors are the want of love.
WILLIAM LAW

2311 Love does not consist in gazing at
each other but in looking together in
the same direction.
ANTOINE DE SAINT-EXUPÉRY

2312 Love does not dominate; it culti-
vates.
JOHANN WOLFGANG VON GOETHE

2313 The Angel who presided at my birth
Said,—"Little Creature, formed for
joy and mirth,
Go love, without the help of any-
thing on earth."
WILLIAM BLAKE

2314 A tale without love is like beef
without mustard: an insipid dish.
ANATOLE FRANCE

2315 Belief in the existence of other
human beings as such is love.
SIMONE WEIL

2316 They love indeed who quake to say
they love.
PHILIP SIDNEY

2317 Man while he loves is never quite
depraved.
CHARLES LAMB

2318 I never could explain *why* I love
anybody, or anything.
WALT WHITMAN

2319 The Bible speaks of a mysterious sin
for which there is no forgiveness:
this great unpardonable sin is the
murder of the "love-life" in a
human being.
HENRIK IBSEN

2320 Love makes obedience lighter than
liberty.
WILLIAM R. ALGER

2321 It is sad not to be loved, but it is
much sadder not to be able to love.
MIGUEL DE UNAMUNO

2322 Love is responsibility of an *I* for a
Thou.
MARTIN BUBER

2323 Love must be learned and learned
again and again; there is no end to
it. Hate needs no instruction, but
waits only to be provoked.
KATHERINE ANNE PORTER

2324 Tell me how much you know of the
sufferings of your fellow men and I
will tell you how much you have
loved them.
HELMUT THIELICKE

2325 Work and love—these are the
basics. Without them there is neuro-
sis.
THEODOR REIK

2326 Love makes everything lovely; hate
concentrates itself on the one thing
hated.
GEORGE MAC DONALD

2327 Love between persons means that
each wants the other to be more
himself.
M.C. D'ARCY, S.J.

MEDITATION

2328 Let the words of my mouth, and the meditation of my heart, be always acceptable in thy sight, O Lord, my strength and my redeemer.
Psalm 19:14

2329 Reverie is the Sunday of thought.
HENRI FRÉDÉRIC AMIEL

2330 Meditation is the soul's perspective glass, whereby, in her long removes, she discerneth God as if he were nearer at hand.
OWEN FELLTHAM

2331 Whatever the world thinks, he who hath not meditated much upon God, the human mind, and the *summum bonum,* may possibly make a thriving earthworm, but will most indubitably make a sorry patriot and a sorry statesman.
GEORGE BERKELEY

2332 Where there is charity and wisdom, there is neither fear nor ignorance. Where there is patience and humility, there is neither anger nor vexation. Where there is poverty and joy, there is neither greed nor avarice. Where there is peace and meditation, there is neither anxiety nor doubt.
FRANCIS OF ASSISI

2333 Meditation is that exercise of the mind by which it recalls a known truth, as some kinds of creatures do their food, to be ruminated upon till all the valuable parts be extracted.
GEORGE HORNE

2334 Those who draw water from the wellspring of meditation know that God dwells close to their hearts. For those who wish to discover the quietude of old amid the hustle and bustle of today's machine civilization, there is no way save to rediscover this ancient realm of meditation. Since the loss of my eyesight I have been as delighted as if I had found a new wellspring by having arrived at this sacred precinct.
TOYOHIKO KAGAWA

2335 Proficiency in meditation lies not in thinking much, but in loving much. It is a way of seeking the divine companionship, the "closer walk." Thus it is that meditation has come to be called "the mother of love."
RICHARDSON WRIGHT

MEEKNESS

(See *Humility, Poor in Spirit*)

2336 "To thine own self be true" is a piece of high-class ethical futility which Shakespeare appropriately puts into the mouth of his own most priceless old dotard. The first condition of attainment in science or art or religion is not loyalty to self, but forgetfulness of self in concentration on the Object; it is truly the meek who possess the earth.
WILLIAM TEMPLE

2337 I'm nobody! Who are you?
Are you nobody, too?
Then there's a pair of us—don't tell!
They'd banish us, you know.

How dreary, to be somebody!
How public, like a frog
To tell your name the livelong day
To an admiring bog!
EMILY DICKINSON

2338 Meekness is love at school, at the school of Christ. It is the disciple learning to know, and fear, and distrust himself, and learning of him who is meek and lowly of heart, and so finding rest to his soul.

JAMES HAMILTON

2339 Selfish men may possess the earth; it is the meek only who inherit it from the heavenly Father, free from all defilements and perplexities of un-righteousness.

JOHN WOOLMAN

2340 Meekness takes injuries like pills, not chewing, but swallowing them down.

THOMAS BROWNE

2341 The best of men is like water;
    Water benefits all things
    And does not compete with them.
It dwells in the lowly places that all disdain—
    Wherein it comes near to the Tao.

In his dwelling, the Sage loves the lowly earth;
In his heart, he loves what is profound;
In his relations with others, he loves kindness;
In his words, he loves sincerity;
In government, he loves peace;
In business affairs, he loves ability;
In his actions, he loves choosing the right time.
    It is because he does not contend
    That he is without reproach.

LAO TZU

2342 The man who said, "Blessed is he that expecteth nothing, for he shall not be disappointed," put the eulogy quite inadequately and even falsely. The truth is, "Blessed is he that expecteth nothing, for he shall be gloriously surprised." The man who expects nothing sees redder roses than common men can see, and greener grass, and a more startling sun.

GILBERT KEITH CHESTERTON

MODESTY

Let another man praise thee, and 2343 not thine own mouth.

Proverbs 27:2

Modesty is to merit what shade is to 2344 figures in a picture; it gives it strength and makes it stand out.

JEAN DE LA BRUYÈRE

The man who is ostentatious of his 2345 modesty is twin to the statue that wears a fig-leaf.

MARK TWAIN

Modesty is always the sign and 2346 safeguard of a mystery. It is explained by its contrary—profanation. Shyness or modesty is, in truth, the half-conscious sense of a secret of nature or of the soul too intimately individual to be given or surrendered.

HENRI FRÉDÉRIC AMIEL

There's a lot to be said for the fellow 2347 who doesn't say it himself.

MAURICE SWITZER

It is easy for a somebody to be 2348 modest, but it is difficult to be modest when one is a nobody.

JULES RENARD

MORALITY

(See *Goodness, Moral Law, Religion and Morality*)

2349 Morality is not properly the doctrine of how we may make ourselves happy, but how we may make ourselves worthy of happiness.

IMMANUEL KANT

2350 It is not, what a lawyer tells me I *may* do; but what humanity, reason, and justice tell me I ought to do.

EDMUND BURKE

2351 To make our idea of morality centre on forbidden acts is to defile the imagination and to introduce into our judgments of our fellow-men a secret element of gusto.

ROBERT LOUIS STEVENSON

2352 If your morals make you dreary, depend upon it, they are wrong. I do not say give them up, for they may be all you have, but conceal them like a vice lest they should spoil the lives of better and simpler people.

ROBERT LOUIS STEVENSON

2353 An Englishman thinks he is moral when he is only uncomfortable.

GEORGE BERNARD SHAW

2354 Conduct is three-fourths of our life and its largest concern.

MATTHEW ARNOLD

2355 Veracity is the heart of morality.

THOMAS HENRY HUXLEY

2356 Morality is a private and costly luxury.

HENRY ADAMS

It is not enough to do good; one 2357 must do it the right way.

JOHN, VISCOUNT MORLEY

An act has no ethical quality what- 2358 ever unless it be chosen out of several, all equally possible.

WILLIAM JAMES

There is but one unconditional com- 2359 mandment, which is that we should seek incessantly, with fear and trembling, so to vote and to act as to bring about the very largest total universe of good which we can see.

WILLIAM JAMES

Nothing is settled until it is settled 2360 right.

ABRAHAM LINCOLN

The health of a community is an 2361 almost unfailing index of its morals.

JAMES MARTINEAU

Morals make characters, not per- 2362 sonalities.

Anonymous

Understanding the rainbow is phys- 2363 ics, but delight in the rainbow is morality.

LIN YUTANG

To him in whose eyes no one is bad, 2364 who can appear good?

MARTIAL

Morality, when vigorously alive, 2365 sees farther than intellect, and provides unconsciously for intellectual difficulties.

JAMES ANTHONY FROUDE

If the moral and physical fibre of its 2366 manhood and its womanhood is not a state concern, the question is, what is?

BENJAMIN N. CARDOZO

2367 The Puritan is never popular, not even in a society of Puritans. In case of a pinch, the mass prefer to be good fellows rather than to be good men.

JOHN DEWEY

2368 The moral good is not a goal but an inner force which lights up man's life from within.

NICOLAS BERDYAEV

NEIGHBORS

2369 The love of our neighbor is the only door out of the dungeon of self.

GEORGE MAC DONALD

2370 Though we do not have our Lord with us in bodily presence, we have our neighbor, who, for the ends of love and loving service, is as good as our Lord himself.

TERESA OF AVILA

2371 All is well with him who is beloved of his neighbors.

GEORGE HERBERT

2372 Love your neighbor, but don't pull down the hedge.

Swiss proverb

2373 Love thy neighbor, even when he plays the trombone.

Jewish proverb

2374 Man becomes a holy thing, a neighbor, only if we realize that he is the

property of God and that Jesus Christ died for him.

HELMUT THIELECKE

OBEDIENCE

We ought to obey God rather than men.   2375

Acts 5:29

Don't listen to friends when the   2376
Friend inside you says "Do this!"

MOHANDAS GANDHI

The eating of the fruit was not   2377
prohibited as being in itself evil but
in order that in this small matter
men should do something for the
sole reason that it was commanded
of God.

THOMAS AQUINAS

To obey is the proper office of a   2378
rational soul.

MICHEL DE MONTAIGNE

Every revelation of God is a de-   2379
mand, and the way to knowledge of
God is by obedience.

WILLIAM TEMPLE

No man ruleth safely but he that is   2380
willingly ruled.

THOMAS À KEMPIS

By obedience we are made a society   2381
and a republic, and distinguished
from herds of beasts, and heaps of
flies, who do what they list and are
incapable of laws.

JEREMY TAYLOR

Obedience is a complicated act of   2382
virtue, and many graces are exer-

cised in one act of obedience. It is an act of humility, of mortification and self-denial, of charity to God, of care of the public, of order and charity to ourselves and all our society, and a great instance of victory over the most refractory and unruly passions.

JEREMY TAYLOR

2383 The life of the world goes on through the will of some one. Some one makes our own life and that of the universe his own inscrutable care. To have a hope of understanding what that will means, we must first carry it out, we must do what is required of us. Unless I do what is required of me, I can never know what that may be, and much less know what is required of us all and of the whole universe.

LEO TOLSTOY

2384 Though he were a Son, yet learned he obedience by the things which he suffered; and being made perfect, he became the author of eternal salvation unto all them that obey him.

Hebrews 5:8–9

OPPORTUNITY

2385 Now it is high time to awake out of sleep: for now is our salvation nearer than when we believed.

Romans 13:11

2386 There is a tide in the affairs of men
Which taken at the flood leads on to
    fortune;
Omitted, all the voyage of their life
Is bound in shallows and in miseries.

On such a full sea are we now afloat,
And we must take the current when
    it serves,
Or lose our ventures.

WILLIAM SHAKESPEARE

A wise man will make more opportunities than he finds. 2387

FRANCIS BACON

Seek the first possible opportunity 2388 to act on every good resolution you make.

WILLIAM JAMES

God often gives in one brief moment that which he has for a long time denied. 2389

THOMAS À KEMPIS

No great man ever complains of want of opportunity. 2390

RALPH WALDO EMERSON

A clash of doctrines is not a disaster—it is an opportunity. 2391

ALFRED NORTH WHITEHEAD

Truly there is a tide in the affairs of men; but there is no gulf-stream setting forever in one direction. 2392

JAMES RUSSELL LOWELL

Behold, I have set before thee an open door, and no man can shut it. 2393

Revelation 3:8

Curse ye Meroz, said the angel of the Lord, curse ye bitterly the inhabitants thereof; because they came not to the help of the Lord, to the help of the Lord against the mighty. 2394

Judges 5:23

Aut disce aut discedite, non sors tertia hic manet—Either learn or depart, 2395 there is no third choice here.

Motto of Winchester College,
England

2396 Do not wait for extraordinary circumstances to do good; try to use ordinary situations.

JEAN PAUL RICHTER

2397 It is less important to redistribute wealth than it is to redistribute opportunity.

ARTHUR H. VANDENBERG

2398 You will never "find" time for anything. If you want time you must make it.

CHARLES BUXTON

2399 Not only strike while the iron is hot, but make it hot by striking.

OLIVER CROMWELL

PATIENCE

2400 I can well wait a century for a reader, since God has waited six thousand years for a discoverer.

JOHANNES KEPLER

2401 Fortune is like the market, where many times, if you can stay a little, the price will fall.

FRANCIS BACON

2402 Beware the fury of a patient man.

JOHN DRYDEN

2403 A patient man will bear for a time, and afterward joy shall spring up unto him.

Ecclesiasticus 1:23

2404 An aged man, whom Abraham hospitably invited to his tent, refused to join him in prayer to the one spiritual God. Learning that he was a fire-worshiper, Abraham drove him from his door. That night God appeared to Abraham in a vision and said: "I have borne with that ignorant man for seventy years; could you not have patiently suffered him one night?"

The Talmud

It takes patience to appreciate domestic bliss; volatile spirits prefer unhappiness.   2405

GEORGE SANTAYANA

Patience is power; with time and patience the mulberry leaf becomes silk.   2406

Chinese proverb

On every level of life from housework to heights of prayer, in all judgment and all efforts to get things done, hurry and impatience are sure marks of the amateur.   2407

EVELYN UNDERHILL

A lot of the road to heaven has to be taken at thirty miles per hour.   2408

EVELYN UNDERHILL

Patience with ourselves is a duty for Christians and the only real humility. For it means patience with a growing creature whom God has taken in hand and whose completion he will effect in his own time and way. . . .   2409

EVELYN UNDERHILL

Perhaps there is only one cardinal sin: impatience. Because of impatience we were driven out of Para-   2410 dise; because of impatience we cannot return.

FRANZ KAFKA

2411 We must wait for God, long, meekly, in the wind and wet, in the thunder and lightning, in the cold and the dark. Wait, and he will come. He never comes to those who do not wait.

FREDERICK W. FABER

2412 Patience is a bitter plant but it bears sweet fruit.

German proverb

2413 It is easy finding reasons why other folk should be patient.

GEORGE ELIOT

2414 "Take your needle, my child, and work at your pattern; it will come out a rose by and by." Life is like that; one stitch at a time taken patiently, and the pattern will come out all right like embroidery.

OLIVER WENDELL HOLMES

2415 Everything comes to him who hustles while he waits.

THOMAS A. EDISON

2416 This is thankworthy, if a man for conscience toward God endure grief, suffering wrongfully. For what glory is it, if, when ye be buffeted for your faults, ye shall take it patiently? but if, when ye do well, and suffer for it, ye take it patiently, this is acceptable with God. For even hereunto were ye called: because Christ also suffered for us, leaving us an example, that ye should follow in his steps.

I Peter 2:19–21

PEACE

Peace is not an absence of war, it is a virtue, a state of mind, a disposition for benevolence, confidence, justice.   2417

BARUCH SPINOZA

The deliberate aim at Peace very easily passes into its bastard substitute, Anesthesia.   2418

ALFRED NORTH WHITEHEAD

We may enjoy abundance of peace if we refrain from busying ourselves with the sayings and doings of others, and things which concern not ourselves. How can he abide long time in peace who occupieth himself with other men's matters, and with things outside himself, and meanwhile payeth little or rare heed to the self within? Blessed are the single-hearted, for they shall have abundance of peace.   2419

THOMAS A KEMPIS

Thou wilt keep him in perfect peace, whose mind is stayed on thee: because he trusteth in thee.   2420

Isaiah 26:3

If it be possible, as much as lieth in you, live peaceably with all men.   2421

Romans 12:18

Thinking about interior peace destroys interior peace. The patient who constantly feels his pulse is not getting any better.   2422

HUBERT VAN ZELLER

If we will have peace without a worm in it, lay we the foundations of justice and good will.   2423

OLIVER CROMWELL

2424 A great many people are trying to make peace, but that has already been done. God has not left it for us to do; all we have to do is to enter into it.

DWIGHT L. MOODY

2425 Peace is rarely denied to the peaceful.

JOHANN VON SCHILLER

2426 If they want peace, nations should avoid the pinpricks that precede cannon shots.

NAPOLEON BUONAPARTE

2427 The grim fact is that we prepare for war like precocious giants and for peace like retarded pygmies.

LESTER B. PEARSON

2428 Peace cannot be kept by force. It can only be achieved by understanding.

ALBERT EINSTEIN

2429 Even peace may be purchased at too high a price.

BENJAMIN FRANKLIN

PERSEVERANCE

2430 No man, having put his hand to the plough, and looking back, is fit for the kingdom of God.

Luke 9:62

2431 Nothing great was ever done without much enduring.

CATHERINE OF SIENA

2432 Be thou faithful unto death, and I will give thee a crown of life.

Revelation 2:10

The difference between persever- *2433* ance and obstinacy is, that one often comes from a strong will, and the other from a strong won't.

HENRY WARD BEECHER

By gnawing through a dike, even a *2434* rat may drown a nation.

EDMUND BURKE

Big shots are only little shots who *2435* keep shooting.

CHRISTOPHER MORLEY

Many are stubborn in pursuit of the *2436* path they have chosen, few in pursuit of the goal.

FRIEDRICH WILHELM NIETZSCHE

To persevere in one's duty and to be *2437* silent is the best answer to calumny.

GEORGE WASHINGTON

Lincoln's road to the White House: *2438*

Failed in business in 1831.
Defeated for Legislature in 1832.
Second failure in business in 1833.
Suffered nervous breakdown in 1836.
Defeated for Speaker in 1838.
Defeated for Elector in 1840.
Defeated for Congress in 1843.
Defeated for Congress in 1848.
Defeated for Senate in 1855.
Defeated for Vice President in 1856.
Defeated for Senate in 1858.
Elected President in 1860.

Anonymous

PERSONALITY

Personality is that being which has *2439* power over itself.

PAUL TILLICH

2440 The term "person" means that which is most perfect in all nature.
THOMAS AQUINAS

2441 Human personality and individuality written and signed by God on each countenance is something altogether sacred, something for the resurrection, for eternal life.
LÉON BLOY

2442 God himself I may declare to be the supreme expression of personality.
GORDON W. ALLPORT

2443 A person makes his appearance by entering into relation with other persons.
MARTIN BUBER

2444 The search for a new personality is futile; what is fruitful is the human interest the old personality can take in new activities.
CESARE PAVESE

PERSPECTIVE

2445 Years ago I was spending a vacation on the coasts of Maine, my companions being a research physician, a geologist, and a professor of astronomy. They talked much of the age of the cliffs we climbed, of the sea life we examined under the physician's microscope, of the vast interstellar spaces. We had as our guide, philosopher, fisherman, and friend a man who listened to our conversation with staring eyes. It was the year of a presidential election, the one in which William Jennings Bryan was making his last desperate effort to become president. Maine was a rock-ribbed Republican state. By and by our Maine friend began to ask questions: Were the rocks all that old? Were we descended, so to speak, from sea worms? Was the universe so unspeakably big? When all had been explained, he sighed heavily and spoke his mind. "Well," he said, "I guess it won't make a powerful lot of difference even if Bryan *is* elected."
CHARLES FISKE

POOR IN SPIRIT

(See *Humility, Meekness*)

"Poor in spirit" refers, not precisely 2446 to humility, but to an attitude of dependence on God and detachment from earthly supports.
RONALD KNOX

"Blessed are the poor in spirit" 2447 means: "Blessed is the man who has realized his own utter helplessness, and who has put his whole trust in God." If a man has realized his own utter helplessness, and has put his whole trust in God, there will enter into his life two things which are opposite sides of the same thing. He will become completely *detached from things,* for he will know that things have not got it in them to bring happiness or security; and he will become completely *attached to* God, for he will know that God alone can bring him help, and hope, and strength. The man who is poor in spirit is the man who has realized that things mean nothing, and that God means everything.
WILLIAM BARCLAY

PRINCIPLES

2448 It is easier to fight for one's principles than to live up to them.
ALFRED ADLER

2449 Nobody ever did anything very foolish except from some strong principle.
WILLIAM LAMB,
Viscount Melbourne

2450 To have doubted one's own first principles is the mark of the civilized man.
OLIVER WENDELL HOLMES, JR.

2451 The value of a principle is the number of things it will explain.
RALPH WALDO EMERSON

2452 Principles always become a matter of vehement discussion when practice is at ebb.
GEORGE GISSING

2453 We may be personally defeated, but our principles never.
WILLIAM LLOYD GARRISON

2454 What we must look for here is, first, religious and moral principles; secondly, gentlemanly conduct; thirdly, intellectual ability.
THOMAS ARNOLD,
to his scholars at Rugby

2455 That is the issue that will continue in this country when these poor tongues of Judge Douglas and myself shall be silent. It is the eternal struggle between these two principles—right and wrong—throughout the world. They are the two principles that have stood face to face from the beginning of time, and will ever continue to struggle.
ABRAHAM LINCOLN

PROGRESS

2456 All that is human must retrograde if it does not advance.
EDWARD GIBBON

2457 Social advance depends as much upon the process through which it is secured as upon the result itself.
JANE ADDAMS

2458 Not to go back is somewhat to advance,
And men must walk, at least, before they dance.
ALEXANDER POPE

2459 The reasonable man adapts himself to the world, but the unreasonable man tries to adapt the world to him—therefore, all progress depends upon the unreasonable man.
GEORGE BERNARD SHAW

2460 Men have learned to travel farther and faster, though on errands not conspicuously improved. This, I believe, is called progress.
WILLIS FISHER

2461 The longer I live, the more keenly I feel that whatever was good enough for our fathers is not good enough for us.
OSCAR WILDE

2462 Belief in progress is a doctrine of idlers and Belgians. It is the individual relying upon his neighbors to do his work.
CHARLES BAUDELAIRE

2463 Fundamental progress has to do with the reinterpretation of basic ideas.
ALFRED NORTH WHITEHEAD

2464 The necessity of rejecting and destroying some things that are beautiful is the deepest curse of existence.
GEORGE SANTAYANA

2465 Every step of progress the world has made has been from scaffold to scaffold, and from stake to stake.
WENDELL PHILLIPS

2466 Without the idea of progress life is a corrupting marsh.
H.G. WELLS

PROPHECY

2467 The prophet is primarily the man, not to whom God has communicated certain divine thoughts, but whose mind is illuminated by the divine spirit to interpret aright the divine acts; and the act is primary.
WILLIAM TEMPLE

2468 The prophets are sent out from the visible mathematics of the glory to proclaim the moral mathematics of the glory. Morality is either the mathematics of power or it is nothing. Their business is to recover mankind—but first the inclusive-exclusive Israel—to an effort to know only the good.
CHARLES WILLIAMS

2469 It has not pleased God to build either the congregation of Israel or the fellowship of the church on prophets. They are the warning, the correction, the voice in the wilderness.
CHARLES WILLIAMS

2470 The question-askers are usually of two kinds. There are, first, the men

of religion, the prophets, of whom only a few exist in any generation, and to whom, since the Reformation, we have decided to pay respect in lieu of attention. Then there are the artists, among whom we should include, of course, all true scientists, educators, and philosophers. On occasion we still listen to them. They are the ones who rowel us out of our sleep. They are the magnificent cockleburs of the human race.
CLIFTON FADIMAN

Prophets were twice stoned—first in 2471 anger; then, after their death, with a handsome slab in the graveyard.
CHRISTOPHER MORLEY

The prophet is to be no mere announcer, he is rather God's agent who by the "word" *accomplishes* what he foretells, whether good or bad. 2472
FLEMING JAMES

Every honest man is a prophet; he 2473 utters his opinion both of private and public matters. Thus, if you go on so, the result is so. He never says, such a thing will happen let you do what you will. A prophet is a seer, not an arbitrary dictator.
WILLIAM BLAKE

PRUDENCE

Prudence is the ability to use the 2474 means towards the universal end of man, that is, happiness.
IMMANUEL KANT

We must not trust every word of 2475 others or feeling within ourselves, but cautiously and patiently try the matter, whether it be of God.

THOMAS À KEMPIS

2476 Prudence versus passion is a conflict that runs through history. It is not a conflict in which we ought to side wholly with either party.

BERTRAND RUSSELL

2477 The simple believeth every word: but the prudent man looketh well to his going.

Proverbs 14:15

2478 Prudence is an attitude that keeps life safe, but does not often make it happy.

SAMUEL JOHNSON

2479 Men are born with two eyes, but with one tongue, in order that they should see twice as much as they say.

CHARLES CALEB COLTON

QUIETNESS

2480 All the troubles of life come upon us because we refuse to sit quietly for a while each day in our rooms.

BLAISE PASCAL

2481 I grew up in the generation of the giants—John R. Mott and his disciples—among whom it was taken for granted that if you were going to live the Christian life at all, you would give at least one hour daily, before the first meal of the day, to

seeking God through his Word and to listening to his voice.

STEPHEN NEILL

It is difficult to be quiet if you have 2482 nothing to do.

ARTHUR SCHOPENHAUER

If we have not quiet in our minds, 2483 outward comfort will do no more for us than a golden slipper on a gouty foot.

JOHN BUNYAN

God gives quietness at last. 2484

JOHN GREENLEAF WHITTIER

Study to be quiet, and to do your 2485 own business.

I Thessalonians 4:11

Give us grace and strength to for- 2486 bear and to persevere. Give us courage and gaiety and the quiet mind, spare to us our friends, soften to us our enemies.

ROBERT LOUIS STEVENSON

Grant, we beseech thee, merciful 2487 Lord, to thy faithful people pardon and peace, that they may be cleansed from all their sins, and serve thee with a quiet mind.

Book of Common Prayer

REALISM

It is a condition which confronts 2488 us—not a theory.

GROVER CLEVELAND

Facts call us to reflect, even as the 2489

tossings of a capsizing vessel cause the crew to rush on deck and to climb the masts.

ALBERT SCHWEITZER

2490 Myson used to say we should not investigate facts by the light of arguments, but arguments by the light of facts; for the facts were not put together to fit the arguments, but the arguments to fit the facts.

DIOGENES LAERTIUS

2491 We are much beholden to Machiavel and others, that write what men do, and not what they ought to do.

FRANCIS BACON

2492 The optimist sees the doughnut. The pessimist sees the hole in the doughnut. The realist eats the doughnut.

Anonymous

his morality. In a thousand ways, some great, some small, but all subtle, we are daily tempted to that great sin.

WILLIAM E. GLADSTONE

RELIGION AND POLITICS

I could not be leading a religious life   2496 unless I identified myself with the whole of mankind, and that I could not do unless I took part in politics. The whole gamut of man's activities today constitutes an indivisible whole. You cannot divide social, economic, political and purely religious work into watertight compartments.

MOHANDAS GANDHI

RELIGION AND MORALITY

2493 If morality was Christianity, Socrates was the Savior.

WILLIAM BLAKE

2494 Teach a child what is wise, that is *morality*. Teach him what is wise and beautiful, that is *religion*.

THOMAS HENRY HUXLEY

2495 There is one proposition which the experience of life burns into my soul; it is this, that a man should beware of letting his religion spoil

RELIGION AND SCIENCE

Ecclesiasticism in science is only   2497 unfaithfulness to truth.

THOMAS HENRY HUXLEY

The religion that is afraid of science   2498 dishonors God and commits suicide.

RALPH WALDO EMERSON

Where it is a duty to worship the   2499 sun it is pretty sure to be a crime to examine the laws of heat.

JOHN, VISCOUNT MORLEY

2500 Science makes impossible any religion but the highest.

B.H. STREETER

REPENTANCE

(See *Healing and Health, Humility, Sin, Shame*)

2501 Repentance—it is always to start over again.

JEAN VIANNEY, the Curé d'Ars

2502 O God, though our sins be seven, though our sins be seventy times seven, though our sins be more than the hairs of our head, yet give us grace in loving penitence to cast ourselves down into the depths of thy compassion.

CHRISTINA ROSSETTI

2503 We make a ladder out of our vices if we trample those same vices underfoot.

AUGUSTINE OF HIPPO

2504 Before God can deliver us we must undeceive ourselves.

AUGUSTINE OF HIPPO

2505 A noble mind disdains not to repent.

ALEXANDER POPE

2506 Man must be lenient with his soul in her weaknesses and imperfections and suffer his failings as he suffers those of others, but he must not be idle, and must encourage himself to better things.

SERAPHIM OF SAROV

2507 You can begin a new life! Only see things afresh, as you saw them before; for in this consists the new life.

MARCUS AURELIUS

2508 It is a great grace of God to practice self-examination; but too much is as bad as too little. Believe me, by God's help we shall advance more by contemplating the Divinity than by keeping our eyes fixed on ourselves.

TERESA OF ÁVILA

2509 Rolling in the muck is not the best way of getting clean.

ALDOUS HUXLEY

2510 Repentance is deep understanding.

The Shepherd of Hermas

2511 A man should never be ashamed to own he has been in the wrong, which is but saying, in other words, that he is wiser today than he was yesterday.

JONATHAN SWIFT

2512 Repentance may begin instantly, but reformation often requires a sphere of years.

HENRY WARD BEECHER

2513 Repentance is another name for aspiration.

HENRY WARD BEECHER

2514 It can take less than a minute to commit a sin. It takes not as long to obtain God's forgiveness. Penitence and amendment should take a lifetime.

HUBERT VAN ZELLER

2515 I saw in secret a man flowing with the tears of thought and repentance, and inwardly he shone like a young tree with all the blossom of May upon it.

THEODOR HAECKER

2516 Sometimes it does us good to make a slip: it keeps us humble. We cannot be conquered so long as we do not lose courage.

FRANCIS DE SALES

2517 When thou attackest the roots of sin, fix thy thought upon the God whom thou desirest rather than upon the sin which thou abhorrest.

WALTER HYLTON

2518 How can we tell when a sin we have committed has been pardoned? By the fact that we no longer commit that sin.

RABBI BUNAM OF PZHYSHA

2519 Repentance is no more than a passionate intention to know things after the mode of heaven.

CHARLES WILLIAMS

2520 For godly sorrow worketh repentance to salvation not to be repented of; but the sorrow of the world worketh death.

II Corinthians 7:10

SACRIFICE

2521 A man came home after the last war with an empty coat sleeve. A tactless neighbor said: "I see you've lost your arm." The veteran answered sharply: "I didn't lose it. I gave it."

Anonymous

2522 The Son of Man *must* suffer. For the manifestation of love, by which it wins its response, is always sacrifice. The principle of sacrifice is that we choose to do or to suffer what apart from our love we should not choose to do or to suffer. When love is returned this sacrifice is the most joyful thing in the world, and heaven is the life of joyful sacrifice. But in a selfish world it must be painful, and the pain is the source of triumph.

WILLIAM TEMPLE

We can offer up much in the large, 2523 but to make sacrifices in little things is what we are seldom equal to.

JOHANN WOLFGANG VON GOETHE

Not even for the highest principles 2524 has anyone the right to sacrifice others than himself.

Anonymous

I shrink to give up my life, and thus 2525 do not plunge into the great waters of life.

RABINDRANATH TAGORE

The essence of man lies in this, in 2526 his marvelous faculty for seeking truth, seeing it, loving it, and sacrificing himself to it.

GIUSEPPE PREZZOLINI

The hope of mankind does not lie in 2527 the action of any corporate body, be it ever so powerful, but in the influence of individual men and women who for the sake of a greater have sacrificed a lesser aim.

KENNETH WALKER

It is only through the mystery of 2528 self-sacrifice that a man may find himself anew.

CARL G. JUNG

2529 Self-preservation is the first law of nature; self-sacrifice the highest rule of grace.

Anonymous

SAINTS

2530 It is easier to make a saint out of a libertine than out of a prig.

GEORGE SANTAYANA

2531 The elect are whosoever will, and the nonelect, whosoever won't.

HENRY WARD BEECHER

2532 The saint is saint, not because he is "good," but because he is transparent for something that is more than he himself is.

PAUL TILLICH

2533 The power of the soul for good is in proportion to the strength of its passions. Sanctity is not the negation of passion but its order. Hence great saints have often been great sinners.

COVENTRY PATMORE

2534 There is only one sorrow, the sorrow of not being a saint.

LÉON BLOY

2535 Grace is indeed required to turn a man into a saint; and he who doubts this does not know what either a man or a saint is.

BLAISE PASCAL

2536 Most saints in the past were created by the people in spite of the priests.

REMY DE GOURMONT

2537 A saint is one who makes goodness attractive.

A.E. HOUSMAN

Nature requires the saint since he 2538 alone knows the miracle of transfiguration; growth and development, the very highest and most sustained incarnation, never weary him.

FRIEDRICH WILHELM NIETZSCHE

A vulgar man cannot be a saint. 2539

RABBI HILLEL

The great painter boasted that he 2540 mixed all his colors with brains, and the great saint may be said to mix all his thoughts with thanks.

GILBERT KEITH CHESTERTON

Many of the insights of the saint 2541 stem from his experience as a sinner.

ERIC HOFFER

The only difference between a saint 2542 and a sinner is that every saint has a past, and every sinner has a future.

OSCAR WILDE

St. Malo would not move his cloak, 2543 because a wren had nested in it; and the other day a professional in a golf championship let go his chance of winning, because he would not play his ball out of a thrush's nest.

HELEN WADDELL

Every saint has a bee in his halo. 2544

E.V. LUCAS

SELF-CONQUEST

And Jacob was left alone; and there 2545 wrestled a man with Jacob until the breaking of the day.

Genesis 32:24

2546   He that is slow to anger is better than the mighty; and he that ruleth his spirit than he that taketh a city.
Proverbs 16:32

2547   It often happens that our passions lie dormant. If, during that time, we do not lay up provision of strength with which to combat them when they wake up, we shall be vanquished.
FRANCIS DE SALES

2548   There is endless room for rebellion against ourselves.
GEORGE MAC DONALD

2549   The best time for you to hold your tongue is the time when you feel you must say something or bust.
JOSH BILLINGS

2550   O Lord, help us to be masters of ourselves, that we may be servants of others.
ALEXANDER PATERSON

SELF-CRITICISM

2551   If the average person were to give a commensurable kicking to the one responsible for most of his troubles, he couldn't sit down for a week.
BUD NELSON

2552   Shortly before Shelley died he had a curious dream, in which he saw his spectral self coming toward his conscious self, and the spectral self suddenly lifted the hood from its brow, and spoke to the conscious self, saying, "Art thou satisfied?"
H.D. ROSENTHAL

The unexamined life is not worth   2553
living.
SOCRATES

It is my custom every night, as   2554
soon as the candle is out, to run over the words and actions of the past day; and I let nothing escape me, for why should I fear the sight of my errors when I can admonish and forgive myself?
I was a little too hot in such a dispute; my opinion might well have been withheld, for it gave offense and did no good. The thing was true; but all truths are not to be spoken at all times. I would I had held my tongue, for there is no contending, either with fools or with our superiors. I have done ill, but it shall be so no more. Habit is a cable; we weave a thread of it every day, and at last we can not break it.
HORACE MANN

SELF-KNOWLEDGE

"Know thyself"? If I knew myself,   2555
I'd run away.
JOHANN WOLFGANG VON GOETHE

Almost all our faults are preferable   2556
to the mthods we resort to to hide them.
FRANÇOIS DE LA ROCHEFOUCAULD

All men are ordinary men; the ex-   2557
traordinary men are those who know it.
GILBERT KEITH CHESTERTON

Train up a child in the way he   2558
should go—and walk there yourself once in a while.
JOSH BILLINGS

2559 Somewhere Oliver Wendell Holmes said that in every "John" there are three Johns: first, there is John as he sees himself; second, there is John as his associates and friends seè him; finally, there is John as God sees him; and it is the Spirit of knowledge alone that gives us this last view of self.
FRANK H. HALLOCK

2560 Other men's sins are before our eyes; our own are behind our backs.
SENECA

each individual himself or herself to guard.
MOHANDAS GANDHI

It is necessary to the happiness of a man that he be mentally faithful to himself. 2567
THOMAS PAINE

My great-grandfather was President of the United States, my grand-father was Senator of Ohio, my father is Ambassador to Ireland, and I am a Brownie. 2568
The young daughter of William Howard Taft III

SELF-RESPECT

2561 It is difficult to make a man miserable while he feels he is worthy of himself and claims kinship to the great God who made him.
ABRAHAM LINCOLN, *to a deputation of Negroes*

2562 Johnson did not strut or stand on tip-toe; he only did not stoop.
JAMES BOSWELL

2563 Few are chosen, for the good reason that few choose themselves.
ALDOUS HUXLEY

2564 He who makes a beast of himself gets rid of the pain of being a man.
SAMUEL JOHNSON

2565 No one can make you feel inferior without your consent.
ELEANOR ROOSEVELT

2566 Self-respect and honor cannot be protected by others. They are for

SERVICE

The service we render for others is really the rent we pay for our room on this earth. 2569
WILFRED GRENFELL

Where I lie down worn out, other men will stand young and fresh. By the steps I have cut they will climb; by the stairs that I have built they will mount. They will never know the name of the man who made them. At the clumsy work they will laugh; when the stones roll they will curse me. But they will mount, and on my work, they will climb, and by my stair. . . . And no man liveth to himself, and no man dieth to himself. 2570
OLIVE SCHREINER

I am only one but still I am one. I cannot do everything but still I can do something; and because I cannot do everything let me not refuse to do the something that I can do. 2571
EDWARD EVERETT HALE

SHAME

(See *Repentance*)

2572 The more things a man is ashamed of, the more respectable he is.
GEORGE BERNARD SHAW

2573 I never wonder to see men wicked, but I often wonder to see them not ashamed.
JONATHAN SWIFT

2574 A hurtful act is the transference to others of the degradation which we bear in ourselves.
SIMONE WEIL

2575 Where there is yet shame, there may in time be virtue.
SAMUEL JOHNSON

SHARING

2576 In a shared fish, there are no bones.
DEMOCRITUS OF ABDERA

2577 There is no savor like that of bread shared among men.
ANTOINE DE SAINT-EXUPÉRY

2578 Goods which are not shared are not goods.
FERNANDO DE ROJAS

2579 Rejoice with them that do rejoice, and weep with them that weep.
Romans 12:15

2580 If somebody goes without *his* daily bread, as happens too often, it is not because God has failed to provide a sufficient quantity of *our* daily bread but because somebody has failed to recognize that it is *ours* and not his own, and has failed to share. This is man's failure, not God's.
CARROLL E. SIMCOX

2581 When a man dies he clutches in his hands only that which he has given away during his lifetime.
JEAN JACQUES ROUSSEAU

SILENCE

2582 The Father uttered one Word; that Word is his Son, and he utters him for ever in everlasting silence; and in silence the soul has to hear it.
JOHN OF THE CROSS

2583 Silence is deep as Eternity, speech is shallow as Time.
THOMAS CARLYLE

2584 Silence is the unbearable repartee.
GILBERT KEITH CHESTERTON

2585 A fool can noght be stille.
GEOFFREY CHAUCER

2586 NOISE, *n.* A stench in the ear. The chief product and authenticating sign of civilization.
AMBROSE BIERCE,
The Devil's Dictionary

2587 A closed mouth catches no flies.
MIGUEL DE CERVANTES

2588 Better to remain silent and be thought a fool than to speak and to remove all doubt.
ABRAHAM LINCOLN

2589 He had occasional flashes of silence

that made his conversation perfectly delightful.

SYDNEY SMITH

2590 Blessed is the man who, having nothing to say, abstains from giving wordy evidence of the fact.

GEORGE ELIOT

2591 Sometimes silence is not golden— just yellow.

Anonymous

SIMPLICITY

2592 Seek simplicity, and distrust it.

ALFRED NORTH WHITEHEAD

2593 It is no good asking for a simple religion. After all, real things are not simple. They look simple, but they are not. The table I am sitting at looks simple: but ask a scientist to tell you what it is really made of— all about the atoms and how the light waves rebound from them and hit my eye and what they do to the optic nerve and what it does to my brain—and, of course, you find that what we call "seeing a table" lands you in mysteries and complications which you can hardly get to the end of. A child saying a child's prayer looks simple. And if you are content to stop there, well and good. But if you are not—and the modern world usually is not—if you want to go on and ask what is really happening— then you must be prepared for something difficult. If we ask for something more than simplicity, it is silly then to complain that the something more is not simple.

C.S. LEWIS

We have exchanged the Washington- 2594 ian dignity for the Jeffersonian simplicity, which was in truth only another name for the Jacksonian vulgarity.

BISHOP HENRY CODMAN POTTER

Simplicity is the most deceitful mis- 2595 tress that ever betrayed man.

HENRY ADAMS

My good Henry Thoreau made this 2596 else solitary afternoon sunny with his simplicity and clear perception. How comic is simplicity in this double-dealing, quacking world. Everything that boy says makes merry with society, though nothing can be graver than his meaning.

RALPH WALDO EMERSON

Blissful are the simple, for they shall 2597 have much peace.

THOMAS À KEMPIS

All great things are simple, and 2598 many can be expressed in a single word: freedom; justice; honor; duty; mercy; hope.

WINSTON CHURCHILL

As people become wise in their own 2599 eyes . . . customs rise up from the spirit of this world . . . till a departure from the simplicity that there is in Christ becomes as distinguishable as light from darkness, to such who are crucified to the world.

JOHN WOOLMAN

Everything should be made as sim- 2600 ple as possible, but not simpler.

ALBERT EINSTEIN

SINCERITY

2601 Sincerity comes directly from the heart. One finds it in very few people; what one usually finds is but a deft pretense designed to gain the confidence of others.

FRANÇOIS DE LA ROCHEFOUCAULD

2602 Weak people cannot be sincere.

FRANÇOIS DE LA ROCHEFOUCAULD

2603 We are not bound to say all we think but we are bound not even to look what we do not think.

GEORGE MAC DONALD

2604 I saw a man pick up a football once at the Rose Bowl, run 65 yards—and 90,000 people cheered; but he ran the wrong way and lost the game. He was the most sincere man I think I have ever seen. I had him right in my field glasses. Boy, he had sincerity on his face as he went down that field. But he was wrong.

BILLY GRAHAM

2605 Sincerity is the highest compliment you can pay. Jones Very charmed us all by telling us he hated us all.

RALPH WALDO EMERSON

2606 The sincere alone can recognize sincerity.

THOMAS CARLYLE

2607 *To Romain Rolland:*
I take it that in your day, as now, people talked with terrible facility about sincerity—especially their own. In *Jean Christophe* you wrote: "Least of all could he forgive her lack of sincerity. He did not know that sincerity is a gift as rare as intelligence or beauty and that it cannot justly be expected of everybody." I hear people saying ever so casually: "I don't pretend to be a saint, but at least I'm sincere." You were right: sincerity is a gift as rare as intelligence or beauty, but every cheap jack supposes that he has barrels of it to spare. And sometimes it is found in lunatics. Henry Mencken once reminded us that the man who shot McKinley was undoubtedly sincere. So: we may find sincerity in the fanatic, crank, or monomaniac. We always find it in the saint. And in whom else?

CARROLL E. SIMCOX

SOCIAL JUSTICE

2608 What mean ye that ye beat my people to pieces, and grind the faces of the poor? saith the Lord God of hosts.

Isaiah 3:15

2609 Disbelief in Christianity is not so much to be dreaded as its acceptance with a complete denial of it in society and politics.

MARK RUTHERFORD

2610 Ill fares the land, to hastening ills a prey,
Where wealth accumulates, and men decay.

OLIVER GOLDSMITH

2611 What is the use of belonging to an empire on which the sun never sets if one has to live in an alley on which the sun never rises?

Anonymous

2612 Anticipate charity by preventing

poverty; assist the reduced fellow-man, either by a considerable gift, or a sum of money, or by teaching him a trade, or by putting him in the way of business, so that he may earn an honest livelihood, and not be forced to the dreadful alternative of holding out his hand for charity. This is the highest step and the summit of charity's golden ladder.

MOSES MAIMONIDES

2613 Almighty God, who hast created man in thine own image; grant us grace fearlessly to contend against evil, and to make no peace with oppression; and, that we may reverently use our freedom, help us to employ it in the maintenance of justice among men and nations, to the glory of thy holy Name; through Jesus Christ our Lord.

Book of Common Prayer

STEWARDSHIP

2614 The two things which, of all others, most want to be under a strict rule, and which are the greatest blessings to ourselves and to others, when they are rightly used, are our time and our money.

WILLIAM LAW

2615 Entirely too much has been said in most churches about the stewardship of money and too little about the stewardship of power. The modern equivalent of repentance is the responsible use of power.

HARVEY COX

2616 You remember that among the Franks whole armies were some-times given baptism at one stroke, and many warriors went into the water with their right hands held high, so that they did not get wet. Then they could say, "This hand has never been baptized," and they could swing their battle axes just as freely as ever. The modern counter-part of that partial baptism is seen in many people who have been baptized, all except their pocket-books. They hold these high out of the water.

HALFORD E. LUCCOCK

Stewardship is what a man does 2617 after he says "I believe."

W.H. GREEVER

SUFFERING

(See *Adversity*)

Suffering passes, but the fact of 2618 having suffered never leaves us.

LÉON BLOY

The tragedy of life is not so much 2619 what men suffer, but rather what they miss.

THOMAS CARLYLE

How little it takes to make life 2620 unbearable: a pebble in the shoe, a cockroach in the spaghetti, a woman's laugh.

HENRY L. MENCKEN

It requires more courage to suffer 2621 than to die.

NAPOLEON BUONAPARTE

It is a glorious thing to be indif- 2622

ferent to suffering, but only to one's own suffering.

ROBERT LYND

2623 The best prayers have often more groans than words.

JOHN BUNYAN

2624 The chief pang of most trials is not so much the actual suffering itself as our own spirit of resistance to it.

JEAN NICOLAS GROU

2625 Unearned suffering is redemptive.

MARTIN LUTHER KING, JR.

2626 Let us be thankful that our sorrow lives in us as an indestructible force, only changing in form, as forces do, and passing from pain to sympathy. To have suffered much is like knowing many languages. Thou hast learned to understand all.

GEORGE ELIOT

2627 It is not ignoble to feel that the fuller life which a sad experience has brought us is worth our own personal share of pain. The growth of higher feeling within us is like the growth of faculty, bringing with it a sense of added strength. We can no more wish to return to a narrower sympathy than a painter or a musician can wish to return to his cruder manner, or a philosopher to his less complete formula.

GEORGE ELIOT

2628 In sick-rooms, in prisons, in dreary, unsympathetic homes, in stores where failure brooded like the first haze of a coming eastern storm, everywhere men have suffered, to some among the sufferers this truth has come. They lifted their heads up and were strong. Life was a new

thing to them. They were no longer the victims of a mistaking chance or of a malignant devil, but the subjects of an educating God.

PHILLIPS BROOKS

SYMPATHY

Then I came to them of the captivity 2629 at Tel-abib, that dwelt by the river Chebar, and I sat where they sat, and remained there astonished among them seven days.

Ezekiel 3:15

Of John Woolman as of Shelley it 2630 might well be said, "He was as a nerve o'er which do creep the else unfelt oppressions of the earth."

VIDA SCUDDER

Sympathy is your pain in my heart. 2631
Anonymous child

Next to love, sympathy is the divin- 2632 est passion of the human heart.

EDMUND BURKE

TEMPERANCE

No man ever repented that he arose 2633 from the table sober, healthful, and with his wits about him.

JEREMY TAYLOR

By his restrictions the master pro- 2634 claims himself.

JOHANN WOLFGANG VON GOETHE

Let nothing be lost, said our Sav- 2635 iour. But that is lost that is misused.

WILLIAM PENN

2636 Put a knife to thy throat, if thou be a man given to appetite.
Proverbs 23:2

2637 Every man that striveth for the mastery is temperate in all things.
I Corinthians 9:25

2638 Abstinence makes the heart grow clearer.
Anonymous

2639 Temperate temperance is best; intemperate temperance injures the cause of temperance.
MARK TWAIN

2640 To go beyond the bounds of moderation is to outrage humanity.
BLAISE PASCAL

2641 Complete abstinence is easier than perfect moderation.
AUGUSTINE OF HIPPO

2642 Temperance and labor are the two best physicians of men.
JEAN JACQUES ROUSSEAU

THANKSGIVING

2643 We bless thee for our creation, preservation, and all the blessings of this life; but above all, for thine inestimable love in the redemption of the world by our Lord Jesus Christ; for the means of grace, and for the hope of glory.
Book of Common Prayer

2644 I own that I am disposed to say grace upon twenty other occasions in the course of the day besides my dinner. I want a form for setting out upon a pleasant walk, for a moonlight ramble, for a friendly meeting, or a solved problem. Why have we none for books, those spiritual repasts—a grace before Milton—a grace before Shakespeare—a devotional exercise proper to be said before reading the Fairy Queen?
CHARLES LAMB

2645 It is probable that in most of us the spiritual life is impoverished and stunted because we give so little place to gratitude. It is more important to thank God for blessings received than to pray for them beforehand. For that forward-looking prayer, though right as an expression of dependence upon God, is still self-centered in part, at least, of its interest; there is something we hope to gain by our prayer. But the backward-looking act of thanksgiving is quite free from this. In itself it is quite selfless. Thus it is akin to love. All our love to God is in response to his love for us; it never starts on our side. "We love, because he first loved us" (I John 4:19).
WILLIAM TEMPLE

2646 Jan Struthers died a few years ago. Since then, attention has been given to a little poem which she had written, and which was read at her funeral. It not only reveals a rare spirit, but also has a bright light to throw on all of life. Here is the verse:

One day my life will end; and lest
Some whim should prompt you to review it,
Let her who knew the subject best
Tell you the shortest way to do it:
Then say: "Here lies one doubly blest."

Say: "She was happy." Say: "She knew it."

That is the sharp point—*"she knew it."* So many people who have so many of the materials of happiness do not *know* it! Instead of really knowing their happiness and being grateful for it, their eyes are roving over the fence to the seemingly greener grass far away. The spirit of thankfulness will help one to know this happiness and save life from being one long-drawn-out sigh.

HALFORD E. LUCCOCK

UNDERSTANDING

2647 I am the master of everything I can explain.

THEODOR HAECKER

2648 To understand oneself is the classic form of consolation; to elude oneself is the romantic.

GEORGE SANTAYANA

2649 If the cultivation of the understanding consists in one thing more than another, it is surely in learning the ground of one's own opinions.

JOHN STUART MILL

2650 Wisdom is the principal thing; therefore get wisdom: and with all thy getting get understanding.

Proverbs 4:7

2651 To put it briefly, the holy things of God cannot truly be laid hold of except by holy persons; and holiness is the result of both divine grace and self-discipline. Both are requisite for the successful theologian.

FRANCIS J. HALL

Understanding is a two-way street.   2652

ELEANOR ROOSEVELT

VOCATION

It is not society's fault that most   2653
men seem to miss their vocation.

GEORGE SANTAYANA

The test of a vocation is the love of   2654
the drudgery it involves.

LOGAN PEARSALL SMITH

Blessed is he who has found his   2655
work; let him ask no other blessedness.

THOMAS CARLYLE

If we find the job where we can be   2656
of use, we are hitched to the star of
the world and move with it.

RICHARD CABOT

We must not forget that our voca-   2657
tion is so to practice virtue that men
are won to it; it is possible to be
morally upright repulsively.

WILLIAM TEMPLE

The vocation of every man and   2658
woman is to serve other people.

LEO TOLSTOY

No human being is meant to be a   2659
carbon copy, a double, an understudy, a *Doppelgänger*, a shadow.
Each must be his own man, much as
this may mean resembling someone
else's. This is not egocentricity or
independence of the herd. It is the
incommunicable response to the
particular summons of God.

HUBERT VAN ZELLER

WISDOM

2660 Wisdom is a loving spirit.
Wisdom of Solomon 1:6

2661 Wisdom is the right use of knowledge. To know is not to be wise. Many men know a great deal, and are all the greater fools for it. There is no fool so great a fool as the knowing fool. But to know how to use knowledge is to have wisdom.
CHARLES H. SPURGEON

2662 Knowledge comes, but wisdom lingers.
ALFRED, LORD TENNYSON

2663 The art of being wise is the art of knowing what to overlook.
WILLIAM JAMES

2664 Nine-tenths of wisdom consists of being wise in time.
THEODORE ROOSEVELT

2665 Wisdom is ofttimes nearer when we stoop than when we soar.
WILLIAM WORDSWORTH

2666 The older I grow the more I distrust the familiar doctrine that age brings wisdom.
HENRY L. MENCKEN

2667 It is easier to be wise for others than for ourselves.
FRANÇOIS DE LA ROCHEFOUCAULD

2668 The only one who is wiser than anyone is everyone.
NAPOLEON BUONAPARTE

2669 The first key to wisdom is assiduous and frequent questioning. For by doubting we come to inquiry, and by inquiry we arrive at truth.
PETER ABÉLARD

2670 Common sense in an uncommon degree is what the world calls wisdom.
SAMUEL TAYLOR COLERIDGE

2671 A man doesn't begin to attain wisdom until he recognizes that he is no longer indispensable.
RICHARD E. BYRD

2672 The good Lord set definite limits on man's wisdom, but set no limits on his stupidity—and that's just not fair!
KONRAD ADENAUER

2673 Every day I hear stupid people saying things that are not stupid.
MICHEL DE MONTAIGNE

2674 The whole secret of remaining young in spite of years, and even of gray hairs, is to cherish enthusiasm in oneself, by poetry, by contemplation, by charity—that is, in fewer words, by the maintenance of harmony in the soul. When everything is in its right place within us, we ourselves are in equilibrium with the whole work of God. Deep and grave enthusiasm for the eternal beauty and the eternal order, reason touched with emotion and a serene tenderness of heart—these surely are the foundations of wisdom.
HENRI FRÉDÉRIC AMIEL

2675 I said, Days should speak, and multitude of years should teach wisdom. But there is a spirit in man: and the inspiration of the Almighty giveth them understanding. Great men are not always wise: neither do the aged understand judgment.

Job 32:7–9

WORK

2676 God give me work
Till my life shall end
    And life
Till my work is done.
WINIFRED HOLTBY, *her epitaph*

2677 When we cannot love our work, let us think of it as thy task, and by our true love to thee make unlovely things shine in the light of thy great love, through Jesus Christ our Lord.
GEORGE DAWSON

2678 To do great work a man must be very idle as well as very industrious.
SAMUEL BUTLER

2679 Nothing is really work unless you would rather be doing something else.
JAMES M. BARRIE

2680 Work is love made visible.
KAHLIL GIBRAN

2681 I like work; it fascinates me. I can sit and look at it for hours.
JEROME K. JEROME

2682 The world is filled with willing people; some willing to work, the rest willing to let them.
ROBERT FROST

2683 The work an unknown good man has done is like a vein of water flowing hidden underground, making the ground green.
THOMAS CARLYLE

Excellence is never granted to man, 2684 but as the reward of labor. It argues, indeed, no small strength of mind to persevere in the habits of industry, without the pleasure of perceiving those advantages which, like the hands of a clock, whilst they make hourly approaches to their point, yet proceed so slowly as to escape observation.
JOSHUA REYNOLDS

The man who rolls up his shirt 2685 sleeves is rarely in danger of losing his shirt.
Anonymous

Genius may conceive, but patient 2686 labor must consummate.
HORACE MANN

Work is the curse of the drinking 2687 classes.
Anonymous

I go on working for the same reason 2688 that a hen goes on laying eggs.
HENRY L. MENCKEN

My father taught me to work, but 2689 not to love it. I never did like to work, and I don't deny it. I'd rather read, tell stories, crack jokes, talk, laugh—anything but work.
ABRAHAM LINCOLN

Happiness, I have discovered, is 2690 nearly always a rebound from hard work.
DAVID GRAYSON

ZEAL

Zeal dropped in charity is good, 2691 without it good for nothing: for it devours all it comes near.

WILLIAM PENN

2692 Dear Crito, your zeal is invaluable, if a right one; but if wrong, the greater the zeal the greater the danger.

SOCRATES

2693 And if you will here stop and ask yourself, why you are not as pious as the primitive Christians were, your own heart will tell you, that it is neither through ignorance, nor inability, but purely because you never thoroughly intended it.

WILLIAM LAW

2694 We are sometimes moved by passion and suppose it zeal.

THOMAS À KEMPIS

It is good to be zealously affected always in a good thing.   2695

Galatians 4:18

Never let your zeal outrun your charity. The former is but human, the latter is divine.   2696

HOSEA BALLOU

The greatest dangers to liberty lurk in insidious encroachment by men of zeal, well-meaning, but without understanding.   2697

LOUIS D. BRANDEIS

The greater state of love is zeal of love, which runs out into excrescences like a fruitful and pleasant tree; or bursting into gums, and producing fruits, not of a monstrous, but of an extraordinary and heroical greatness.   2698

JEREMY TAYLOR

VI

The End

Then cometh the end, when he shall have delivered up the kingdom to God, even the Father; when he shall have put down all rule and all authority and power.

I Corinthians 15:24

Then said Mr. Valiant-for-truth, "I am going to my Father's; and though with great difficulty I am got hither, yet now I do not repent me of all the trouble I have been at to arrive where I am. My sword I give to him that shall succeed me in my pilgrimage, and my courage and skill to him that can get it. My marks and scars I carry with me, to be a witness for me that I have fought His battles who now will be my rewarder." When the day that he must go hence was come, many accompanied him to the riverside, into which as he went he said, "Death, where is thy sting?" And as he went down deeper, he said, "Grave, where is thy victory?" So he passed over, and all the trumpets sounded for him on the other side.

John Bunyan

BEREAVEMENT

2699 Our attitude to all men would be Christian if we regarded them as though they were dying, and determined our relation to them in the light of death, both of their death and of our own. A person who is dying calls forth a special kind of feeling. Our attitude to him is at once softened and lifted on to a higher plane. We then can feel compassion for people whom we did not love. But every man is dying, I too am dying and must never forget about death.

NICOLAS BERDYAEV

2700 Each of us bears in his soul as it were a little graveyard of those whom he has loved. They sleep there, through the years, untroubled. But a day cometh,—this we know,—when the graves shall reopen. The dead issue from the tomb and smile with their pale lips—loving, always—on the beloved, and the lover, in whose breast their memory dwells, like the child sleeping in the mother's womb.

ROMAIN ROLLAND

2701 Strange that I did not know him then,
　　That friend of mine!
I did not even show him then
　　One friendly sign;

But cùrsed him for the ways he had
　　To make me see
My envy of the praise he had
　　For praising me.

I would have rid the earth of him
　　Once in my pride. . . .
I never knew the worth of him
　　Until he died.

EDWIN ARLINGTON ROBINSON

But, oh, for the touch of a vanished 2702 hand,
And the sound of a voice that is still!

ALFRED, LORD TENNYSON

Now he is dead, wherefore should I 2703 fast? can I bring him back again? I shall go to him, but he shall not return to me.

II Samuel 12:23

Half the interest of my life seems to 2704 have gone when I cannot look forward any more to his dear voice of welcome or to the letters which were my greatest happiness. For now there is no one to venerate, no one to work for, or to think about while working. I always knew that I was leaning on these feelings too much, but I could not try to prevent them; and so at last I am left with a loneliness that can never be filled.

GEORGE ROMANES,
after the death of Charles Darwin

It is very sad to lose your child just 2705 when he was beginning to bind himself to you; and I don't know that it is much consolation to reflect that the longer he had wound himself up in your heartstrings, the worse the tear would have been, which seems to have been inevitable sooner or later. One does not weigh and measure these things while grief is fresh, and in my experience a deep plunge into the waters of sorrow is the hopefullest way of getting through them on one's daily road of life again. No one can help another very much in these crises of life; but love and sympathy count for something.

THOMAS HENRY HUXLEY

2706 Sorrow makes us all children again, destroys all differences of intellect.
RALPH WALDO EMERSON

2707 And the king was much moved, and went up to the chamber over the gate, and wept: and as he went, thus he said, O my son Absalom, my son, my son Absalom! would God I had died for thee, O Absalom, my son, my son!
II Samuel 18:33

2708 Blessed are they that mourn; for they shall be comforted.
Matthew 5:4

2709 'Tis only when they spring to heaven that angels
Reveal themselves to you; they sit all day
Beside you, and lie down at night by you
Who care not for their presence, muse or sleep,
And all at once they leave you, and you know them!
ROBERT BROWNING

2710 He has out-soared the shadow of our night;
Envy and calumny and hate and pain,
And that unrest which men miscall delight,
Can touch him not and torture not again;
From the contagion of the world's slow stain
He is secure, and now can never mourn
A heart grown cold, a head grown grey in vain.
PERCY BYSSHE SHELLEY

2711 Depart, O Christian soul, out of this world,

In the Name of God the Father Almighty who created thee.
In the Name of Jesus Christ who redeemed thee.
In the Name of the Holy Ghost who sanctifieth thee.
May thy rest be this day in peace, and thy dwelling-place in the paradise of God.
Book of Common Prayer

COMMUNION OF SAINTS

The union of men with God is the   *2712*
union of men with one another.
THOMAS AQUINAS

God forbid that in a higher state of   *2713*
existence she should cease to think of me, to long to comfort me, she who loved more than words can tell.
AUGUSTINE OF HIPPO, *of his mother*

There is   *2714*
One great society alone on earth:
The noble Living and the noble Dead.
WILLIAM WORDSWORTH

May I gently suggest that all of us   *2715*
need to update our image of our own beloved dead? If we have ever found ourselves thinking, or even saying: "*Now* she understands"; "*Now* he'll know it all," then we are on the right track. For we are groping after the conviction that the dead are truly alive, and moving with us into the future but with much clearer eyes. If we think of them in the biblical image as "a cloud of witnesses," they are not just

spectators from a distance of one, ten, fifty, or four hundred years; they are contemporaries cheering us on. We sing their songs, and they are singing ours. And in our efforts to steer the right course, to win through to the fulfilment God has planned for us, their vote is being cast all the time on the side of love, of courage, of hope, of justice, of integrity and faith.

DAVID H.C. READ

2716   O blest communion, fellowship divine!
　　We feebly struggle, they in glory shine;
　　Yet all are one in thee, for all are thine.

WILLIAM WALSHAM HOW

2717   My grandfather, I'm told, used to say that he "looked forward to having some very interesting conversations with St. Paul when he got to heaven." Two clerical gentlemen talking at ease in a club! It never seemed to cross his mind that an encounter with St. Paul might be rather an overwhelming experience even for an Evangelical clergyman of good family. But when Dante saw the great apostles in heaven they affected him like *mountains.* There's lots to be said against devotions to saints; but at least they keep on reminding us that we are very small people compared to them. How much smaller before their Master?

C.S. LEWIS

2718   So part we sweetly in this troublous world
　　To meet with joy in sweet Jerusalem.

WILLIAM SHAKESPEARE

To him that is joined to all the living there is hope.   2719

Ecclesiastes 9:4

They that love beyond the world cannot be separated by it. Death is but a crossing the world, as friends do the seas; they live in one another still.   2720

WILLIAM PENN

Humanity is one in Christ, men are branches of one vine, members of one body. The life of each man enlarges itself infinitely into the life of others, the communion of saints, and each man in the church lives the life of all men in the church; each man is humanity. He belongs not only to that part of humanity which, living on earth at the moment, stands before God in prayer and labor, for the present generation is only a page in the book of life. In God and in his church there is no difference between living and dead, and all are one in the love of the Father. Even the generations yet to be born are part of this one divine humanity.   2721

SERGIUS BULGAKOV

DEATH

The souls of the righteous are in the hand of God, and there shall no torment touch them.   2722.
In the sight of the unwise they seemed to die: and their departure is taken for misery,
And their going from us to be utter destruction: but they are in peace.
For though they be punished in the

sight of men, yet is their hope full of immortality.

And having been a little chastised, they shall be greatly rewarded: for God proved them, and found them worthy for himself.

Wisdom of Solomon 3:1–5

2723   Rejoice not over thy greatest enemy being dead, but remember that we die all.

Ecclesiasticus 8:7

2724   The last enemy that shall be destroyed is death.

I Corinthians 15:26

2725   This reasonable moderator, and equal piece of justice, death.

THOMAS BROWNE

2726   We all labor against our own cure, for death is the cure of all diseases.

THOMAS BROWNE

2727   The event of death is always astounding; our philosophy never reaches, never possesses it; we are always at the beginning of our catechism; always the definition is yet to be made. What is death?

RALPH WALDO EMERSON

2728   Life levels all men: death reveals the eminent.

GEORGE BERNARD SHAW

2729   There the wicked cease from troubling; and there the weary be at rest.

Job 3:17

2730   Death is the side of life which is turned away from us.

RAINER MARIA RILKE

2731   I would let death seize upon me while I am tending my cabbages.

MICHEL DE MONTAIGNE

Death, be not proud, though some   2732
have called thee
Mighty and dreadful, for thou art
not so,
For those whom thou think'st thou
dost overthrow,
Die not, poor death, nor yet canst
thou kill me.

JOHN DONNE

I came from God, and I'm going   2733
back to God, and I won't have any
gaps of death in the middle of my
life.

GEORGE MAC DONALD

You will be dead so long as you   2734
refuse to die.

GEORGE MAC DONALD

I depart from life as from an inn,   2735
and not as from my home.

MARCUS TULLIUS CICERO

Men fear death as children fear to   2736
go in the dark; and as that natural
fear in children is increased with
tales, so is the other.

FRANCIS BACON

There is a moment in every man's   2737
life when he has to make ready for a
departure, and at last the moment
comes for him to leave his earthly
home, and to give an account of his
labor. May every one of us then be
able to say: I have not darkened
immortal souls with suspicion or
fear, I have been frank, loyal and
trustful; I have looked those who
did not share my ideals straight in
the eyes and treated them with
brotherly affection, in order not to
impede the carrying out of God's
great purpose, in his good time—a
purpose which must bring about the
fulfilment of the divine teaching and

command of Jesus, "that we may all be one."

POPE JOHN XXIII

2738 Let me die the death of the righteous, and let my last end be like his!

Numbers 23:10

2739 Yea, though I walk through the valley of the shadow of death, I will fear no evil: for thou art with me.

Psalm 23:4

2740 Precious in the sight of the Lord is the death of his saints.

Psalm 116:15 (AV)

2741 He will swallow up death in victory; and the Lord God will wipe away tears from off all faces.

Isaiah 25:8

2742 Lord, now lettest thou thy servant depart in peace, according to thy word.

Luke 2:29

Next to the Blessed Sacrament itself, your neighbor is the holiest object presented to your senses. If he is your Christian neighbor he is holy in almost the same way, for in him also Christ *vere latitat*—the glorifier and the glorified, Glory Himself, is truly hidden. 2746

C.S. LEWIS

May God deny you peace, but give you glory! 2747

MIGUEL DE UNAMUNO

If ye be reproached for the name of Christ, happy are ye; for the spirit of glory and of God resteth upon you. 2748

I Peter 4:14

Christ in you, the hope of glory. 2749

Colossians 1:27

When Christ, who is our life, shall appear, then shall ye also appear with him in glory. 2750

Colossians 3:4

GLORY

2743 Grace is but glory begun, and glory is but grace perfected.

JONATHAN EDWARDS

2744 We thank thee . . . for the means of grace, and for the hope of glory.

Book of Common Prayer

2745 And the Word was made flesh, and dwelt among us, and we beheld his glory, the glory as of the only begotten of the Father, full of grace and truth.

John 1:14

HEAVEN AND HELL

Heaven is God and God is in my soul. 2751

ELISABETH DE LA TRINITÉ

Heaven is under our feet as well as over our heads. 2752

HENRY DAVID THOREAU

Happiness in heaven means that evey man can do what he wills because he has perfect love. In this aeon, certainly, there is no man who is not horror-stricken at the thought that men do what they will. For nowadays such men exist—but they 2753 pride themselves upon being good haters.

THEODOR HAECKER

2754 Heaven proceeds forever *from* me outward to all things, and not *to* me from coffee and custard.

RALPH WALDO EMERSON

2755 In the future life we'll have enjoyment of every kind and the whole earth will be adorned with many trees and all things that are pleasant to look at. If we have our Lord God we'll have enough. We'll be children of God.

MARTIN LUTHER

2756 Heaven is not to be looked upon only as the reward, but as the natural effect, of a religious life.

JOSEPH ADDISON

2757 To my friend, in recollection of his son, and my son, who, by the grace of God, have the privilege of being boys throughout eternity.

CALVIN COOLIDGE,
*his inscription in a friend's book after
the death of Calvin Coolidge, Jr.*

2758 Since I am coming to that holy room,
Where with thy choir of saints forevermore,
I shall be made thy music; as I come
I tune the instrument here at the door
And what I must do then, think here before.

JOHN DONNE

2759 All the way to heaven is heaven.

CATHERINE OF SIENA

2760 How far away is heaven? It is not so far as some imagine. It wasn't very far from Daniel. It was not so far off that Elijah's prayer, and those of others could not be heard there. Christ said when ye pray say, "Our Father, who art in heaven." Men full of the Spirit can look right into heaven.

DWIGHT L. MOODY

2761 On earth there is no heaven, but there are pieces of it.

JULES RENARD

2762 The main object of religion is not to get a man into heaven, but to get heaven into him.

THOMAS HARDY

2763 One day, in my despair, I threw myself into a chair in the consulting-room and groaned out: "What a blockhead I was to come out here to doctor savages like these!" Whereupon Joseph quietly remarked: "Yes, Doctor, here on earth you are a great blockhead, but not in heaven."

ALBERT SCHWEITZER

2764 For the only air of the soul, in which it can breathe and live, is the present God and the spirits of the just: that is our heaven, our home, our all-right place . . . We shall be God's children on the little hills and in the fields of that heaven, not one desiring to be before another any more than to cast that other' out; for ambition and hatred will then be seen to be one and the same spirit.

GEORGE MAC DONALD

2765 Eternal form shall still divide
The eternal soul from all beside,
And I shall know him when we meet.

ALFRED, LORD TENNYSON

2766 Let us think much of rest,—the rest which is not of indolence, but of powers in perfect equilibrium. The rest which is as deep as summer midnight, yet full of life and force as summer sunshine, the sabbath of Eternity. Let us think of the love of God, which we shall feel in its full tide upon our souls. Let us think of that marvelous career of sublime occupation which shall belong to the spirits of just men made perfect; when we shall fill a higher place in God's universe, and more consciously, and with more distinct insight, co-operate with God in the rule over his creation.

FREDERICK W. ROBERTSON

2767 If you insist on having your own way, you will get it. Hell is the enjoyment of your own way forever. If you really want God's way with you, you will get it in Heaven, and the pains of Purgatory will not deter you, they will be welcomed as means to that end.

DANTE ALIGHIERI

2768 When the world dissolves, all places will be hell that are not heaven.

CHRISTOPHER MARLOWE

2769 Hell is truth seen too late—duty neglected in its season.

TRYON EDWARDS

2770 Men are not in Hell because God is angry with them: they are in wrath and darkness because they have done to the light which infinitely flows forth from God as that man does to the light of the sun who puts out his own eyes.

WILLIAM LAW

2771 Are there not, however, many passages in the New Testament which speak of the endless torment of the lost? No; as far as my knowledge goes there is none at all. There are sayings which speak of being cast into undying fire. But if we do not approach these with the presupposition that what is thus cast in is indestructible, we shall get the impression, not that it will burn for ever, but that it will be destroyed.

WILLIAM TEMPLE

Annihilation is an everlasting punishment, though it is not unending torment.   2772

WILLIAM TEMPLE

The hell to be endured hereafter, of 2773 which theology tells, is no worse than the hell we make for ourselves in this world by habitually fashioning our characters in the wrong way.

WILLIAM JAMES

We make a great mistake if we 2774 connect with our conception of heaven the thought of rest from work. Rest from toil, from weariness, from exhaustion—yes; rest from work, from productiveness, from service—no. That abundant and increasing vitality of spirit and of body which is poured into the saints from the glorified Christ, that life from the very source of life, is not to be spent in idle harping upon harps of gold, reclining on clouds, or wandering aimlessly through the paradise of God, clad in white robes and with crowned heads. These apocalyptic pictures are symbols of a bliss which passes words; but there is another side to the picture, which is too often forgotten in our anticipations of the life to come.

"They rest not day and night";
"they serve God day and night";
"his servants shall do him service."
B.F. WESTCOTT

2775 I ponder "What is hell?" I maintain it is the suffering of not being able to love.
FYODOR DOSTOEVSKY

2776 When we preach on hell, we might at least do it with tears in our eyes.
DWIGHT L. MOODY

2777 In thy presence is fulness of joy; at thy right hand there are pleasures for evermore.
Psalm 16:11 (AV)

2778 Thine eyes shall see the king in his beauty: they shall behold the land that is very far off.
Isaiah 33:17

2779 In my Father's house are many mansions.
John 14:2

2780 Here we have no continuing city, but we seek one to come.
Hebrews 13:14

2781 We, according to his promise, look for new heavens and a new earth, wherein dwelleth righteousness.
II Peter 3:13

2782 God shall wipe away all tears from their eyes; and there shall be no more death, neither sorrow, nor crying, neither shall there be any more pain: for the former things are passed away.
Revelation 21:4

IMMORTALITY

Winter is on my head but eternal spring is in my heart. The nearer I approach the end, the plainer I hear around me the immortal symphonies of the world to come. For half a century I have been writing my thoughts in prose and verse; but I feel that I have not said one-thousandth part of what is in me. When I have gone down to the grave I shall have ended my day's work; but another day will begin the next morning. Life closes in the twilight but opens with the dawn. 2783
VICTOR HUGO

Our dissatisfaction with any other solution is the blazing evidence of immortality. 2784
RALPH WALDO EMERSON

The seed dies into a new life, and so does man. 2785
GEORGE MAC DONALD

No young man believes he shall ever die. 2786
WILLIAM HAZLITT

If individuals live only seventy years, then a state, or a nation, or a civilization, which may last for a thousand years, is more important than an individual. But if Christianity is true, then the individual is not only more important but incomparably more important, for he is everlasting and the life of a state or a civilization, compared with his, is only a moment. 2787
C.S. LEWIS

What is our life but a succession of preludes to that unknown song 2788

whose first solemn note is sounded
by Death?

ALPHONSE DE LAMARTINE

2789 Those who hope for no other life are
dead even for this.

JOHANN WOLFGANG VON GOETHE

2790 The average man does not know
what to do with this life, yet wants
another one that will last forever.

ANATOLE FRANCE

2791 Immortality is the glorious discovery of Christianity.

WILLIAM ELLERY CHANNING

2792 Surely God would not have created
such a being as man, with an ability
to grasp the infinite, to exist only for
a day. No, no, man was made for
immortality.

ABRAHAM LINCOLN

2793 Life is the childhood of immortality.

DANIEL A. POLING

2794 Divine Wisdom, intending to detain
us some time on earth, has done
well to cover with a veil the prospect
of the life to come; for if our sight
could clearly distinguish the opposite bank, who would remain on this
tempestuous coast of time?

MME. GERMAINE NECKER DE STAËL

2795 I have never seen what to me
seemed an atom of proof that there
is a future life. And yet—I am
strongly inclined to expect one.

MARK TWAIN

2796 There is, I know not how, in the
minds of men, a certain presage, as
it were, of a future existence; and
this takes the deepest root, and is

most discoverable, in the greatest
geniuses and most exalted souls.

MARCUS TULLIUS CICERO

You must know that I should not 2797
love you half so well, if I did not
believe you would be my friend to
eternity. There is not room enough
for friendship to unfold itself in such
a nook of life as this.

WILLIAM COWPER,
in a letter to Lady Hesketh

I loved you, Evelyn, all the while! 2798
    My heart seemed full as it
could hold;
There was place and to spare for the
    frank young smile,
    And the red young mouth, and
the hair's young gold.
So hush,—I will give you this leaf to
    keep:
    See, I shut it inside the sweet
cold hand!
There, that is our secret: go to sleep!
    You will wake, and remember,
and understand.

ROBERT BROWNING

Here in this world He bids us come, 2799
there in the next He shall bid us
welcome.

JOHN DONNE

I am used to this body, Lord, 2800
    even though it depreciates
every year.
How could I play a harp
    or shovel coal without it?
What could I possibly do
    for an eternity
        without fingers or eyes or
legs?
If there is spiritual work,
    teach me how to do it now.
. . . .

You will have to learn
    how to use spiritual tools:
      love,
        patience,
          and laughter.
ROBERT HALE

2801 Your heart shall live for ever.
Psalm 22:26

2802 Fear not them which kill the body, but are not able to kill the soul.
Matthew 10:28

2803 I am the resurrection, and the life: he that believeth in me, though he were dead, yet shall he live: and whosoever liveth and believeth in me shall never die.
John 11:25–26

2804 This corruptible must put on incorruption, and this mortal must put on immortality.
I Corinthians 15:53

JUDGMENT

2805 Every man's work shall be made manifest: for the day shall declare it, because it shall be revealed by fire; and the fire shall try every man's work of what sort it is.
I Corinthians 3:13

2806 Only our concept of time makes it possible for us to speak of the Day of Judgment by that name; in reality it is a summary court in perpetual session.
FRANZ KAFKA

2807 Those consequences which follow from our actions or characters by the operation of God's laws are his judgments upon us.
WILLIAM TEMPLE

There ain't no throne, and there 2808
ain't no books,
    It's 'Im you've got to see;
      It's 'Im, just 'Im, as is the judge
    Of blokes like you and me.
      And boys, I'd rather frizzle up
    In the flames of a burning 'ell
Than stand and look into 'Is face
And 'ear 'Is voice say, "Well?"
G.A. STUDDERT-KENNEDY

For judgment I am come into this 2809
world.
John 9:39

Nay, even to the true servants of 2810
Christ, the prospect is awful. "The righteous," we are told, "will scarcely be saved" (I Peter 4:8). Then will the good man undergo the full sight of his sins, which on earth he was laboring to obtain, and partly succeeded in obtaining, though life was not long enough to learn and subdue them all. Doubtless we must all endure that fierce and terrifying vision of our real selves, that last fiery trial of the soul (I Cor. 3:13) before its acceptance, a spiritual agony and second death to all who are not then supported by the strength of him who died to bring them safe through it, and in whom on earth they have believed.
JOHN HENRY NEWMAN

Behold, I come quickly; and my 2811
reward is with me, to give every man according as his work shall be.
Revelation 22:12

LAST WORDS

2812 See in what peace a Christian can die!

JOSEPH ADDISON

2813 Beautiful!

ELIZABETH BARRETT BROWNING

2814 So this is death—well . . .

THOMAS CARLYLE

2815 I know now that patriotism is not enough; I must have no hatred and no bitterness toward anyone.

EDITH CAVELL, *English nurse, executed by Germans in World War I*

2816 The issue is now clear. It is between light and darkness and everyone must choose his side.

GILBERT KEITH CHESTERTON

2817 Glory to God for all things!

JOHN CHRYSOSTOM

2818 It is very beautiful over there.

THOMAS A. EDISON

2819 I see Mother.

CHARLES W. ELIOT

2820 Welcome, Sister Death!

FRANCIS OF ASSISI

2821 Shall not the Judge of all the earth do right?

JAMES ANTHONY FROUDE

2822 Amen.

WILLIAM E. GLADSTONE

2823 More light!

JOHANN WOLFGANG VON GOETHE

2824 May God forgive him! I want him in heaven.

MARIA GORETTI, *11, fatally stabbed while resisting the advances of a 19-year-old youth*

2825 I am so happy, I am so happy.

GERARD MANLEY HOPKINS

2826 Let us cross over the river and rest under the shade of the trees!

GENERAL THOMAS "STONEWALL" JACKSON

2827 I stick by Almighty God—He alone is, all else is death. Don't call this dying; I am just entering upon life.

HENRY JAMES, SR.

2828 It is so good to get home.

WILLIAM JAMES

2829 I love you, dear, but the Lord is my Life and my Light.

COVENTRY PATMORE, *embracing his wife*

2830 I love everybody. If ever I had an enemy I should hope to meet and welcome that enemy in heaven.

CHRISTINA ROSSETTI

2831 'Tis well.

GEORGE WASHINGTON

2832 The best of all is this—God is with us.

JOHN WESLEY

LIFE ETERNAL

2833 Eternal life and survival are not the same; and yet they are related to each other. Eternal life is a quality of ultimate reality; survival is a quantitative measure of duration. Eternal life belongs to the conception of reality as a kingdom of values; survival conceives human existence as a page of history.

WILLIAM RALPH INGE

2834 This is life eternal, that they might know thee the only true God, and Jesus Christ, whom thou hast sent.

John 17:3

2835 We know that we have passed from death to life, because we love the brethren.

I John 3:14

2836 Verily, here must the spirit rise to grace, or else neither the body nor it shall there rise to glory.

LANCELOT ANDREWES

2837 There really are two ideas, life which goes on and life which has some quality or value in it which lifts it above time. We might use "everlasting" for the first idea and "eternal" for the second.

W.R. MATTHEWS

2838 Your enjoyment of the world is never right till every morning you awake in Heaven; see yourself in your Father's Palace; and look upon the skies, the earth, and the air, as Celestial Joys: having such a reverend esteem of all, as if you were among the Angels. The bride of a monarch in her husband's chamber, hath no such causes of delight as you.

THOMAS TRAHERNE

2839 The life of faith does not earn eternal life; it is eternal life. And Christ is its vehicle.

WILLIAM TEMPLE

The presentation of the Gospel to 2840 the worldly minded always suffers under this disability, that the world confidently believes it to be something quite different from what it is. It cannot "see" it. . . . So men think of eternal life as the everlasting happiness of a still self-centred soul. But it is nothing of the kind. It is fellowship with God in which our souls, so far as they are self-centred, can find no happiness.

WILLIAM TEMPLE

It is eternity now, I am in the midst 2841 of it. It is about me in the sunshine.

RICHARD JEFFERIES

Just as the wave cannot exist for 2842 itself, but is ever a part of the heaving surface of ocean, so must I never live my life for itself, but always in the experience which is going on around me.

ALBERT SCHWEITZER

I have often wondered at the unac- 2843 countableness of man in this, among other things, that though he loves changes so well, he should care so little to hear or think of his last, great, and best change too, if he pleases. Being, as to our bodies, composed of changeable elements, we, with the world, are made up of, and subsist by revolution: but our souls being of another and nobler nature, we should seek our rest in a more enduring habitation. The truest end of life is to know the life that never ends.

WILLIAM PENN

PARADISE

2844 He said unto Jesus, Lord, remember me when you comest into thy kingdom. And Jesus said unto him, Verily I say unto thee, To day shalt thou be with me in paradise.
Luke 23:42–43

2845 Can there be Paradise for any while there is Hell, conceived as unending torment, for some? Each supposedly damned soul was born into the world as a mother's child, and Paradise cannot be Paradise for her if her child is in such a Hell.
WILLIAM TEMPLE

2846 The souls of Christ's disciples go to the invisible place determined for them by God and there dwell awaiting the Resurrection.
IRENAEUS

2847 I heard a voice from heaven saying unto me, Write, Blessed are the dead which die in the Lord from henceforth: Yea, saith the Spirit, that they may rest from their labors; and their works do follow them.
Revelation 14:13

2848 O Lord, support us all the day long of this troublous life, until the shadows lengthen, and the evening comes, and the busy world is hushed, and the fever of life is over, and our work is done. Then in thy mercy grant us a safe lodging, and a holy rest, and peace at the last forever.
JOHN HENRY NEWMAN

2849 Truly Jerusalem name we that shore,
Vision of peace that brings joy evermore;
Wish and fulfilment can sever'd be ne'er,
Nor the thing prayed for come short of the prayer.

There, where no troubles distraction can bring,
We the sweet anthems of Sion shall sing;
While for thy grace, Lord, their voices of praise
Thy blessed people eternally raise.
PETER ABÉLARD

2850 'Tis sweet, as year by year we lose Friends out of sight, in faith to muse How grows in Paradise our store.
JOHN KEBLE

2851 "Today thou shalt be with me" (Lk. 23:43). Jesus, then, was going that day to paradise. He and the penitent had been together on Golgotha, and would be together in the Garden of the Lord. Jesus at his death went into the state of the dead. "He descended," as the Creed has it, "into Hell"—into Hades, as the Greeks called it, into Sheol, as the old Hebrews would have said. And lo! it was no longer Hell or Sheol, no longer a dark cavernous prison, but a garden, the Garden of happy souls, the Garden of the Lord. It was no longer a prisonhouse from which there was no escape, but the antechamber of heaven, the waiting-place of souls expecting their resurrection. "He went and preached to the spirits in prison" (I Peter 3:19) and converted their prison into a place of liberty and joyful hope.
B.F. WESTCOTT

2852 The Bible tells us only one thing—

only one—about the dead who have passed out of our sight. They are with God. How simple that is! How sufficient it becomes! How cheap and tawdry, as we dwell on it, it makes the guesses and conceits with which men try to make real to themselves what the dead are doing! They are with God. Their occupations are ineffable. No tongue can tell their new, untasted joy. The scenery in the midst of which they live speaks to the spirit with voices which no words born of the senses can describe. But companionship and care,—those are the precious, those are the intelligible things. The dead are with God. O you who miss even today the sound of the familiar voices, the sight of the dear, familiar faces, believe and be more than satisfied with that.

PHILLIPS BROOKS

SECOND COMING

2853 I hope the last day will not be long delayed. The darkness grows thicker around us, and godly servants of the Most High become rarer and more rare. Impiety and licentiousness are rampant throughout the world, and we live like pigs, like wild beasts, devoid of all reason. But a voice will soon be heard thundering forth: "Behold, the bridegroom cometh!" God will not be able to bear this wicked world much longer, but will come, with the dreadful day, and chastise the scorners of his Word.

MARTIN LUTHER

2854 In power the Kingdom was established when Christ was lifted up upon the Cross. From that moment it is true that "He cometh with clouds"; that is present fact. He reigns from the Tree. But not all have eyes to perceive; and the time when "every eye shall see him" is still future, and this is the truth in the expectation of a Return or Second Coming.

WILLIAM TEMPLE

2855 Behold, he cometh with clouds; and every eye shall see him, and they also which pierced him: and all kindreds of the earth shall wail because of him.

Revelation 1:7

2856 The signs of his coming have repeatedly appeared in successive generations—such as wars and rumors of wars, famines, pestilences and earthquakes, and disturbances in the heavens, all indicating the transitoriness of cosmic and human conditions. They show the irreversible progress of this world's things towards their cataclysmic end, but do not determine the date of that end . . . When regarded in the large time perspectives of the divine drama, they signify that it is truly "at hand." This is the thought that Christ meant to write upon our minds in terms never to be obliterated or reduced in admonitory meaning.

FRANCIS J. HALL

2857 Watch ye therefore: for ye know not when the master of the house cometh, at even, or at midnight, or at the cockcrowing, or in the morning: lest coming suddenly he find you sleeping.

Mark 13:35–36

2858 When Christ appears in the clouds he will simply be manifesting a metamorphosis that has been slowly accomplished under his influence in the heart of the mass of mankind.

PIERRE TEILHARD DE CHARDIN

2859 Almighty God, give us grace that we may cast away the works of darkness, and put upon us the armor of light, now in the time of this mortal life, in which thy Son Jesus Christ came to visit us in great humility; that in the last day, when he shall come again in his glorious majesty to judge both the quick and the dead, we may rise to the life immortal, through him who liveth and reigneth with thee and the Holy Ghost, now and ever.

Book of Common Prayer

Good night! good night!
Far flies the light;
But still God's love
Shall flame above,
Making all bright.
Good night! Good night!

Victor Hugo

Indexes

INDEX OF SOURCES

1152; saints 2541; success and failure 1357.

Hofmannsthal, Hugo von friendship 929.

Holland, Josiah Gilbert body and soul 374.

Holmes, Oliver Wendell Bible 64; brotherhood 388; humility 2172; patience 2414; weakness 1404.

Holmes, Oliver Wendell, Jr. action 1820; bigotry 764; change 403; experience 1959; faith 1984; greatness 2067; joy 2233; philosophy 1211; principles 2450; tradition 1794.

Holtby, Winifred work 2676.

Hooker, Richard church 1517; goodness 2037; reverence 299; sacraments 1779; tradition 1802.

Hoover, Herbert war and peace 1384.

Hopkins, Gerard Manley *Creation*; last words 2825.

Hopkins, Mark Jesus 1659; revolution 1299.

Horne, George meditation 2333.

Hough, Lynn Harold atonement 1490; preaching 1747.

Housman, A.E. God and his creation 154; saints 2537.

How, William Walsham communion of saints 2716.

Howe, Edgar W. gluttony 942; home 1020.

Howe, Nathaniel martyrdom 1691.

Hubbard, Elbert criticism 832; gossip 943; laws 1098; optimism and pessimism 1178; sin 1332; success and failure 1363.

Hubbard, Frank McKinney adversity 1839.

Hügel, Friedrich von action 1821; concern 1890; Holy Spirit 185.

Hugh of St. Victor knowledge 1068.

Hugo, Victor Bible 67, *Finis, God,*

happiness 2095, immortality 2783, men and women 502.

Humphrey, Hubert H. law 1101.

Hungarian proverb fall of man 879.

Hunt, Leigh sleep 624.

Hunter, John E. salvation 1792.

Hutchins, Robert Maynard humor 2190.

Huxley, Aldous bigotry 762; Devil 431; experience 1954; good and evil 458; ignorance 1043; Lord's Prayer 1683; music 1177; repentance 2509; self-respect 2563; truth and falsehood 661.

Huxley, Julian S. words 1444.

Huxley, Thomas Henry bereavement 2705; Bible 59; education 864; freedom 1997; goodness 2036; humility 2187; knowledge 1063; morality 2355; religion and morality 2494; rich and poor 1305.

Hyde, William de Witt *Life in the Spirit.*

Hylton, Walter repentance 2517.

Ibn Gabirol, Solomon angels 327; compassion 1884; hate 1003.

Ibn Ezra, Moses hate 1001; leadership 1106.

Ibsen, Henrik love 2319.

Iino, Norimoto conversion 1532.

Inge, William Ralph animals 335; freedom 2000; Gospel 1600; government 959; humor 2200; Jesus 1644; life eternal 2833; tradition 1800.

Ingelow, Jean prayer 239.

Ingersoll, Robert G. men and women 507; nature 552; religion 274.

Irenaeus paradise 2846; salvation 1783.

Irish proverb experience 1957.

Irving, Washington change 410; knowledge 1076.

Keats, John body and soul 377.
Keble, John paradise 2850.
Keller, Helen adversity 1842; God's word 135.
Kelly, Father theology 303.
Kempis, Thomas à adversity 1831; Bible 65; criticism 831; cross 1547, 1548; following Christ 1585; grace 1615; judging others 1050; joy 2231; obedience 2380; opportunity 2389; peace 2419; prudence 2475; simplicity 2597; temptation 1367; zeal 2694.
Kennedy, Edward M. reconciliation 1762.
Kennedy, John F. government 960; revolution 1303.
Kennedy, Robert F. idealism 2204.
Kepler, Johannes patience 2400.
Kettering, Charles F. ignorance 1044; past, present, and future 594.
Keynes, John Maynard money 1163.
Kierkegaard, Søren greatness 2075; prayer 249.
King, Martin Luther, Jr. justice 2268; suffering 2625; violence 1376.
Kingsley, Charles action 1818; dissatisfaction 1936; freedom 1995; growth 2084.
Kipling, Rudyard knowledge 1071; sin 1338.
Kirk, Kenneth E. Jesus 1630.
Kirk, Russell Jesus 1657.
Knox, John God and man 164.
Knox, Ronald ecclesiasticism 1554; humor 2192; poor in spirit 2446.
Koretser Rabbi, The prayer 252.
Korzybski, Alfred sin 1340.
Krutch, Joseph Wood custom 840.

Lacordaire, Jean Jesus 1653.
Laertius, Diogenes realism 2490.
Lake, Kirsopp faith 1979.

Lamartine, Alphonse de grief 981; immortality 2788.
Lamb, Charles love 2317; thanksgiving 2644.
Lamb, William, Viscount Melbourne principles 2449.
Lanier, Sidney music 1172.
Lao Tzu judging others 1052; leadership 1108; meekness 2341.
Latham, Peter Mere common sense 805.
Latimer, Hugh Devil 433.
Lavater, Johann Kasper order 565.
Law, William heart 2128; heaven and hell 2770; love 2310; prayer 260; pride 1259; stewardship 2614; worldliness 1449; zeal 2693.
Lawrence, Brother Holy Spirit 195; prayer 257.
Lawrence, D.H. belief 51; freedom 1994; justice 2272.
Leavitt, H.H. fasting 1990.
Lec, Stanislaw J. God and his creation 146.
Lee, Robert E. duty 1939; gentility 2011; war and peace 1382.
Leo I, Pope eucharist 1564.
Lerner, Max power 605.
Leopardi, Giacomo nature 546.
Lewis, C.S. atonement 1489; belief 45; Bible 68; brokenness 1845; chastity 1869; communion of saints 2717; daily living 1931, 1932; fall of man 881; glory 2746; grace 1621; Holy Trinity 200; immortality 2787; Incarnation 1629; Lord's Prayer 1681; preaching 1750; sex 613; simplicity 2593; sin 1333.
Lichtenberg, Georg Christoph belief 38; blessings 359; humor 2189; judging others 1059.
Lincoln, Abraham blessings 358; criticism 833; duty 1940; God's judgments 106; God's providence 115; God's will 130; gov-

saints 2535; temperance 2640; theology 300.

Paterson, Alexander self-conquest 2550.

Patmore, Coventry last words 2829; saints 2533; words 1436.

Paton, Alan acceptance 1812; humility 2186; liking and loving 2301.

Pavese, Cesare joy 2237; personality 2444; religion 267.

Pearson, Lester B. peace 2427.

Péguy, Charles God and man 161; government 953, 954, 955.

Pelikan, Jaroslav tradition 1798.

Penn, William church 1522; communion of saints 2720; ends and means 871; humility 2169; knowledge of God 205; law 1092; life eternal 2843; parenthood 575; religion 277; temperance 2635; temptation 1365; truth and falsehood 656; zeal 2691.

Percy, William Alexander peace of God 236.

Perry, Bliss resurrection 1776.

Peter of Alcántara love for God 226.

Peter the Lombard atonement 1488.

Petit-Senn, John pleasure 1222.

Pfister, Oscar Jesus 1641.

Phelps, William Lyon following Christ 1582; gentility 2008.

Phillips, J.B. Holy Spirit 196.

Phillips, Wendell heart 2129; humility 2178; progress 2465; revolution 1294.

Pitt, William humor 2191; manners 1130.

Pittenger, Norman preaching 1741.

Pius XI, Pope education 870.

Plato justice 2257; politics 1237.

Pliny the Elder home 1014.

Plotinus beauty 348; *Creation.*

Plunkett, Joseph Mary cross 1546.

Plutarch words 1447.

Poling, Daniel A. immortality 2793.

Poole, Mary Pettibone laughter 1083.

Pope, Alexander anger 743; forgiveness 1593; honesty 2137; hope 2144; judging others 1054; *Man*; pride 1254; progress 2458; repentance 2505.

Porter, Katherine Anne love 2323.

Potter, Henry Codman simplicity 2594.

Pound, Ezra animals 338.

Prestige, G.L. Holy Trinity 202.

Prezzolini, Giuseppe sacrifice 2526.

Quarles, Francis God and man 165; heart 2122; world 680.

Quayle, William A. preaching 1754.

Quick, Oliver C. Incarnation 1637.

Quintilian, Marcus Fabius theology 304.

Rabelais, François conscience 416.

Ramakrishna, Sri God and man 176.

Rauschenbusch, Walter Christianity 1514.

Raven, Charles E. brokenness 1843.

Read, David H.C. communion of saints 2715.

Reid, James reconciliation 1761.

Reik, Theodore love 2325.

Renan, Ernest Jews 496.

Renard, Jules heaven and hell 2761; modesty 2348.

Reynolds, Joshua work 2684.

Richard of Chichester following Christ 1577.

Richardson, Alan God's word 133.

Richter, Jean Paul attributes of God 21; character 786; family 448; forgiveness 1594; opportunity 2396; revenge 1276.

Rickenbacker, Eddie courage 1906.

Rilke, Rainer Maria death 2730; hope 2152; love 2306; marriage 1136.

Robbins, Howard Chandler ascension of Christ 1480.

INDEX OF BIBLE PASSAGES

INDEX OF SUBJECTS

All references are to numbers of the quotations in the book and not to pages. The hyphenated pair of numbers in italics indicates the quotations specifically assigned to the given category—*e.g.* the quotations 1806 through 1813 are under the heading "acceptance." The other numbers are references to quotations on the same subject under other headings.

ACKNOWLEDGMENTS

Grateful acknowledgment is made to publishers and individuals for permission to reprint sections from the following copyrighted material:

The Apostle's Creed For Everyman by William Barclay. Used by permission of Harper & Row, Publishers, Inc. Published in England as *The Plain Man Looks at the Apostle's Creed* by William Collins Sons & Co., Ltd.

Christian Faith and Life by William Temple. Used by permission of SCM Press, Ltd.

The Christianity of Main Street by Theodore O. Wedel. Copyright 1950 by Theodore O. Wedel. Used by permission of Macmillan Publishing Co., Inc., and Macmillan, London and Basingstoke.

"A Christmas Carol" from *The Collected Poems of G. K. Chesterton.* Used by permission of Dodd, Mead & Company and Miss D. E. Collins and Eyre Methuen Ltd.

The Cocktail Party by T. S. Eliot. Copyright 1950 by T. S. Eliot. Used by permission of Harcourt Brace Jovanovich, Inc., and Faber & Faber, Ltd.

Considerations by Hubert van Zeller. Used by permission of Templegate Publishers and Sheed & Ward, Ltd.

The Divine Milieu by Pierre Teilhard de Chardin. English translation [by Bernard Wall] copyright © 1960 by William Collins Sons & Co., Ltd., London, and Harper & Row, Publishers, Inc., New York. Used by permission.

The End of Man by Austin Farrer. Copyright trustees of Katherine Farrer deceased 1973. Used by permission of Wm. B. Eerdmans Publishing Co. and the Society for Promoting Christian Knowledge.

The Epistle to the Romans by Karl Barth, translated by Edwyn C. Hoskyns. Used by permission of Oxford University Press.

An Expanding Faith by David H. C. Read. Used by permission of Wm. B. Eerdmans Publishing Co.

From Skepticism to Faith by Charles Fiske. Copyright 1934 by Harper & Row, Publishers, Inc. Used by permission.

God Was in Christ by D. M. Baillie. Copyright, 1945, by Charles Scribner's Sons. Used by permission of Scribner's and Faber & Faber, Ltd.

Lust: Trafficing in the bodies
of others

Not so much "finding" the right
person as "being" the right
person.

Instead of "God-like"
We want to act "like God"

Better to act "unto a "feeling"
Than to "feel" unto an "act"